OXFORD WORLD'S CLASSICS

ON OBLIGATIONS

MARCUS TULLIUS CICERO (106–43 BC) was the son of a Roman knight from Arpinum, some 70 miles (112 km.) south-east of Rome. He rose to prominence through his eloquence at the bar and in the Senate; but, without hereditary connections or military achievements, he lacked a solid power-base; and so, in spite of strenuous manœuvres, he failed to reconcile the youthful Pompey and later Octavian (Augustus) to the senate. In the Great Civil War of 49, he could have joined Caesar, but he refused and was eventually murdered at the insistence of Antony, whom he had castigated in his *Philippics*. But although Cicero was ultimately a political failure, he became for long periods of Europe's history not only a symbol of constitutional government but also a model of literary style. More important still, he is recognized as the main vehicle for the transmission of Hellenistic philosophy to the West. As a historian of thought, his discussions of philosophical systems were judicious. But in political theory, where he purported to be describing a constitution or framing laws, his conservatism tended to outweigh his intellectual open-mindedness. Hence, in his vision of political life, he remained above all an old-fashioned Roman.

P. G. WALSH is Emeritus Professor of Humanity at the University of Glasgow. His publications include Apuleius, *The Golden Ass* (Oxford World's Classics, 1995), Cicero, *The Nature of the Gods* (Oxford World's Classics, 1998), Boethius, *The Consolation of Philosophy* (Oxford World's Classics, 1999), Petronius, *The Satyricon* (Oxford World's Classics, 1997), *The Roman Novel* (1970, 1995), and *Livy, his Historical Aims and Methods* (1961, 1995).

OXFORD WORLD'S CLASSICS

*For over 100 years Oxford World's Classics have brought
readers closer to the world's great literature. Now with over 700
titles—from the 4,000-year-old myths of Mesopotamia to the
twentieth century's greatest novels—the series makes available
lesser-known as well as celebrated writing.*

*The pocket-sized hardbacks of the early years contained
introductions by Virginia Woolf, T. S. Eliot, Graham Greene,
and other literary figures which enriched the experience of reading.
Today the series is recognized for its fine scholarship and
reliability in texts that span world literature, drama and poetry,
religion, philosophy and politics. Each edition includes perceptive
commentary and essential background information to meet the
changing needs of readers.*

OXFORD WORLD'S CLASSICS

CICERO

On Obligations

Translated with an Introduction and Notes by
P. G. WALSH

OXFORD
UNIVERSITY PRESS

OXFORD

UNIVERSITY PRESS

Great Clarendon Street, Oxford OX2 6DP

Oxford University Press is a department of the University of Oxford.
It furthers the University's objective of excellence in research, scholarship,
and education by publishing worldwide in

Oxford New York

Athens Auckland Bangkok Bogotá Buenos Aires Cape Town
Chennai Dar es Salaam Delhi Florence Hong Kong Istanbul Karachi
Kolkata Kuala Lumpur Madrid Melbourne Mexico City Mumbai Nairobi
Paris São Paulo Shanghai Singapore Taipei Tokyo Toronto Warsaw

with associated companies in Berlin Ibadan

Oxford is a registered trade mark of Oxford University Press
in the UK and in certain other countries

Published in the United States
by Oxford University Press Inc., New York

First published 2000
First published as an Oxford World's Classics paperback 2001
Reissued 2008

British Library Cataloguing in Publication Data

Data available

Library of Congress Cataloging in Publication Data

Cicero, Marcus Tullius.
[De officiis. English]
On obligations / Cicero; translated with an introduction and notes by P. G. Walsh.
(Oxford world's classics)
Includes bibliographical references (p.   ) and index.
1. Ethics, Ancient.   I. Walsh, P. G. (Patrick Gerard)   II. Title.
PA6308.D5 W26   2000
171'.2—dc21   99–056114

ISBN 978–0–19–954071–6

23

Typeset in Ehrhardt
by Jayvee, Trivandrum, India
Printed and bound in Great Britain by
Clays Ltd, Elcograf S.p.A.

Acknowledgements

This translation is based on the authoritative OCT of M. Winter-bottom. In grappling with the text, I have regularly consulted the well-turned Loeb version of Walter Miller (1913) and the rendering of E. M. Atkins (Cambridge 1991). The annotations have benefited from the helpful explanations by M. T. Griffin and E. M. Atkins in the Cambridge volume, but above all from the recent commentary of A. R. Dyck, so thorough and comprehensive in its scope that it must be accounted a major contribution to Ciceronian studies. I should like to thank those scholars who offered helpful criticisms of the specimen translations which I submitted to the Press, and especially Professor Donald Russell, who read through the entire translation and improved it immeasurably. Finally, I express my gratitude yet again to Hilary O'Shea for her unobtrusive advice and encouragement.

P.G.W.

Contents

Abbreviations

Introduction

I. THE POLITICAL BACKGROUND

Cicero informed his friend Atticus in a letter dated 25 October 44 BC that he had embarked on a philosophical treatise to be entitled *De officiis* and addressed to his son Marcus. By 5 November he further reports that he has completed the first two books. He had worked at speed, dashing them off in less than four weeks. October–November 44 is the secure date for the composition of the work.[1]

The *De officiis* is of all Cicero's philosophical works the one most deeply affected by his experiences of Roman public life; these range from the period of his boyhood up to his enforced retirement from politics following Julius Caesar's victory in the Great Civil War and the assassination of the dictator a year later on the Ides of March 44 BC. The final months between March and October 44 are vividly documented by his correspondence with Atticus, to whom he wrote almost every day. The letters illuminate the contents of the treatise at many points, and the sombre mood in which Cicero contemplated the death-throes of the republic; the first two of the *Philippics*, the speeches composed against Mark Antony (the first delivered on 2 September, and the second never delivered but sent to Atticus on 25 October) provide further evidence from his own pen.[2]

Though Caesar publicly rejected the title *rex* and rebuffed Mark Antony's attempt to crown him, the crowd of honours which he accepted—dictatorship for life, oaths of loyalty from all senators, his head on the coinage, and other kingly prerogatives—intensified the feelings of alienation among traditionalists of philosophical bent.

---

[1] For the secure dates, see *Att.* 15. 13. 6, 16. 11. 4. For the speculative date of commencement, see M. Fiévez, *Latomus* 12 (1953), 261–74 (arguing for some time between 9 and 23 October 44 BC).

[2] The correspondence is exploited in several recent studies of Cicero; see the bibliography for those of Mitchell, Rawson, Shackleton Bailey, and Stockton. For the *Philippics*, see the edition with accompanying translation of Shackleton Bailey, *Philippics* (Chapel Hill 1986).

Caesar had always treated Cicero generously in victory, but he was well aware of the revulsion which these honours had aroused in him. 'I have no doubt that he utterly loathes me', he is alleged to have commented a few days before his assassination. Throughout the *De officiis* Caesar as the *bête noire*, the man who has brought down the Roman republic, repeatedly surfaces.[3]

Cicero took no part in the murder of Caesar, but his immediate reaction was one of jubilation, to be replaced by feelings of frustration and deepening pessimism as the conspirators allowed Antony as surviving consul to seize the initiative. When Caesar's bequest of 300 sesterces to each citizen was announced, and when Antony's funeral speech provoked public disorder, Brutus and Cassius, elected praetors before the assassination, were afraid to appear in Rome; in mid-April Antony had them exempted from their duties, and they retired elsewhere in Italy.[4]

In the weeks following Caesar's assassination, Antony as the dominant consul (Dolabella, Cicero's son-in-law, had been confirmed as his colleague on 17 March) was a model of moderation, seeking good relations with Cicero and other senior senatorials. But in mid-April the youthful Gaius Octavius, great-nephew of Julius Caesar who had named him as his heir, crossed to Italy from Greece to claim his inheritance. He was in no hurry to proceed to Rome, preferring to remain in Campania to confer with (among others) his stepfather Lucius Philippus, and Cicero who was resident at Puteoli. He treated Cicero with deference; the elder statesman at this stage underrated the youth just turning nineteen, who now following his formal adoption was to be known as Caesar Octavianus (hence 'Octavian'). It is perhaps significant that there is no allusion to the young man in the *De officiis*.

Octavian's arrival in Rome in early May roused Antony to more incisive action. He had already exploited the publication of Caesar's *acta* to gain support by extending privileges to provincial communities, and at the end of April he had journeyed to Campania to superintend the land-allocations to Caesar's veterans. On his return to

---

[3] For the honours conferred on Caesar, see Suetonius, *Iulius* 76. Caesar's comment on Cicero, *Att.* 14. 1. 1–2. The passages in *De officiis* denigrating Caesar, 1. 26, 45, 112; 2. 27 ff.; and above all 3. 82 ff.

[4] For detailed accounts of the months following the Ides of March, see E. Rawson, *CAH* 9[2], ch. 12 and the studies of Cicero listed in n. 2.

Rome in late May he brought with him a large number of veterans, an act which convinced Cicero that the rule of law was to be replaced by the rule of force. In early June he secured the provinces of Cisalpine Gaul and Gallia Comata (the areas of Transalpine Gaul not yet incorporated into the province) with four legions to be transferred from Macedonia. Cicero's relations with him had always been uneasy since 49 BC, when Antony, left in charge of Italy during Caesar's absence, had refused Cicero leave to quit Italy; again in 48 BC Cicero had deemed it prudent to remain in Brundisium pending Caesar's return rather than to expose himself to Antony's arbitrary domination. Cicero now had his suspicions confirmed that Antony was ruthlessly continuing Caesar's policies of undermining the republic and the rule of law; though he never cites him by name in this treatise, oblique allusions to him and his followers are legion, and the *Second Philippic* is a sustained indictment of his policies.[5]

Cicero increasingly felt that there was to be no role for him in politics. Even before the Ides of March he had contemplated an extended visit to Athens to supervise the education of his son Marcus, who was studying under the Peripatetic philosopher Cratippus. The assassination of Caesar caused him to put off this plan in order to support his friend Brutus. Between April and June he moved restlessly between his country-houses at Puteoli, Astura, and Tusculum. Finally he decided to quit Italy; he set out on the first leg of his journey from the port of Pompeii to Sicily. But after his ship put out for Greece, it was forced to turn back by contrary winds. As he lingered at Leucopetra, news of a possible accommodation between Antony and the so-called liberators, reinforced by outspoken criticisms of his departure, induced him in a fit of patriotic fervour to return to Italy. There a meeting with Brutus at Velia hardened his determination to return to Rome. He entered the city amidst scenes of great enthusiasm on 31 August, and on 2 September delivered the *First Philippic*.[6]

The speech, couched in moderate language, reviews Antony's political record since the Ides of March: his initial measures, including abolition of the dictatorship, had brought renewed hope for the

---

[5] For criticisms of Antony and his followers in this treatise, see 1. 57; 2. 3, 28; 3. 2.

[6] Cicero's decision to return from Sicily to Rome, *Att.* 16. 7. 1 ff.; his meeting with Brutus, 16. 7. 5, *Phil.* 1. 9; his return to Rome greeted with acclaim, Plutarch, *Cic.* 43. 5.

republic, but the month of June had heralded a decisive change. Antony's measures were going far beyond Caesar's decrees; Cicero hints at financial corruption, and openly asserts that Antony is seeking excessive power with the intimidation of senate and magistrates. Antony was absent when this brave attack on him was delivered, but report of it roused him to fury. As a later *Philippic* makes clear, his scurrilous riposte on 19 September blamed Cicero for all the political disasters of the previous twenty years. Cicero retired to Puteoli to frame an extended reply in similarly abusive terms. The speech was too explosive ever to be delivered; it was sent to Atticus on 25 October, with the request that it be circulated at his friend's discretion. Atticus suggested some amendments, to which Cicero replied on 5 November; the speech was presumably published after Antony had left Rome for his province of Cisalpine Gaul at the end of November. Thus it is clear that Cicero worked on this speech immediately prior to his composition of *De officiis*, and its imprint on the philosophical treatise is apparent.[7]

2. CICERO AS PHILOSOPHER[8]

The *De officiis* was composed as postscript to the series of philosophical works which Cicero wrote in the two-year period between the last months of 46 BC and the end of 44, when his life in politics had been effectively foreclosed. His interest in philosophy had dated from his teens in Rome, where he enjoyed acquaintance with eminent philosophers—Phaedrus the Epicurean, Diodotus the Stoic, Philo and Antiochus the Academics. Later, during his sojourn abroad in 79–77 BC, he studied in Athens with Antiochus (now head of the Academy there), with the Epicureans Zeno of Sidon and Phaedrus, and with Pupius Piso, a Peripatetic. He later journeyed to the cities of Asia and to Rhodes. At Smyrna he held discussions with the exiled Roman Stoic Rutilius Rufus, but his more important

---

[7] Antony's scurrilous speech, *Phil.* 11; Cicero's dispatch of the *Second Philippic* to Atticus, *Att.* 15. 13. 1; response to his suggested amendments, *Att.* 16. 11. 1 ff. (followed by his announcement of progress on *De officiis*).

[8] More detail of this section in the Oxford World's Classics edition of *The Nature of the Gods* (Oxford 1998), pp. xviiff., with bibliography. Add now J. G. F. Powell (ed.), *Cicero the Philosopher* (Oxford 1995).

encounter with Stoicism was at Rhodes in the person of the versatile scholar Posidonius, whose name was to loom large throughout Cicero's philosophical corpus. These early studies led Cicero to profess allegiance to the Academic school, and to the end of his life he stoutly defended this connection. But in *De officiis* he adopts in ethics a consistently Stoic stance, exploiting the freedom permitted by his school to embrace teachings which appear to him probable at particular times and in particular circumstances.[9]

Though on his return to Rome his energies were concentrated primarily on achieving his rise to eminence in the courts and in politics, he maintained his interest in philosophy by voluminous reading during such leisure hours as he could spare. But in 58 BC he was forced into exile when indicted by the tribune Clodius for executing citizens without trial when repressing the Catilinarian conspiracy. Though he was able to return to Rome from Macedonia after a year and a half when his banishment was repealed in August 57, his political impotence in the face of the so-called First Triumvirate of Caesar, Pompey, and Crassus, which was renewed at Luca in 56, left him with abundant leisure for studies. His other great scholarly enthusiasm besides philosophy, the theory and practice of oratory, led him to publish three books of *De oratore* first, but it is notable that this work contains an extended discussion of the connection between oratory and philosophy.[10]

Between 54 and 51 BC he followed this work with two treatises on political philosophy, *Republic* and *Laws*. Plato's shadow looms over both these titles, though it is notable that whereas Plato's *Republic* is a prescription for justice in a Utopian state, Cicero's vision is rooted in the historical existence of the Roman constitution; he considers this to be closer to the ideal than Plato's hypothetical republic, which is criticized on various counts. Hence Cicero draws on other more pragmatic discussions, including that of the historian Polybius who was an avid admirer of the Roman constitution. Like the *Republic*,

[9] J. Glucker and P. Steinmetz (independently of each other) have argued that Cicero switched allegiance from Philo's scepticism to Antiochus' 'Old Academy' in the 50s BC, but reverted to the scepticism of Carneades and Philo in 45 BC. Their views are documented and opposed by W. Gorler in *Cicero the Philosopher* (see n. 8), 85 ff., arguing for Cicero's consistent scepticism ('an inner conflict, sometimes painfully felt, between scrupulous reason and edifying ideals').

[10] For the relationship between oratory and philosophy, see *De oratore* 3. 56 ff.

Cicero's *Laws* have come down to us in a fragmentary state, but enough has survived to indicate that the proposals for legislation underpin the constitution described in *Republic*. The limitations of Cicero's political vision were to be cruelly exposed within a few years by the advent of the Great Civil War in 49 BC; the religious measures proposed indicate the importance which he attached to religious ritual for the stability of the state. As in the *De officiis* later, he abandons the sceptical standpoint of the Academics to propound the Stoic doctrine of natural law, arguing that a rational Providence governs the world and imposes a general law of behaviour on all mankind. Individual communities legislating for their peculiar concerns need not follow such natural law in all respects, but its principles should underlie all civil legislations in the main.[11]

Cicero was still at work on the *Laws* when he was appointed governor of Cilicia. He left Rome in the spring of 51 BC, leaving the treatise unfinished. En route to his province he met the Peripatetic philosopher Cratippus at Mitylene; this encounter may have encouraged him to recommend Cratippus as tutor to his son Marcus, for he later acclaimed him as 'on a par with the most eminent Peripatetics'. On his return from a busy tour as governor, he put in at Athens in 50 BC to renew acquaintance with the Stoic Aristus, brother of Antiochus, and with other resident philosophers.[12]

Cicero's support for Pompey and the senatorial rump against Caesar in the Great Civil War inevitably meant that on his return from Greece he was precluded from politics, and accordingly he devoted himself to a life of scholarship. As before in the 50s, he gave preference first to rhetoric; a series of oratorical works flowed from his pen in late 47 and 46 BC—*Brutus*, a history of Roman oratory,

[11] For an excellent account of the *Republic* and the *Laws* see the Oxford World's Classics edition by Jonathan Powell and Niall Rudd (Oxford 1998), pp. xv–xxxi. Also M. Schofield, 'Cicero's Definition of Res Publica' in *Cicero the Philosopher* (n. 8), 82, conceding the myopic nature of Cicero's political vision, but saluting the *Republic* as 'a lucid and original analysis of what makes a government legitimate . . . an elected aristocracy of men of energy and judgment as the best way for a sovereign people to manage its affairs'. For the relation between natural law and civil law as discussed in this treatise, see especially 3. 69.

[12] The *Laws* may have been completed after Cicero returned from Cilicia; see *Fam.* 9. 2. 5 (April 46 BC). Macrobius, *Saturnalia* 6. 4. 8 quotes from 'the fifth book of *De legibus*', but we possess only Books 1–2 complete and 3 fragmentary. For Cratippus as Marcus' tutor, see this treatise, 1. 1; for Cicero's high opinion of him, *Div.* 1. 5. The encounter with Aristus and with other philosophers at Athens, *Att.* 5. 20. 3, 7. 1. 1.

Orator, an analysis of the ideal form of oratory, and two minor treatises. But by early and mid-46 he had already embarked simultaneously on philosophical studies, with the aim of instructing a wider circle of Romans in this central branch of Greek literary culture.[13]

The programme which he undertook is summarized at the beginning of Book 2 of his *De diuinatione*, composed in the spring of 44 BC. He explains there that he had begun with the *Hortensius*, an exhortation to the study of philosophy, on which he was working in late 46 and early 45. The work has not survived, but it has won fame because Augustine acknowledges it as having converted him to the study of philosophy. This was followed by the *Academica*, a work on epistemology. He composed a first version in two books (*Catulus* and *Lucullus*), but then he revised it extensively in four books. A single book from each of the two versions has survived and comprises the modern text. Book 1 is the first book of the later version and treats the Academic doctrine of the probable; Book 2 is the second book of the first edition, and concerns itself mainly with the different approaches of Carneades and Antiochus to scepticism.[14]

Having cleared the ground with this preliminary investigation of the theory of knowledge, Cicero next turned to ethics, the branch of philosophy universally regarded in Hellenistic Athens as the most important. In the *De finibus* he discussed in five books the differing views of the main schools on the highest ends which mankind should seek. He followed this with the *Tusculan Disputations*, again in five books, to investigate how mortals should attain happiness. Death, pain, mental disturbance, irrational emotions are to be disregarded; the pursuit of virtue is the recipe for happiness.[15]

Cicero next turned his attention to physics and the related discipline of theology. In *The Nature of the Gods*, composed in three books, he devoted the first book to the doctrines of Epicurus, and after rapidly dismissing them, he applied the rest of the treatise to an extended discussion of Stoic theology, confessing at the close

---

[13] Philosophical studies under way, *Fam.* 9. 2. 5 (April 46); *Fam.* 11. 27. 5 (?August? 46).

[14] Augustine's acknowledgement, *Conf.* 3. 7. On Carneades and Antiochus, see below, p. xxxii f.

[15] There is now an Oxford Classical Text of *De finibus*, ed. L. D. Reynolds (Oxford 1998). A. E. Douglas has edited *Tusculan Disputations* 1, and 2 and 5 (with translations, Warminster 1985, 1989).

of the treatise that the Stoic theory 'seemed to come more closely
to a semblance of the truth'. He complemented this investigation
with two works which are a continuation of the study of Stoic
theology, *On Divination* and *On Fate* (this last has not survived
complete).[16]

While working on *De diuinatione* and *De fato*, Cicero turned to
what he doubtless regarded as more exhilarating themes, in the sense
that they allowed him to dwell more on Roman and personal concerns. The three topics of old age, friendship, and glory all reappear
in the *De officiis*. In the *De senectute*, donning the persona of old Cato,
he recommends to his friend Atticus and to himself (both now in
their sixties) a continuing busy life guided by practice of the four cardinal virtues. Again in *De amicitia* the central spokesman is a prominent Roman, Laelius the loyal friend of the celebrated Scipio
Aemilianus and a wise Stoic. The third of these treatises, *De gloria*,
has a particularly close connection with the present work. Unfortunately it has not survived, but there is a long disquisition on glory in
the *De officiis*, and given Cicero's tendency to incorporate in his last
philosophical work reminiscences of earlier ones, it appears likely
that the gist of the lost treatise has been reproduced here.[17]

Thus the *De officiis* comes as the climax of a lifelong enthusiasm
for philosophy, and in particular after intensive reflection on its central concerns as viewed by the spokesmen of the Hellenistic schools.
It will be clear that Cicero is no professional academic. 'These works
do not attempt, and therefore should not be expected, to make the
same kind of appeal as, for instance, the epistemological and metaphysical speculations that were fashionable in the last century . . .
These writings deal with the kind of philosophy which concerns
man as a political and social being.' Though his approach to problems is less sophisticated than that of modern philosophers, he
dealt with issues of perennial concern, in ways comprehensible to
those unschooled in, or impatient with, the abstruse discussion
characteristic of the discipline today.[18]

---

[16] There is a text and translation of *De fato* by R. W. Sharples (Warminster 1991).

[17] For old age in the present treatise, 1. 122–3, 149; friendship, 1. 43, 120; 2. 30–1; glory,
2. 31 ff.

[18] The citation is from A. E. Douglas, 'Cicero the Philosopher' in *Cicero* (ed. T. A. Dorey,
London 1964), 136. Similar sentiments by J. G. F. Powell in *Cicero the Philosopher* (n. 8
above), 1–4.

3. *DE OFFICIIS*: TITLE, CONTENT, AUDIENCE

For the first two books of this treatise, Cicero followed closely the work of the Stoic philosopher Panaetius. It was therefore understandable that he should adopt Panaetius' title as well, which was *Peri tou kathēkontos*, 'Concerning the appropriate'. This was the regular Stoic expression to categorize ethical behaviour; it had been employed as a title by the three venerable Stoic heads Zeno, Cleanthes, and Chrysippus before Panaetius, and it was pressed into service again by his successors Hecato and Posidonius. It had therefore acquired the status of a specialized Stoic term, 'appropriate behaviour directed towards virtue'.[19]

When Cicero in rendering this title employed the Latin word *officium* ('service', 'friendly office'), it inevitably lacked the nuance of the Greek. That at any rate was the reaction of Cicero's friend Atticus, whose long residence in Greece and interest in philosophy lent him enviable expertise. From Cicero's correspondence we infer that he demurred at the use of the word in the political sense of 'obligation to the state'. Cicero spiritedly defended his choice: 'There is no doubt in my mind that we use *officium* for the Greeks' *kathekon* . . . or else give me something better.'[20] Cicero may have been implying that it was the most appropriate expression for the philosophical concept in the different social ambience of Rome.

Equally hazardous as translation from the Greek into Latin is the rendering of the Latin into English. 'On Duties' is inadequate, since the word duty need not have a moral connotation; in army-life, for example, 'duties' can include cleaning out the latrines. I prefer the rendering 'On Obligations', while being conscious that the latinate word has a clumsier ring.

Cicero followed Panaetius' programme in structuring the treatise in three books. The first deals with honourable conduct (*honestum*), the second with what is useful (*utile*), and the third with potential conflicts of interest between the two. As Cicero explains, Panaetius initially expressed the intention of handling the third theme, but never actually did so; Cicero himself repairs the omission, though with assistance from other sources.

---

[19] For details of earlier and subsequent Stoic treatises with the same title, see Dyck, 4.
[20] *Att.* 16. 14. 3.

In Book 1, Cicero employs 'the honourable' (*honestum*) synonymously with *uirtus* (Stoic virtue, the only good at which we are to aim). The *honestum* has four subdivisions from which all obligations stem. These are in essence the four cardinal virtues expounded by Plato of wisdom, justice, courage, and temperance, but the Stoics have expanded these concepts. In Panaetius' discussion, (or in Cicero's brief adaptation of it, 1. 18–19), the obligations falling under wisdom are wholly concerned with the pursuit of knowledge and concern for the truth. Here a long-standing controversy raises its head: are we to seek knowledge for its own sake because in Aristotle's words 'All men by nature desire to know', or should our pursuit of learning be harnessed to the pursuit of virtue? In this dispute between Peripatetics and Stoics, Cicero is here strongly influenced by the Stoic view, condemning research into 'matters not merely arcane and taxing, but also unprofitable' (elsewhere he redresses the balance by greater sympathy for the Peripatetic view; see 1. 18n.). Here the worthy studies which he praises all contribute to the study of nature or to life in the community, and so are consonant with Stoic aims. The Stoic emphasis on service to the community also surfaces here; Cicero enthusiastically endorses it, since it squares with his own order of priorities in which private scholarship was undertaken only when political activity was ruled out. He raises this question of the order of priorities between public service and private study again at 1. 153 ff. (where for the first time he offers the useful distinction between wisdom (*sapientia*) and prudence (*prudentia* or practical wisdom, 'knowledge of things to be sought and things to be avoided'). Such *prudentia* is valuable in our participation in public life; 'knowledge and contemplation of the world of nature would be feeble and unfulfilled if no practical action were to flow from it.' So in general the life of learning should find its justification in service to the community (1. 155–6).[21]

The second of the cardinal virtues, justice, is in the Stoic scheme expanded to embrace beneficence or generosity, a virtue which looms large in Aristotle's treatment of the virtues in the *Nicomachean Ethics*.[22] The principles of just behaviour and the obligations it

---

[21] For the cardinal virtues in Plato, see *Rep.* 427d ff., and 1. 13n. below. Aristotle's words, *Metaphysics* 1. 1. The Peripatetic–Stoic dispute is outlined in my *GR* article (see 1. 18–19n.) with bibliography.

[22] *Nic. Eth.* 1120a ff.

entails are first outlined (1. 20–41), followed by the role of beneficence as adjunct to justice (1. 42–60). Two principles for just behaviour are first laid down: no person should suffer harm at the hands of
another unless he is an aggressor, and all men should observe the
common good; in all relations good faith (*fides*) is the foundation of
justice. Obligations towards individuals are twofold: we must refrain
from directly harming them, and we should not stand idly by when
wrongs are perpetrated on others. The roots of injustice are
analysed: occasionally fear, more often greed, and more often still
lust for dominance and fame (Julius Caesar is cited as a heinous
example). Occasions when apparent injustices are justified are presented: for example, failure to keep promises when they would harm
the parties, or when they are extracted by trickery. Finally there is a
section on obligations in warfare, an important early contribution to
'Just War' theory. Due warning and demands for satisfaction must
first be served; wars should be fought only 'for the purpose of living
peaceably without suffering injustice'; and the defeated should be
spared unless they have committed monstrosities.

The section on beneficence (1. 42–60) is based largely on Aristotle's *Nicomachean Ethics*. Generosity to one must not involve harm
to another (a further attack on Caesar is made here); our giving
should not go beyond our means; the worthiness of the recipient and
his needs should dictate our approach. Gifts which cost nothing
should be freely bestowed even on strangers in view of the fellowship
existing among the whole human race. At this point haste of composition leads Cicero to diverge disconcertingly from his theme of
appropriate generosity to delineate the degrees of fellowship from
the broadest to the most intimate, beginning with the human race in
general and passing successively to nation, local community, circle of
friends, and kin. He justifies this excursus by following it with the
desirable priorities in dispensing obligations. Somewhat illogically,
in view of what precedes, he joins country to parents as the rightful
recipients of our first obligations, followed by lesser kin and friends
with the same moral ideals as ours. He emphasizes, however, that we
must show discrimination by taking account of circumstances;
experience rather than precept is the better guide.

Following Panaetius, Cicero posits as the third of the four virtues
from which our obligations derive magnanimity or greatness of soul
(1. 61–92), a wider concept than Plato's courage. He stresses at the

outset that this virtue looks to the welfare of the community rather than the prestige of the individual; in this sense magnanimity takes justice as its guide. The desire for glory often leads to acts of injustice (Cicero had discussed the topic of glory in general in the lost *De gloria*, but the gist of it is probably reproduced in this treatise at 2. 31 ff.). The magnanimous man will be indifferent to all except the acquisition of virtue, and he will shoulder the most exacting tasks; the language of Stoicism looms large here, for greed, pleasure, glory, and disturbing emotions are to be repressed to gain mental equilibrium. Cicero here introduces the contrasting lives of the academic in retirement and the busy politician; the secluded life of retirement is justifiable in certain circumstances, but not if this is the (Epicurean) aim of avoiding or even denigrating the toils of public life, which is the higher calling. Cicero is concerned also to stress that military achievement does not beckon the magnanimous man more than the life of politics; Greek examples (presumably cited by Panaetius) are complemented by appropriate Roman parallels, Cicero himself numbered among them. Equanimity and foresight, both marks of the magnanimous man, are indeed required more in civil administration than in warfare, in which headstrong ambition for glory may overshadow the common welfare. Throughout this section, the qualities desirable in the ideal statesman rather than the obligations required of him are paraded; there is an obvious link between the two, but the focus is blurred.

The last and lengthiest of the discussions of the four subsidiary virtues is concerned with the concept of the fitting (1. 93–151), which has replaced Plato's virtue of temperance. We are to presume that Cicero has bowed to Panaetius' arrangement here, but the substitution is a curious one, not least because 'the fitting' is for a Roman an aesthetic rather than a moral concept, though the Stoics may have visualized it differently. More seriously, and Cicero concedes this at the outset, there is no compelling reason for associating the fitting more with temperance than with the three previous virtues, though Cicero strives to do so. Several of the topics raised in this section (for example, seemly dress and deportment, and appropriate housing) are remote from moral obligation which is Cicero's claimed topic.

Cicero ranges widely in his discussion of the fitting, and many of his topics do embrace the obligations to exercise the temperance demanded by reason. We are to discipline ourselves by promoting seemly wit and banishing unseemly obscenity; our lifestyle should eschew base pleasures and embrace sobriety. We should rest content with our natural endowments rather than attempt to imitate those of others; we should work hard at what suits us best, though chance or parental example may dictate our choice of career. Different stages in life, differences of rank or social status impose different obligations. Our bodily functions and physical habits generally, and the language we employ to describe these, should be seemly; and activity on the stage, in the baths, on the exercise ground, and in the public streets should observe due decorum. Conversation at an informal level should be subject to 'rules' in the same way as public speaking; we should try to exclude the vicious emotions which the Stoics condemn from our conversation as from our behaviour generally. As leading citizens, we should ensure that our residences are suitably spacious, but we should avoid excessive expenditure on them. As a final observation, Cicero lists the trades and professions which worthy individuals must avoid, and contrasts with them the more respectable occupations appropriate to the middle class (but by implication not to sons of senators).

In the final section of the first book (1. 152–60), Cicero deals with an issue omitted by Panaetius: granted that obligations stem from all four cardinal virtues (temperance here appears as the fourth), which should be given priority? In offering his solution, Cicero distinguishes between wisdom and knowledge; wisdom embraces concern for the community, which is the sphere of justice, so that whereas wisdom is the first of the virtues absolutely, justice comes first in practical application. Its obligations are higher than those of acquiring knowledge. However, many individuals who have devoted themselves to scholarship have contributed to the public good by educating their pupils for public service, and have thus applied their faculties to the benefit of mankind. In considering the relative claims of obligations stemming from justice and those demanded by temperance, Cicero concludes that there are some acts so degrading that no appeal to the common good can justify them. Finally, in adjudicating between conflicting duties in community-claims governed by justice, Cicero puts obligations to the gods first, those to country second, those to parents third, and those to others fourth. This list of priorities is not wholly consistent with the rankings at 1. 58.

After twin apologias for philosophical study and adherence to the Academics, Cicero embarks in Book 2 on consideration of the useful. (I render *utile* as 'useful' rather than 'expedient' to avoid the derogatory sense of 'politic rather than just'.) Implicit throughout the discussion of the useful is what is useful for political advancement. He begins with the bald assertion of what he is to argue in Book 3, that the useful is always identical with the honourable.

Cicero first assembles the elements in the world which promote the benefit of human life (2. 11–30), following Aristotle's categories of inanimate things, brute beasts, and our fellow-men. Cicero has already rehearsed in *The Nature of the Gods* the benefits extracted by human skill from inanimate things and from the brute beasts (2. 150ff.). He hymns human skills in establishing communities which bestow lasting benefits, but he also signals the destructive tendencies of fellow-men which impede civilized life. Hence the wisdom and virtue of outstanding individuals must be harnessed for the guidance of communities. In gaining the support of our fellow-men, affection is a stronger bond than fear, as the recent history of Rome demonstrates.

How then are we to win that affection? Here Cicero dilates on the usefulness of glory, and how to attain it (2. 31–51). We must gain the affection, trust, and admiration of men for our achievements and merits; these include contempt for death, pain, pleasure, and all except virtue. Concern for justice is particularly important; history demonstrates that men renowned for a combination of justice and prudence are chosen to rule. Glory is initially gained most easily in warfare. Modesty and familial piety are useful traits, and close association with respected elders inspires confidence. But the greatest glory is gained by eloquence in political assemblies, and more particularly in the courts, where speeches for the defence are more advisable than those for the prosecution. Above all, innocent persons should never be indicted on capital charges.

Beneficence—generosity with money, and secondly with personal help—is next discussed as a means of winning favour; the second is the nobler of the two (2. 52–85). So far as outlays of money are concerned, Cicero adheres to Aristotelian precepts (see 1. 42–60, with nn.), to which he attaches Roman examples. A distinction is made between extravagant financing of public feasts and shows for momentary prestige, and generosity in relieving the urgent needs of individual citizens. Cicero qualifies his criticism of expenditure on public shows by conceding that some such outlays were necessary at Rome if worthy men were to advance their political careers. He expresses approval also of funding for construction-works like harbours and aqueducts. Private generosity he recommends as a service to the community which wins general applause; he includes hospitality, notably to foreign visitors, under this heading.

The second type of beneficence, personal services, is visualized by Cicero as offered predominantly in the lawcourts, involving legal expertise, eloquence, and friendly contacts. Such assistance is to be given to worthy recipients without payment; the needy will be more rewarding persons to assist, for the wealthy often resent patronage, and fail to return favours. Service to the community at large is then considered; Cicero argues (with recent confiscations by Caesar in his mind) that the primary responsibility here is the protection of private property, and the avoidance of imposing property-taxes—a notorious blindness to the social injustice endemic in the Roman state. He laments the national decline from incorruptibility to widespread greed, associating with this the clamour for agrarian reform and the cancellation of debts. As regularly, Cicero complements Greek examples adduced by Panaetius (here the case of Aratus of Sicyon, narrated at length) with others from nearer home, notably Cicero's own successful resistance to cancellation of debts in the face of the agitation of Catiline.

Cicero concludes the second book with brief mention of the usefulness of healthy living and of money (2. 86–7), and discussion of comparisons between different types of usefulness (2. 88–9).

The third and final book is devoted to the conflict between the honourable and the apparently useful—'apparently', because Cicero argues throughout that the intrinsically useful is identical with the honourable. After his self-deprecating Introduction explaining his attitude to leisure (3. 1–6), he first seeks to clarify the attitude of his source Panaetius: he had expressed the intention of handling the conflict, but had never got round to it (3. 7–13).

The discussion proper begins with the distinction between 'perfect' obligations which only the Stoic sage could fulfil, and the 'intermediate' or second-level obligations which ordinary mortals can practise (3. 14–18); he intends to concentrate on the second. He formulates a rule for proceeding when the apparently useful appears to conflict with the honourable (3. 19–39). This rule is derived from the Stoics, and Cicero strenuously defends his right as an Academic to adopt the doctrine of another school. The rule is that our fellowship with all other men forbids us to exploit any person for our own profit. This principle is at the root of all law, international and civil, because it is inherent in natural law. Cicero takes the argument further by stating that it is more natural to be active in helping others than to live in secluded retirement. What is useful to us individually is what is useful to the human community. We are not to restrict our obligations to kin or to fellow-citizens, and to exploit the rest of the world. We must invoke this rule when we examine the apparently useful; if it contains a shameful element, it must be rejected, even if there is no danger of our reprehensible conduct ever coming to light. The famous anecdote of Gyges is adduced to underline this.

The central section of the book (3. 40–95) examines the claims of the apparently useful against the demands of justice. It is legitimate to protect our own interests, but not if this damages another. Even the demands of friendship must not override the canons of justice. Politicians must not advance the interests of the state by wronging other communities or by adopting other dishonourable policies. On commercial transactions Stoics were divided in their views about the morality of *caveat emptor*, but Cicero is emphatic that a vendor should declare any defects in his wares, and malicious fraud is to be forbidden. The civil law will ensure this in most cases, but in others decisions have to be taken on the basis of natural law. Even so-called 'good men' have been guilty of dishonesty in pursuit of the apparently useful, and recent years have witnessed signal examples of corruption in high places; Marius, Pompey, and above all Caesar are singled out. Cicero appends to this discussion some hypothetical instances of the apparently useful drawn from the Stoic Hecato. He also raises the issue once again of whether promises and agreements need always be kept (cf. 1. 31–2), specifying instances when they should not be.

Cicero next discusses the apparently useful in relation to the third virtue of magnanimity (3. 96–115). The supreme example is Regulus; he takes as historical the legend that after capture by the Carthaginians, Regulus was sent to Rome to negotiate the return of noble prisoners to Carthage, having sworn an oath to return to torture and death if his visit was unsuccessful. Cicero raises and answers a series of objections to Regulus' decision to go back. Is there any need to keep an oath? Yes, for justice and good faith demand it. Could Jupiter have inflicted an evil for breaking the oath greater than the pain Regulus inflicted on himself? Answer: pain is not an evil. But is the base behaviour of breaking an oath to be considered a great evil? Yes, for nothing is so repulsive as dishonour. Is not a promise made to a faithless people invalid? Fidelity must be observed if an oath made to an enemy was sworn with the intention of keeping it; examples are adduced of such fidelity from earlier Roman history. Why did he consent to travel to Rome if he intended to argue against the release of the Carthaginian prisoners? Because the senate rather than he himself had the authority to decide the issue. In short, for a Roman a sworn oath was the most binding pledge possible; Cicero offers further historical examples to underline this.

Finally, the apparently useful is discussed against the fourth virtue. Cicero again compromises between the fitting and temperance by calling it 'propriety, restraint, moderation, self-control, and temperance' (3. 116–20). An attack is mounted on the Epicureans, whose doctrine of pleasure as the chief end cannot be reconciled with temperance, and on other philosophers (perhaps reforming Academics) who argue for pleasure combined with virtue as life's chief aim to be sought.

Cicero addressed his treatise to his son Marcus, who was studying at Athens under the Peripatetic Cratippus. Roman fathers, especially those of the governing class, took a close interest in the education of their sons. Earlier, Cicero had not only appointed tutors for Marcus, but had on occasion taken over his education himself.[23] After Pompey's defeat at Pharsalus in 48 BC (young Marcus served with some distinction as commander of one of Pompey's cavalry contingents), and after Caesar pardoned father and son, Cicero persuaded young Marcus to follow his own example, and to further his education at Athens. The young man set out in May 45 BC.[24]

---

[23] For tutors, see *Q.F.* 2. 4. 2 (Tyrannio as teacher of the 8-year-old Marcus); *Q.F.* 3. 3. 4 (Paeonius teaches him as an 11-year-old); *Att.* 6. 1. 12 (Dionysius teaches the 14-year-old). Cicero himself tutored Marcus at 11 (*Q.F.* 3. 4. 6) and 15 (*Att.* 8. 4. 1). See M. van den Bruwaene, *Nova et vetera* 15 (1933), 53ff.

[24] *Att.* 15. 15. 4.

Young Marcus did not however settle enthusiastically to his studies in rhetoric and philosophy, after his brief experience of a more active life; there is evidence that he might have preferred to campaign with Caesar in Spain. Reports soon reached his father via Atticus (who increasingly shouldered the supervision of Cicero's domestic affairs) that he was not buckling down; the young man received in May 45 BC a letter of remonstration from Atticus, which was penned 'not too harshly, but not too mildly'. In April of the following year his father explains his anxiety to go to Athens—'to give my Cicero some steadying support'. The chief evidence for Marcus' scholastic progress at this time comes from a letter which he wrote to Tiro, his father's freedman and secretary, written perhaps in August: he claims to spend all his days and many of his evenings in the company of Cratippus, his tutor in philosophy, and to be practising his declamation in Greek. But simultaneously he confesses that on instructions from his father he has dismissed Gorgias, his tutor in rhetoric; Plutarch reveals that the reason for the dismissal was because Gorgias was taking him into haunts of low pleasure and drinking-parties.[25]

Cicero's anxiety about his son's academic progress and playboy tendencies is reflected at several points in this treatise, written shortly after his decision not to confront his son in Athens. At the beginning of the first book, he urges him to work hard at his philosophy, and at oratorical studies in both Greek and Latin; later in the book he expresses the hope that his son will walk in his father's footsteps and emulate his achievements (1. 77). In the second book, he expresses this aspiration still more emphatically: since Marcus is the son of a famous father, the eyes of all are on him in their expectation of great achievements (2. 44). Cicero pointedly remarks that at Marcus' age he was already translating works from Greek into Latin (2. 87). He expresses the hope that his son is concentrating particularly on those studies which will promote an honourable political career in emulation of his father (3. 5–6). At the close of the treatise he voices the pious hope that his son is enjoying his studies, and with a hint of asperity assures him that he will be especially dear to his father if he profits from his advice (3. 121).

---

[25] For Marcus' notion of serving in Spain, *Att.* 12. 7. 1; Atticus' letter to him, cf. *Att.* 13. 1. 1; Cicero's motive for going to Athens, *Att.* 14. 13. 4; Marcus' letter to Tiro, *Fam.* 16. 21 (cf. Plutarch, *Cic.* 24. 8).

Given this evidence of concern for his son's future (Marcus' later career would have satisfied his father's ambitions for him, for after the amnesty of 39 BC Marcus rose to the consulship of 30 BC and subsequently became proconsul of Asia), there is no doubt that the *De officiis* was composed mainly for the benefit of his son. But Cicero visualized Marcus as representative of the young men of senatorial families in whose hands lay the political future of Rome. In this sense the guidelines for political advancement and for appropriate behaviour in office are addressed to a whole generation which would outlive the political corruption of Mark Antony, and might bend to the task of restoring the republic. His able nephew Quintus, whom he claimed to have converted to sound political judgement,[26] was one obvious example. In this sense the *De officiis* stands outside the series of philosophical works which Cicero had composed for the cultural instruction of his contemporaries. They were a rounded survey of the doctrines of the main Hellenistic schools in the three branches of philosophy—epistemology, physics, and ethics. Though this treatise can be attached to *De finibus* and *Tusculans* as a further contribution to the understanding of Stoic ethics, it is more directly a political manifesto, addressed much more closely to the concerns of a Rome still reeling from the effects of the Roman revolution engineered by Julius Caesar.

4. THE SOURCES

In his introduction to the first book, Cicero states: 'At this particular time in my enquiry, I follow the Stoics chiefly, not translating them but following my usual procedure of drawing from their wells as much as, and in whatever way, my judgement and inclination dictate.' Later in the treatise he explains how an Academic can justify this choice of sources: he claims that on the subject-matter of this work the Old Academy voiced views similar to those of the Stoics, and more important, Academics claimed discretion to adopt whatever doctrines appeared most probable at a particular time. His explanation of how he exploited the Stoic sources is noteworthy. While repeatedly praising his source for the first two books,

Panaetius ('that most earnest of Stoics ... the eminent philosopher'),
he does not hesitate to amend, curtail, and supplement his account.
In this spirit he criticizes him for failing to define obligation; he
regards his division of the topic into three sections as inadequate,
and expands his discussion into five; he criticizes him for being long-
winded; and he states that though he has followed him closely, he has
made amendments to his account. Finally, Cicero appended historical examples at many points which postdated the life of Panaetius
and which he garnered from his own experience. This treatise is the
richest of the philosophical writings in this respect.[27]

Panaetius' work *On the Fitting*, the sole source for the first two
books, has unfortunately not survived; we are dependent chiefly on
Cicero for our knowledge of its content. Panaetius, born in the later
180s BC of a high-born family at Rhodes, imbibed his Stoicism at
Athens from Diogenes of Babylon and Diogenes' successor as head
of the Porch, Antipater of Tarsus. After returning to Rhodes, where
he held the priesthood of Poseidon Hippios at Lindos, he moved to
Rome in the 140s BC, and became an influential figure in the cultural
circle of Scipio Aemilianus, who in this treatise is cited as 'his pupil
and friend'; Panaetius' praise of Aemilianus' refusal to be corrupted
by greed is a further indication of their harmonious relationship. He
subsequently seems to have divided his teaching between Rome and
Athens until he succeeded Antipater as head of the Stoa in Athens
about 129 BC, a position which he held until his death about twenty
years later. As a philosopher, he showed some independence from his
Stoic predecessors, notably in his rejection of the doctrine of cyclical
conflagration and rebirth of the universe in favour of Aristotle's
thesis of the eternity of matter.[28]

Panaetius also showed originality in discussion of practical ethics.
One notable doctrine, reflected in this treatise, is that of the four
roles with which nature has endowed us: our status as rational beings
raised above the brute beasts, our individuality which distinguishes
each of us from other humans, the peculiar role which circumstances
impose on us, and the special part which we each map out for

---

[27] For his statement of intent to use Stoic sources, 1. 6; his apologia for using them, 3. 20; his
criticisms of Panaetius, 1. 7; 1. 9; 2. 16; 3. 7–8.

[28] For bibliography specifically on Panaetius, see Long–Sedley 2. 494; add M. Pohlenz,
RE 18. 3, 418. More general accounts in Rist, *Stoic Philosophy*, ch. 10; Sandbach, *The Stoics*,
ch. 8; A. Erskine, *The Hellenistic Stoa* (London 1990), 150ff.

ourselves. We are to take account of these four personae when we decide on the lifestyle best suited to us.[29]

On the Fitting was composed in three books, comprising discussion of the honourable (*kalon*) and the useful (*sumpheron*); the contrasting lengths in Cicero's treatment of the two concepts suggest that Panaetius devoted two books to the honourable and the third to the useful. The structure of Cicero's first book, with the four subdivisions of the honourable into the virtues of wisdom/prudence, justice, magnanimity, and the fitting, must be based on Panaetius' scheme; likewise in the second book Cicero followed the outline of Panaetius' treatment, but with greater independence, notably in the section on the attainment of glory, for which Cicero could draw on his own *De gloria*, now lost. At the outset of his work, Panaetius had declared his intention of adding a further book to clarify the relationship between the honourable and the useful, but as Cicero recounts at tedious length, he inexplicably failed to do so. So did Cicero compose his final book as an original contribution, or did he seek guidance from elsewhere?

Some scholars suggest that Cicero, writing at speed and presumably looking for a guide to provide an apposite structure, has turned to Posidonius, for he too wrote a work called *On the Fitting*, a work which Cicero has cited already in Book 1. Posidonius of Apamea (*c.* 135–*c.* 50 BC) had been a pupil of Panaetius at Athens; later he took up residence in Rhodes, where Cicero in 78 BC studied under him, and thereafter remained an enthusiastic student of his work. He would not, however, have had at his fingertips Posidonius' views on such a recherché topic as the relationship between the honourable and the useful; accordingly he wrote to an acquaintance to request a summary of the content of Posidonius' work *On the Fitting*, which he duly received. But he expresses disappointment at Posidonius' brief treatment of the topic, the more so as Posidonius had written that 'no topic in the whole of philosophy is as vital as this'.[30]

It seems probable, therefore, that Cicero derived only marginal assistance from Posidonius, and at 3. 34 he claims that he will complete the rest of his work 'with no props to lean on, battling it out by

---

[29] Cf. 1. 107; 1. 110ff.; 1. 114ff., with the commentary of Long–Sedley, i. 427–8.

[30] For bibliography on Posidonius, Long–Sedley, ii. 494. For general accounts of his ethics, Rist, ch. 11; Sandbach, ch. 8. For Cicero's attempts to obtain Posidonius' discussion of the topic of Book 3 and his disappointment, see 3. 8 and n.

myself; for since Panaetius there has been no treatment of this topic—at any rate not one which met my approval from my scrutiny of the works which have come into my hands'. The decision to tackle the task unaided lasted only up to 3. 63, where he quotes from Hecato of Rhodes, a Stoic pupil of Panaetius who flourished about 100 BC. Hecato wrote a substantial work *On the Fitting*, for Cicero cites extensively from the sixth book at 3. 89–93. Hecato's work may have been composed as an imaginary dialogue between the two heads of the Stoa, Diogenes and Antipater, under whom Panaetius had studied; Diogenes is represented as the more permissive and Antipater the more rigorous when confronted with hypothetical situations which they can turn to advantage without transgression of the laws. Hecato's stance appears to incline towards the views attributed to Diogenes; Cicero has little time for him on this issue at least.[31]

5. THE HELLENISTIC SCHOOLS AND ETHICAL THEORY

Underlying Cicero's attempt to define ideals of public behaviour— for this is the purpose of the *De officiis*—is the Hellenistic debate about the Chief Good which is the subject of the *De finibus*. Cicero himself was attached to the Academics; his addressee Marcus claims allegiance to the Peripatetics; Cicero consistently argues the case of the Stoics, and with vehemence rejects the thesis of the Epicureans. It will be useful to outline the ethical theory of these four main schools as Cicero interpreted them. All agree that human beings seek happiness, but they differed in their conception of where and how such happiness is to be sought.

The Stoics consistently argue that virtue is the only good, and non-virtue is the only evil. We are to strive to attain virtue (in this treatise consistently called 'the honourable') by living in harmony with nature under the guidance of reason. Everything else in the world, including such advantages as good health, wealth, noble birth, is indifferent. But orthodox Stoics conceded that such advantages are 'things preferred', whereas their opposites (ill-health, poverty, low birth, etc.) are 'things not preferred'. Virtue is to be

---

[31] See 3. 63.

attained by following reason (*logos*), another term for the Stoic deity, and by excising the vicious emotions of appetite/lust, fear, grief, and low pleasure. Only the few truly wise, such as Hercules and Socrates, can succeed in attaining it; the rest must be content to aspire to it. Panaetius, the outstanding representative of the Middle Stoa, sought to soften this rigorous view that virtue is out of reach of the rank and file; he adapted the Stoic ethic to meet their needs, distinguishing between 'absolute' obligations which can be met only by the sage, and 'intermediate' ones which are within the reach of ordinary persons. This is the view which Cicero finds congenial (3. 13 ff.); throughout this treatise the Stoic ethic which he recommends is that propounded by Panaetius. He has little time for the moral casuistry which was developed by the later Stoic Hecato; he abides by the traditional Stoic view accepted by Panaetius that only the action which is virtuous or honourable can be beneficial.[32]

The Peripatetics, whose influence following the deaths of Aristotle and his successor Theophrastus had declined for almost two centuries, gained new strength in the first century BC under Andronicus of Rhodes; Aristotle's writings emerged at that time from obscurity, and the *Nicomachean Ethics* stimulated discussion about the Chief Good among the rival schools. In his long discussion on virtue, Aristotle posited and distinguished between moral and intellectual virtue. Moral virtue he defines as the mean between extremes; so the virtue of courage is the mean between cowardice and rashness, temperance that between self-indulgence and puritanism ('insensibility'), liberality that between prodigality and miserliness, magnificence that between vulgarity and niggardliness, and so on. The essential object of moral virtue is control over pleasures. Intellectual virtue is the exercise of the contemplative reason seeking the truth through the five branches of knowledge—the scientific, artistic, practical, intuitive, and philosophic. For Aristotle such use of the contemplative reason is the highest good, being the exercise exclusive to humans by which they seek perfect happiness. Aristotle does not, however, consider the combination of intellectual and moral virtue as the only good; pleasure, for example, is a good (though some individual pleasures are bad), and so is friendship which can

---

[32] The classic text on Stoic ethics is Cicero, *Fin.* 3. 16–76. For modern discussions, see e.g. Long, *Hellenistic Philosophy*, 179 ff.; Sandbach, ch. 3.

imply virtue. Cicero is however justified in assuring his son that though for the Peripatetics virtue is not the only good, they certainly designate it as the chief good.[33]

Though the Academics always claimed allegiance to the tradition of philosophy inaugurated by Socrates and Plato, the views of the school shifted so frequently that the sole justification for the claim was the continuing practice of exploiting the Socratic technique of probing the doctrines of rival schools. In the third century under Arcesilaus they appropriated the standpoint of the Sceptics ('Examiners'), whose negative procedure was to analyse and rebut the teachings of others, insisting that no objective truth could be attained, and that belief should accordingly be suspended and tranquillity sought from such agnosticism. This sceptical stance was maintained in the second century under the president of the Third Academy Carneades. When he came under pressure to offer a rationale by which we should order our lives, he resorted to the doctrine of probability; certain things can be assumed to be true under particular circumstances. This allowed him to approve different notions of the Chief Good at different times: Cicero depicts him at one moment as defending the combination of 'the honourable and the pleasurable' (so *Acad.* 2. 139), and at another 'the enjoyment of the primary things of nature', a view which he upheld 'for the purpose of argument' (*Fin.* 5. 20).

This modified scepticism was continued by Philo, who succeeded to the headship of the Academy in 110–109 BC, and who escaped the disturbances of the Mithridatic wars in 88 BC by moving to Rome, where the young Cicero became an enthusiastic pupil. Philo's insistence on the impossibility of certain knowledge, a position modified by accepting the doctrine of probability, became Cicero's consistent viewpoint. When Antiochus of Ascalon became head of the Academy in 79–78 BC (Cicero attended his lectures in Athens), he argued that Philo's scepticism was untrue to the authentic tradition of the school; he himself was reverting to the doctrines of the Old Academy. In that spirit he sought a closer rapprochement with the Stoics; as Cicero expresses it, 'He was called an Academic, but if he had changed a very few things, he would have been the most genuine of

---

[33] For guidance in analysing the *Nicomachean Ethics*, see Ross, Aristotle, ch. 7. For Cicero's claim that for the Peripatetics virtue is the chief good, see 3. 35.

Stoics.' (*Acad.* 2. 132). Antiochus further argued that the Stoics were at one with the Peripatetics in substance, differing merely in the terms they used (Cicero, *N.D.* 1. 16). This attempt by Antiochus to achieve a reconciliation between the three schools has affected Cicero's presentation in this treatise; he is concerned to stress the similarities between them to his son, so that both may have an agreed philosophical base from which to view the world of contemporary politics. As an Academic, he can reconcile his approach with both the sceptical tradition of Carneades and Philo, and the eclecticism of Antiochus, notably at 2. 8 and 3. 19–20.[34]

For the Epicureans, pleasure is the chief good: 'We say that pleasure is the beginning and end of living happily.' Some pleasures, however, cause pain; we are to indulge only those pleasures which are not outweighed by attendant pain. But the master's teachings undoubtedly gave prominence to the physical pleasures of food and sex. Pleasure of the soul in its anticipation of the future bodily pleasure ranks higher than the physical pleasure itself. The study of philosophy (Epicurus adopted the atomist theory of Democritus, and taught that the soul as well as the body decomposes at death into its constituent atoms, and hence that there is no need to fear death) helps us to attain the chief good. It teaches us to live a life free of mental strain, which is achieved by withdrawing from public life, for such political activity makes for jealousies and other emotional disturbances. In this sense Epicureanism is self-centred, but as Cicero reluctantly admits in this treatise, its adherents find room in their ethical scheme for the practice of some virtues (3. 118).

Cicero devotes the first two books of his *De finibus* to the Epicurean doctrine of pleasure as the chief good. Here and elsewhere he demonstrates his antipathy to the school by over-emphasis on the cruder aspects of physical pleasure, and an unwillingness to concede the subtler aspects of its doctrines. 'Cicero is clearly unsympathetic to Epicurus . . . he finds it difficult to make consistent sense of him, but he is not predisposed to try too hard.' It is largely through his influence that Epicureanism has gained its modern sense of vulgar hedonism.[35]

---

[34] On the approach of the Academics, see C. L. Stough, *Greek Skepticism* (Berkeley 1969) and M. F. Burnyeat (ed.), *The Skeptical Tradition* (Berkeley 1983).

[35] The initial citation is from the *Letter to Menoeceus* (128), Epicurus' own summary of his ethical doctrine. For the final quotation, see J. C. B. Gosling and C. C. W. Taylor, *The Greeks*

6. SUBSEQUENT INFLUENCE OF THE TREATISE

The *De officiis* gained wide currency in Roman circles not long after his death. In the form in which it has come down to us, its many signs of hasty composition suggest that Cicero's resumption of political activity in December 44 BC precluded him from undertaking any work of revision; more probably it was circulated unchanged on his instructions by his secretary Tiro. Horace and Ovid could safely have advertised their knowledge of it after the disgrace and death of Mark Antony (Plutarch claims that when the emperor Augustus came upon one of his grandsons reading one of Cicero's works, he ran his eye over it and exclaimed: 'A wise man, my boy, and a true patriot!'); but the alleged echoes in their poetry are insufficiently specific to guarantee direct dependence. Clearly, however, many of the 'Memorable Deeds and Words' collected by Valerius Maximus in the reign of Tiberius stem directly from this treatise; there is little doubt that Seneca exploited it in his *De beneficiis*, written in the reign of Nero; and the Elder Pliny in his *Natural History*, composed in the reign of Vespasian, not merely delivers an encomium of Cicero, but claims that the *De officiis* should not only be read daily, but also committed to memory. Severus Alexander (emperor AD 222–235), so his biographer claims, would settle down after military campaigning or civil administration to read Plato's *Republic* and Cicero's *De republica* and *De officiis*. The lexicon of Nonius Marcellus (*De compendiosa doctrina*) contains numerous citations from this treatise, providing useful evidence not only of its continuing circulation in the early fourth century but also of fourth-century textual readings to be weighed against those in the Carolingian manuscripts copied half a millennium later.[36]

Christian writers of the second and third centuries in the West were much more reluctant than their Greek counterparts to give houseroom to the pagan classics. But the picture began to change in the fourth century as an increasing number of natural leaders in society

---

on Pleasure (Oxford 1982), 382 ff. For a modified defence of Cicero's reporting of Epicurean ethics in the *De finibus*, see M. C. Stokes in *Cicero the Philosopher* (n. 8 above), ch. 5.

[36] Scholars note the resemblance between Cicero's account of Regulus (3. 100 ff.) and Horace, *Odes* 3. 5, and Ovid, *Ars Amatoria* 3 (the section on fitting behaviour), but the story was well-worn in literature before Cicero's time (see 3. 100 n.).

turned aside from service to the state to evangelize on behalf of the Church; *Romanitas* thus began to make way for Christian humanism. From this time on until the end of the eighteenth century Cicero played a unique role in the formation of ethical values in the West, and the *De officiis* became the most influential of his philosophical writings.

The first Christian writer to exploit the *De officiis* in the interests of the Church was Lactantius (*c.* AD 240–320), who became a Christian convert at the age of about sixty. Of his works of Christian apologetic, the most important as reflecting the influence of our treatise was the *Divine Institutes* (*c.* AD 305–13). Lactantius addressed it to educated contemporaries to commend the truths of Christianity as a guide to the good life. There are no fewer than forty-two citations of the *De officiis* in it; Lactantius evidently believed that the incorporation of such non-Christian testimonies would be a most effective recommendation of Christian morality. Most of the quotations occur in Book Six ('De uero cultu'); many are cited inaccurately, an indication that the work was so familiar to Lactantius that he reproduced the text from memory. Indeed, when he brought out a second edition of the *Divine Institutes*, he corrected a number of the misquotations. He did not of course uncritically commend all Cicero's teaching. For example, whereas Cicero claims that all philosophers maintain that God is never angry (see 3. 102), Lactantius argues in his *De ira Dei* against this thesis of God's impassibility. But his repeated recourse to the Ciceronian treatises, and to *De officiis* above all, has rightly earned him the title of 'the Christian Cicero'.[37]

The most conspicuous debt owed to the *De officiis* by Patristic writers in the West is to be found in the *De officiis* of Ambrose (339–97). Unlike Lactantius, he was born into a Christian family (his sister Marcellina was a nun), but like Lactantius he had enjoyed a traditional Roman education; after the death of his father, Praetorian Prefect at Trier, his mother took her children back to Rome, where in his education Cicero was 'le maître de sa jeunesse'. His treatise on the obligations of his clergy, based on sermons delivered at Milan after he had been consecrated bishop there by popular acclaim, draws on two main sources, the bible and Cicero's treatise. The biblical influence becomes the stronger as the work progresses, but

[37] R. M. Ogilvie, *The Library of Lactantius* (Oxford 1978), 69.

Cicero's presence is conspicuous throughout. At the outset Ambrose describes how his treatise, divided like Cicero's into three books, originated:

While meditating on this psalm [sc. Ps. 39], the idea of writing *De officiis* occurred to me. Though certain students of philosophy have written on this subject, for example, Panaetius and his son [he refers to his pupil Posidonius] among the Greeks, and Tullius among the Latins, I did not consider it irrelevant to my charge as well to write on this subject. Just as Tullius wrote to educate his son, so I too have written for the formation of you my sons. (1. 23–4)

Some notion of the extent to which Ambrose based his work on Cicero may be gathered from the Appendix to Winterbottom's edition of Cicero, which lists over eighty parallels in Ambrose's first book, thirty in Book 2, and nearly forty in Book 3. The reason for this communion of souls is not hard to seek: Ambrose, a traditional Roman and ex-governor of Liguria-Aemilia, was attracted to the high ethical content introduced by Cicero from his Stoic source. Ambrose 'was in many respects a Stoic himself, predisposed to think on Stoic lines'. Naturally enough, however, his formation as a Christian leads him to diverge in places from the Stoic ethic. Thus, though he agrees that virtue is the highest good, he identifies it with the Christ-God who is loving goodness itself. He modifies the Stoic teaching on the cardinal virtues, and introduces charity as a Christian addition. He rejects the Stoic thesis that while respecting the rights of others, we are justified in asserting our own; the good man must think not of his own rights, but of his obligations. He caps Cicero's examples of honourable conduct with biblical exemplars; thus after mention of Fabricius' chivalrous gesture towards Pyrrhus, he adds: 'Let us return to our Moses, and gather examples as superior in nobility as they are earlier in time' (Cic. 3. 86; Ambrose 3. 91–2).[38]

Though the other giants of fourth-century Christian humanism, Jerome and Augustine, were ardent Ciceronians and reveal an

---

[38] For Cicero and Ambrose, see Ivor Davidson's forthcoming commentary on Ambrose, *De officiis* (Oxford 2000); M. Testard, *Saint Ambroise, Les Devoirs I* (Paris 1984), 22 ff. with earlier bibliography at 28 n. 4. Winterbottom's catalogue of parallels is in his OCT of *De officiis* 170 ff., acknowledging Testard, *Les Devoirs II* (Paris 1992), 233 ff. For Ambrose's Stoic sentiments, see F. Homes Dudden, *The Life and Times of St Ambrose* (Oxford 1935), ii. 551 ff., and in general, E. K. Rand, *Founders of the Middle Ages* (Cambridge, Mass. 1928), ch. 3.

acquaintance with the *De officiis*, their writings are not such as might have exploited extended citation of the treatise; moreover, in later life both were increasingly reluctant to register approval of secular writings. The same is even truer of Gregory the Great (540–610), who airs his disapproval of secular literature: 'The same mouth cannot sing the praises of Jupiter and those of Christ.' During the four centuries between the death of Ambrose and the beginning of the Carolingian age, only occasional references to the work are found. Boethius, another ardent Ciceronian, occasionally echoes it in his *Consolation of Philosophy*; the *Formula honestae uitae* of Martin of Braga (*c.*520–80) discusses the four virtues round which Cicero structures the first book of *De officiis* (some scholars, however, argue against direct consultation of Cicero, claiming a lost work of Seneca's as Martin's direct source); and the Venerable Bede (*c.*673–735) is known to have copied excerpts from the work.

The Carolingian renaissance laid the groundwork for the increasing popularity of *De officiis* in the high Middle Ages. It was copied at several centres in both France and Germany. Lupus of Ferrières (805–62), the leading humanist of the age, procured a copy from Tours to add to his monastic library; the western Frank Hodoard laid claim to the title of the leading Ciceronian of the age by appending to his celebrated *florilegium* (anthology) extracts from several of Cicero's philosophical works, including the *De officiis*.[39]

By the early twelfth century the study of ethics was becoming a central concern in a society deeply troubled by the evidences of financial and sexual corruption both within and outside the Church, and by the violence pervading western society. Ethical texts were increasingly incorporated into the curriculum of the seven liberal arts in the cathedral schools and those of the regular canons. It is true that they continued the old Roman tradition of pedagogy, so that the teaching laid more emphasis on the Latinity than on the significance of the content. But Roman writers like Horace and Quintilian had stressed the importance of such literary study for the inculcation of morality, so that the addition to the curriculum of *De officiis* as

---

[39] For Lupus Servatus, M. L. W. Laistner, *Thought and Letters in Western Europe*, *A.D. 500–900* (Ithaca, NY, 1957), 255. For Hadoard, Manitius, *Gesch. d. lat. Literatur des Mittelalters*[2] (Munich 1955), 479.

prescribed, for example, by Alexander Neckham at Cirencester had more than a purely literary significance.[40]

One of the most intriguing adaptations in the twelfth century of the *De officiis* is the *Moralis philosophia de honesto et utili* of Hildebert of Lavardin (1056–1133). Hildebert, earlier bishop of Le Mans and later archbishop of Tours, was the leading literary figure of the day and an accomplished poet. His treatise is closely based on the structure of *De officiis*. His *Quaestio I* discusses the honourable under its four main subheadings as in Cicero, but preferring *temperantia* rather than 'the fitting' as the fourth. In *Quaestio II* he ranks the four virtues in order of their importance, diverging from Cicero by putting temperance first and prudence last. In *Quaestio III* he analyses the useful, in *IV* he compares the things that are useful, and in *V* he discusses 'the war between the useful and the honourable', closely adhering to Cicero's judgements throughout. But two features make his treatment distinctive among its more prosaic contemporaries. First, he glosses the Ciceronian themes with apposite quotations from Terence, Horace, Lucan, Sallust, and Seneca, as well as from later authors, thereby demonstrating his wide knowledge of Roman literature. Second, at the close of the prose-treatise he appends a lengthy composition in elegiac couplets which in effect is reduplication of the main lines of Cicero's treatise in verses. No more impressive demonstration of the twelfth-century renaissance of Classical learning can be imagined.[41]

Peter Abelard (1079–1142) was the first twelfth-century philosopher to introduce the writings of secular authorities into moral theology; he was 'the first to put the human virtues on the theological map'. In his *Dialogue between a Philosopher, a Jew, and a Christian*, which he presented as a dream-sequence, the Philosopher praises Abelard as one of the few scholars who can combine the insights of secular wisdom with knowledge of Judaic law and Christian revelation. In the discussion of virtue which follows, there is a division between the four categories of prudence, justice, courage, and temperance as in Cicero's treatment in the first Book. These had been briefly analysed by the youthful Cicero in his *De inventione* (2. 53 ff.),

---

[40] See D. E. Luscombe, 'Twelfth-century Ethics', in his edition of *Peter Abelard's Ethics* (Oxford 1971), pp. xvff.

[41] For Hildebert's treatise, see *PL* 171, 1007 ff.

a work widely read in the twelfth century; it is therefore possible that this rather than *De officiis* is Abelard's source. The *Ethics* of Abelard, being concerned more narrowly with problems of Christian morality and notably with the thesis that intention rather than performance makes an act good or evil, does not turn to Cicero for guidance.[42]

The school of Chartres was especially prominent in such ethical discussion; a work entitled *Moralium dogma philosophorum*, attributed (but dubiously) to William of Conches (*c.*1080–1154) gained wide currency, being translated into the vernaculars later in the century. In essence it is a *florilegium* of biblical and philosophical texts, the latter including extracts from *De officiis*; its purpose was to teach summarily the ethics of Cicero and Seneca, focusing especially on the relationship between the honourable and the useful. Another substantial analysis of Cicero's central thesis that the honourable and the useful are identical is found in the writings of John of Salisbury, a former pupil of both Peter Abelard and William of Conches. John's *Policraticus*, a disquisition on government divided between criticism of the *mores* of contemporary courts (Books 1–6) and an exhortation to virtue (Books 7–8), discusses the four cardinal virtues in the second part of the work. A celebrated theme in the *Policraticus* is the justification of tyrannicide, of which John is conventionally regarded as the first medieval apologist. Cicero had laid great emphasis upon this in justification of the assassination of Julius Caesar; in this treatise John writes: 'It is not merely lawful, but even right and just to slay a tyrant' (3. 15). The topic is resumed at greater length in Book 8 (17–23), where John qualifies his earlier adhesion to the Ciceronian thesis with arguments from moral theology.

Alan of Lille (*c.*1128–1203), the philosopher-poet whose *Anti-claudianus* and *De planctu Naturae* reflect his impressive range of Latin learning, wrote in the 1170s a treatise entitled *On Vices and Virtues and the Gifts of the Holy Spirit*. As the title indicates, Alan here discusses the relationship between the cardinal virtues which he found treated in *De officiis* and the Christian virtues deriving from Isaiah and other biblical sources. His conclusion is that the cardinal virtues are not necessarily inferior to the biblical virtues; everything depends on the use to which they are put. More tangentially, the influence of *De officiis* is observable in the satirical work of Jean de

---

[42] On Abelard and Cicero, Luscombe, pp. xxvff.

Hanville. His *Architrenius* ('The Archweeper'), composed about
1184, describes how a weak-willed youth complains of human infirm-
ities. He determines to seek out Lady Nature to lay his complaint
before her; en route he visits a brothel, a house of gluttony, and the
bustle of Paris. When he presents himself before Lady Nature, she
bestows on him the figure of Moderation to be his wife. In the course
of his pilgrimage he is given wholesome advice by various Greek and
Roman sages. Prominent among them is Cicero, who exhorts him
(6. 11) to avoid the prodigality condemned in the *De officiis* (1. 42 ff.).
The influence of Cicero's treatise can be seen at other points of the
poem. The ever-widening circulation of *De officiis* at this time is
reflected in its inclusion in the encyclopaedic composition of the
Dominican Vincent of Beauvais (*c.* 1190–1264). The section entitled
Speculum doctrinae contains extracts from it, and the *Speculum
historiale* includes a summary of it.

But perhaps the most obvious manifestation of the popularity of
De officiis among the schoolmen of the twelfth and thirteenth centuries is its frequent appearance in the *Summa Theologiae* of Thomas
Aquinas. Aquinas was heir to a series of earlier disquisitions on the
virtues, including the *Summa de bono* of his teacher Albertus Mag-
nus, the *Summa de virtutibus* of his fellow-Dominican Guillaume
Peyraut, and the *Summa de bono* of Philip the Chancellor. All these
scholastics had exploited Cicero's philosophical writing, so that
some of Aquinas' citations may have been obtained at second hand.
Aquinas subordinated Cicero and his other Latin sources (notably
Seneca and Macrobius) to his main authority Aristotle ('The
Philosopher'), whose work had been made available in Latin translation by Grosseteste; none the less, *De officiis* occupies a prominent
place in this section of the *Summa*.[43]

Before turning to the four cardinal virtues individually, Aquinas
considered the nature of virtue in general. Here *De officiis* is cited in
two articles, first in his observation that the virtues overlap with each
other, and second in discussion of when it is licit to abandon
community-affairs in order to turn to divine observance. In his
analysis of the individual virtues, he finds nothing germane to his

---

[43] For Aquinas' formative predecessors, see R. A. Gauthier, *Magnanimité* (Paris 1951) ch. 5.
The *Summa Theologiae* is most conveniently consulted in the 60-volume Blackfriars ed. (Latin
and English).

discussion in Cicero's brief account of wisdom/prudence, but *De officiis* is cited several times in Aquinas' treatment of justice. He quotes Cicero's definition, repeats his observation that men are called good when they are just, and cites also Cicero's definition of beneficence. Later, Cicero's cautionary words about lavish giving, and on the importance of keeping promises made to an enemy, are quoted. But the most interesting of these citations under justice concern the morality of buying and selling: Aquinas quotes with approval Cicero's condemnation of deceitful practices when defects in a vendor's wares are concealed.[44]

In Aquinas' discussion of courage, the *De officiis* does not initially loom large, though he cites Cicero's observation that civil achievements are often greater than those in war; he also quotes approvingly the view that justice ranks higher as a virtue than courage. But when magnanimity as part of courage is the focus, Cicero's treatment becomes much more prominent. Aquinas quotes the statements that magnanimity is the quality of a brave man, that freedom from anxiety is a mark of magnanimity, that the magnanimous man despises externals; he also cites the less endearing qualities where Caesar was in Cicero's mind, that the magnanimous man seeks to dominate the political arena, and that he covets personal glory.[45]

When Cicero turned to the fourth subdivision of the honourable, he substituted Panaetius' 'the fitting' for the traditional virtue of temperance, though he associated it more closely with temperance than with the earlier three virtues. Aquinas reverts to temperance, but responds to Cicero's incorporation of the aesthetic aspect by harnessing citations from the *De officiis* to underline this. There are also citations to signify Aquinas' approval of Cicero's identification of the useful with the honourable. Subsequently Aquinas' discussion of temperance is concerned largely with ecclesiastical discipline—for example, the rules for fasting, and again transgressions condemned as sins by the Church; Cicero naturally does not appear in these chapters.[46]

---

[44] For Aquinas' discussion of virtue in general, see *ST* 1a2ae 55–67 (Blackfriars edn. vol. 23); citations of *De officiis* at 61. 4–5 (= *Off.* 1. 68, 1. 71). On justice, 2a2ae 57–122 (Blackfriars edn. vols. 37–41): citations of *De officiis* at 58. 2–3, 11–12; 61. 1; 71. 3; 77. 1, 3 (on buying and selling).

[45] For Aquinas on courage, see *ST* 2a2ae 123–40 (Blackfriars edn. vol. 42); citations of *Off.* are at 123. 5, 12; 129. 5, 7; 131. 2; 132. 2.

[46] Aquinas on temperance, 2a2ae 141–54 (Blackfriars edn. vol. 43); citations of *Off.* at 141. 2, 3; 145. 2.

Dante (1265–1321), who straddles the period between the Middle Ages and the Renaissance, shows close familiarity with the *De officiis*, especially the first book. This is already apparent in the prose works. In the *De monarchia*, in which Dante advocates a universal monarchy dispensing temporal power side by side with the exercise of spiritual authority by the Pope, there are two citations from *De officiis* 1. 38; in the *Convito* there are half-a-dozen quotations, mostly though not all from Book 1. More significant is the influence of Cicero's treatise on the *Divina Commedia*. The *basso Inferno* is divided into the three bottommost circles. Those guilty of violence are consigned to Circle VII; those guilty of deceit, more perverted because they have abused man's gift of reason, are plunged into Circles VIII and IX according to the degree of their guilt. The source is clearly *De officiis* 1. 41: 'There are two ways of inflicting injustice, by force or by deceit . . . Both are utterly alien to human beings, but deceit is the more odious.' As an eminent Dantean scholar observes, 'We unhesitatingly maintain that Dante derived this first fundamental principle of his Classification of Sins from Cicero.' The same critic has identified several other echoes of the *De officiis* in both the *Inferno* and the *Paradiso*.[47]

With the birth of the Italian Renaissance in the fourteenth century, Cicero's influence enters its most glorious era, and the *De officiis* is his most widely read book. The early humanists at Arezzo and Padua immersed themselves in the literature of Classical Rome, with the ambition of adapting both content and form to their own society. Petrarch (1304–74) was the leader in this revival of Classical learning. In his adolescence Cicero (and Virgil) had been his consolation; and when in 1341 he accepted the laurel crown of the poet on the Roman Capitol, he raised the cry of 'Back to antiquity'. But he had been ordained priest at Avignon in 1326, and initially at least his Christian formation retained a powerful hold on him. Thus in his *Secretum* (1342–3), a dialogue between Augustine and himself, he synthesizes Stoic ethics with Christian teaching in such a way as to omit doctrines opposed to Christianity.[48]

[47] For the influence of *Off.* on Dante, see E. Moore, *Studies in Dante: First Series, Scripture and Classical Authors in Dante* (Oxford 1955), 258 ff., 353. The citation is from Moore, *Studies in Dante, Second Series, Miscellaneous Essays* (Oxford 1968), 158.

[48] For Petrarch as heir to the heritage of Classical Rome and notably to Cicero, see R. R. Bolgar, *The Classical Heritage and its Beneficiaries* (Cambridge 1954), ch. 6; also *The Cambridge*

Later, however, he focused his attention more on the secular concerns of political philosophy. Perhaps the most compelling evidence of the influence of *De officiis* is his celebrated letter to Francesco da Carrara (1373). Cicero's discussion of justice had been divided between the principle of not inflicting harm on others and the practice of beneficence. In the first section, the indispensable requirements of justice included keeping one's word and avoiding cruelty and violence. The leader who carries out these injunctions will be loved and admired; affection rather than fear is the key to the acquisition of glory. All these Ciceronian precepts of the *De officiis* are incorporated by Petrarch in his dissertation on the ideal form of princely government.[49]

Petrarch set in train a series of disquisitions on political philosophy inspired by Cicero's treatise. Leonardo Bruno (1369–1444) in his *Laudatio Florentinae urbis* argued that what animated the institutions of the city was the emphasis on republican liberty and the assertion of that *virtus* which is the central concern of the *De officiis*; he cites Cicero's maxim that 'praise for moral excellence (*virtus*) accrues entirely to the active life'. Poggio Bracciolini (1380–1459) in his *De nobilitate* constructs a dialogue between Niccolò Niccoli and the elder Lorenzo de' Medici, in which Lorenzo's espousal of Aristotle's doctrine of nobility is countered by Niccolò's preference for Roman writers, notably 'our Cicero'. The second half of the fifteenth century spawned a large number of manuals of advice to princes on how to govern. Pontano (1426/9–1503) in his *De principe* incorporates Cicero's ideal of decorum, prescribing how a prince should dress, speak, and comport himself (cf. *Off.* 1. 126 ff.). By contrast Machiavelli in his celebrated *Il principe* (1513) diverges from the Ciceronian tradition; he acknowledges that liberality, clemency, inspiring affection, and keeping faith are admirable traits, but stresses that *Realpolitik* finds it necessary to discard them. A willingness to use force on occasion is vital to good government. It is safer to be feared than loved. The successful ruler will not hesitate to

History of Renaissance Philosophy (ed. Charles B. Schmitt and Quentin Skinner, Cambridge 1988), ch. 12. On the *Secretum*, Denys Hay, *The Italian Renaissance* (Cambridge 1962), 82 ff.; Kenelm Foster, *Petrarch, Poet and Humanist* (Edinburgh 1984), 161 ff., arguing for a later date of composition in 1351–3.

[49] The letter to Francesco is in the Basle ed. (1556) of the complete works, (repr. Ridgewood 1964), 421–4; I take this reference from Skinner, *The Cambridge History* (n. 52), 411–12.

break his word if necessary. Machiavelli thus deliberately stood
Cicero's precepts on their heads. His knowledge of *De officiis* is put
to more positive use in his *Discorsi* on Livy's first ten books, chiefly in
the citations of instructive exemplars of effective and of disastrous
government.[50]

Across the Alps, the popularity of the treatise was demonstrated
when it became (with *Paradoxa Stoicorum*) the first printed Latin
text at Mainz in 1465. It was frequently republished thereafter, and
widely read by the German and the French humanists. But the outstanding Ciceronian scholar of the next generation was Erasmus of
Rotterdam (1466/9–1536), who published his own edition with
commentary of the *De officiis* in Paris in 1501. In one of its many
reprints, he enthusiastically praises its 'golden books', which he
describes as 'the godlike fount with its divisions into four streams.
Drinking from it gives you not just fluency of speech, but immortality'. (The praise is repeatedly echoed in the longest of Erasmus'
Colloquies, *The Religious Banquet*, in which the hero Eusebius
remarks: 'Speaking frankly among friends, I cannot read Cicero's
De senectute, De amicitia, De officiis . . . without sometimes kissing the
book and blessing that pure heart.') Another illustrious editor of
De officiis was the German humanist and Lutheran reformer Philip
Melanchthon (1497–1560). After establishing the work in the curriculum of the humanist schools which he founded, he moved into
university teaching, where he devoted virtually all of his Latin
courses to Cicero. A generation later Hugo Grotius (1583–1645), a
graduate of Leiden, composed his celebrated *De iure belli ac pacis* in
three books, a work which draws on several of Cicero's philosophical
works, but above all on *De officiis*.[51]

Meanwhile the England of the humanists Colet and More,
Linacre and Lily was absorbing the masterpieces of Greece and
Rome. The *De officiis* was prescribed reading at the University of
Oxford from 1517, and Ciceronian studies flourished likewise at
Cambridge from the same era. By the second half of the sixteenth
century the treatise formed part of the curriculum in the grammar

---

[50] See Skinner's chapter in *The Cambridge History* (n. 52), 418 ff., 435 ff. On the *Discorsi*, see
MacKendrick, 203.

[51] On Erasmus and Cicero, Dyck, 44 f.; for the citation from *Colloquies*, see *Collected Works
of Erasmus* (Toronto 1997), 192 (and cf. 184). On Melanchthon, Bolgar (n. 52), 344; on
Grotius, MacKendrick, 265 f.

schools as well. Similar developments took place in the Scotland of John Mair and George Buchanan, whose *De iure regni* echoes *De officiis* on the justification of tyrannicide; in the ancient university foundations of St Andrews, Glasgow, and Aberdeen, the work was included in sixteenth-century curricula, and Cicero was read in the schools in Aberdeen, Edinburgh, and Glasgow.[52]

Though seventeenth-century works on political philosophy (notably those of John Milton and John Locke) reflect the continuing influence of *De officiis*, it is in the following century in the Age of the Enlightenment that the treatise gained still higher acclaim. Montesquieu (1689–1755) in his correspondence declares that in his youth 'Le traité *Des offices* m'avait enchanté, et je le prendais pour mon modèle', adding that perusal of Cicero's work induced him to abandon his own plan of writing such a work on *les devoirs*. Montesquieu's celebrated *De l'esprit des lois* is inspired throughout by Cicero's *De legibus* and *De officiis*.[53]

Frederick the Great of Prussia (1712–86), an enthusiastic patron of literature, commissioned Christian Garve to translate *De officiis* into German, and he wrote in glowing terms to his friend Voltaire about the treatise: 'C'est le meilleur ouvrage de morale qu'on ait écrit et qu'on écrira.' Voltaire himself was equally ecstatic: in one of his fictional letters which he ascribes to Memmius, the Epicurean addressee of Lucretius' poem, and which he mischievously claims was 'found by admiral Sheremelot in the Vatican and translated from the Russian rendering by Voltaire', the *De officiis* receives warm praise.[54]

The chief debt which David Hume (1711–76) owes to Cicero is to the latter's *The Nature of the Gods*; but in his *Dialogues concerning Natural Religion* his Catalogue of Virtues derives from the first book of *De officiis*, which, he confesses, 'I had in my eye in all my

[52] See M. L. Clarke, *Classical Education in Britain 1500–1900* (Cambridge 1959), chs. 1–2 for England, ch. 11 (rather thin) for Scotland. For Buchanan's *De iure regni*, I. D. MacFarlane, *Buchanan* (London 1981), 401.

[53] On Cicero and Montesquieu, see Zielinski, *Cicero in Wandel der Jahrdunderte*[4] (Leipzig 1920), 315–16. The citation is from *Correspondance de Montesquieu* (ed. F. Gebelin and A. Morize, Bordeaux 1914), 2. 314, cited by Dyck, 46. For the numerous parallels with Cicero in *De l'esprit*, see MacKendrick, 277.

[54] For the citation of Frederick, see Zielinski, 307, with other similar expressions of enthusiasm. For Voltaire's tribute, see G. Highet, *The Classical Tradition* (Oxford 1949), 328, 655.

reasonings'. His fellow-Scot Adam Smith (1723–90) also draws on the treatise in his *Theory of Moral Sentiments* for his discussion of political regulations based on expediency, and in his *Wealth of Nations*, where he considers enlightened self-interest.[55]

Immanuel Kant (1724–1804) was a good Latin scholar, and hardly needed the help of Christian Garve's translation to grapple with the content of *De officiis*, but Garve's rendering and subsequent published reflections on Cicero's treatise acted as a spur, or rather an irritant, as he developed his own ethical views. In particular he was critical of Cicero's Stoic thesis that ethical norms derive from natural instinct, arguing that they are based on reason rather than nature. None the less, Kant's formulation of the categorical imperative (the behest of conscience as the ultimate moral law) derives in part from the Stoic doctrine of the common humanity which all men share, and which is lent great emphasis in *De officiis* (3. 26).[56]

Fashions in intellectual thought change almost as incomprehensibly as fashions in dress; it would be all too easy to illustrate this from the recent shifts in literary criticism. In the history of philosophy, nothing is so surprising as the fall of Cicero from his high pinnacle in the Age of Enlightenment to the neglect and even contempt which befell him in the nineteenth century. The root cause was the soaring admiration for the history and literature, philosophy and art of fifth- and fourth-century Athens; Hellenistic studies did not receive the same concentration of interest. Roman literature in general was less highly regarded, and Roman philosophy had even less appeal since its focus of interest lay in the Hellenistic schools. In so far as Cicero's works attracted scholarly notice, they were usually visualized as conduit-pipes for the transmission of Greek thought; the synthesis of Greek philosophical ideas with Roman traditional beliefs which they presented attracted the engaged interest of some notable scholars, but they were few. Moreover, Cicero's role as statesman, while the death-throes of the Roman republic were being played out, received withering condemnation from the influential pen of the leading historian of his era, Theodore Mommsen, an admirer of Caesar; his savage criticism extended to condemnation of Cicero's philosophy, on

---

[55] See MacKendrick, 280 ff. on Hume and Adam Smith.
[56] On Cicero and Kant, Dyck, 47–8, MacKendrick 283 ff.

which he was less qualified to pontificate. Study of Cicero's letters and speeches survived in the curricula of all universities and most grammar-schools, because they provided vital testimony for historical study, but the philosophical works were increasingly excluded from the educational establishments and from the libraries of non-specialists.

This unhappy neglect was carried over into the first half of the twentieth century, but more recently there have been encouraging signs of revived interest in Ciceronian philosophy. An important factor has been the upsurge of interest in Hellenistic philosophy in Europe and in North America; since Cicero is a major source (in many areas *the* major source) he is increasingly read and increasingly respected. Moreover, Cicero the statesman has attracted several notable studies in recent years, and they have presented a fairer and more sympathetic assessment of his overall achievement; these studies have included respectful tributes to the philosophical endeavours of a man who in his sixties buckled down to address the perennial questions of the nature of the universe and of man's presence in it.

Summary of the Text

BOOK I. THE HONOURABLE

1-10   *Introduction*: Exhortation to his son to study obligation above all. C. will discuss it under three headings, the honourable, the useful, and possible conflict between the two.

11-17   *Obligations* are imposed by nature's bestowal of reason on humankind. They stem from the honourable, subdivided into four cardinal virtues.

18-19   *Wisdom*: The search for truth is to promote happiness and useful knowledge. It should not divert us from service to the community.

20-41   *Justice* (and Injustice): Two principles: No one should harm another; communal and private interests should both be maintained.
The foundation of justice is good faith.
Two forms of injustice: that inflicted by fear, greed, ambition for power; that passively permitted by abrogation of duty to community.
Some obligations can legitimately be renounced.
Some injustices are committed by legal casuistry.
Obligations in warfare.

42-60   *Beneficence* as adjunct to Justice: Three rules for generous giving. Different categories of human fellowship dictate the order of priorities.

61-92   *Magnanimity*: Courage is 'the virtue which champions the right'.
The power-hungry who practise injustice do not possess magnanimity.
The magnanimous man is indifferent to externals and assumes taxing tasks. He must avoid greed, base pleasures, love of money; be chary of glory.

Retirement from public life licit in certain circumstances.
The military sphere is not more glorious than the civil sphere.
Obligations of political leadership: concern for all sections of the community, affability, a sense of equity, openness to advice.

93–151 *The fitting* and concomitant virtues: It overlaps all four cardinal virtues, but is most relevant to temperance.
Our appetites to be restrained by reason, and to accord with nature.
Our fourfold role dictating our conduct: as humans superior to beasts; as individuals with unique characteristics; as dictated by circumstances; as governed by lifestyles chosen prior to manhood.
Factors affecting our choice of career.
Different obligations of youth, old age, position in society.
Observance of the fitting in dress, deportment, conduct, mentality, and speech (public and private).
The suitable type of residence for a political leader.
Principles of behaviour: reason to govern impulse; careful thought on future projects; maintaining the bearing of a gentleman.
Awareness of the appropriate moment and method of action.
The importance of seeking advice from men of learning and experience.
Suitability and unsuitability of different professions and occupations.

152–60 *Comparison between the virtues, and priority in obligations.*
Service to the community (= justice) takes precedence over knowledge.
But such service is performed by teaching and by writing.
Obligations under temperance occasionally override community interests.
Recipients of obligations in descending order of preference: gods, country, parents, others.

BOOK 2. THE USEFUL

Note on the Text

Since the *De officiis* was first published at Mainz in 1465, at least two dozen notable editions have appeared; since 1969 alone, in spite of the general neglect of the treatise, four have appeared in addition to C. Atzert's 1963 revision of the Teubner text: those of K. Büchner (Latin-German² Zurich 1964), P. Fedeli (Milan 1965), M. Testard (Paris 1965–70), and M. Winterbottom (Oxford 1996). Over the centuries others have published textual observations in monographs and articles, most recently A. R. Dyck in his impressive *Commentary* (Ann Arbor 1993). Though argument still continues over details, the modern editions mentioned, together with the Loeb of W. Miller (1913), present a basically agreed text.

I have benefited from having Winterbottom's edition to hand, and my translation renders his text virtually throughout. As he explains in his Preface, the text rests on a handful of Carolingian manuscripts; they separate into two families. The more reliable of the two comprises four ninth- or tenth-century copies; the other has one tenth-century manuscript which has unfortunately lost many of its leaves, but its readings can be recovered from two fifteenth-century copies, and for the lost section 2. 25–51, from the thirteenth-century Bernensis 104. Somewhat surprisingly, the frequent citations of the treatise by the Church Fathers Lactantius and Ambrose in the fourth century, and by the lexicographer Nonius Marcellus of the same era, add little to the restoration of what Cicero actually wrote.

The major problem which confronts the editor of today is that of possible interpolations. Explanatory glosses made their way into the text by the Carolingian age, in some cases as early as the fourth century. Since Cicero composed his treatise in haste, conservative critics argue that what appear to be banal repetitions can be attributed to slapdash authorship. I have been guided by Winterbottom throughout; excluded passages are indicated in the text by square brackets, and explanations where they seemed desirable have been appended in the notes.

Note on the Translation

The warning words *Traduttore traditore* (or, as Voltaire has it in his *Essay on Epic Poetry*, 'Translations increase the faults of a work, and spoil its beauties') are especially salutary to the reader, no less than to the translator, of a treatise on the history of ideas. The hazards are redoubled in the case of the *De officiis*, since Cicero was adapting for a Roman audience philosophical theory originally composed in Greek.

The problems begin with the title. As noted in the Introduction (§ 3), Cicero was himself criticized for rendering Panaetius' title as *De officiis*. Most modern translators entitle the work *On Duties*, but this expression (especially the plural) has increasingly shaken off its moral sense to mean 'tasks to be performed', or even 'taxes to be paid'; hence my preference for 'obligations'. Problems similarly arise when translating the two central concepts of *honestum* and *utile*. The Loeb translator (whose eloquent version deserves more recognition than modern scholars accord it) renders *honestum* as 'moral goodness', but Cicero was translating the Greek *to kalon*, which bears an aesthetic as well as a moral sense, and connotes a public rather than a private virtue; 'the honourable' expresses this more closely. As for *utile*, the usual rendering is 'expedient', but since that English expression can bear the derogatory sense of 'politic', it is safer to use the prosaic adjective 'useful'.

So far as the four cardinal virtues are concerned, Cicero names the first as 'sapientia et prudentia'. I render *prudentia* (literally 'foresight') as 'prudence' throughout, in the spirit of the definition at 1. 153 of 'knowledge of things to be sought and things to be avoided'. I translate the fourth, *decorum*, again prosaically, as 'the fitting' which seems to me closer than 'propriety' or 'seemliness' in view of the definitions at 1. 97 and 1. 111.

Another area of difficulty lies in Roman politics. I render *boni* as 'good men', though conscious that like *optimates* it often has for Cicero a political nuance, referring to those senatorials of conservative bent who seek what he regards as the good of the state. Again, *populares*, the label attached to politicians who sought by vote-catching the support of the commons, has for Cicero a derogatory ring; hence my rendering 'people-pleasers'. There are useful explanations of other peculiarly Roman concepts in Griffin and Adkins, pp. xliv–xlvii, but the reader is warned of the inadequacy of the English language to render these with close precision.

Select Bibliography

Entries marked with an asterisk contain fuller bibliographies relevant to that section.

I. MODERN EDITIONS AND COMMENTARIES

ATZERT, C. (4th edn., Leipzig 1963).
BÜCHNER, K. (Latin–German, 2nd edn., Zurich 1964).
* DYCK, A. R. (Commentary only, Ann Arbor 1996).
FEDELI, P. (Milan 1965).
GUNERMANN, H. (Latin–German, 2nd edn., Stuttgart 1992).
HOLDEN, H. A. (8th edn., Cambridge 1899).
MILLER, W. (Loeb, Cambridge, Mass. 1913).
SABBADINI, R. (Turin 1889; repr. 1956).
TESTARD, M., 2 vols. (Paris 1965–70).
* WINTERBOTTOM, M. (2nd edn., Oxford 1996).

2. TRANSLATIONS INTO ENGLISH

The first rendering into English was by R. Whytynton ('Bothe in Latyn tongue and englishe', London 1534). Modern translations are:

MILLER, W. (Loeb, Cambridge, Mass. 1913).
HIGGINBOTHAM, J. (California 1967).
EDINGER, H. G. (New York 1974).
GRIFFIN, M. T., and ATKINS, E. M. (Cambridge 1991).

(There are translations of Book 2 in Cicero, *On the Good Life* (Harmondsworth 1971), and of Book 3 in Cicero, *Selected Works* (Harmondsworth 1969), both by Michael Grant.)

3. ARTICLES AND MONOGRAPHS ON *DE OFFICIIS*

ANNAS, J., 'Cicero on Stoic Moral Philosophy and Private Property', in Griffin and Barnes (see § 7).

* DYCK, A., *A Commentary on Cicero's* De officiis (Ann Arbor 1996).
LAKS, A., and SCHOFIELD, M. (eds.), *Justice and Generosity* (Cambridge 1995).
MACKENDRICK, P., *The Philosophical Books of Cicero* (London 1989), 232 ff., 362 ff.
WINTERBOTTOM, M., 'The Transmission of Cicero's *De officiis*', *CQ* 43 (1993), 215 ff.

4. PANAETIUS

Text: VAN STRAATEN, M., *Panaetii Rhodii fragmenta* (3rd edn., Leiden 1962).
ASTIN, A. E., *Scipio Aemilianus* (Oxford 1967).
* ERSKINE, A., *The Hellenistic Stoa: Political Thought and Action* (London 1990).

5. CICERO THE STATESMAN

DOREY, T. A. (ed.), *Cicero* (London 1964).
GELZER, M., *Cicero* (Wiesbaden 1969).
HABICHT, C., *Cicero the Politician* (Baltimore 1990).
* MITCHELL, T. N., *Cicero, the Senior Statesman* (New Haven 1991).
RAWSON, E., *Cicero, a Portrait* (London 1975).
SHACKLETON BAILEY, D. R., *Cicero* (London 1971).
—— *Philippics* (text and trans., Chapel Hill, NC 1986).
STOCKTON, D., *Cicero, a Political Biography* (Oxford 1971).

6. CICERO THE PHILOSOPHER

(Bibliographical Survey in *CW* 51 (1958))
CLARKE, M. L., *The Roman Mind* (London 1954).
DOUGLAS, A. E., 'Cicero the Philosopher', in Dorey (ed.), *Cicero* (London 1964), ch. 6.
—— *Cicero* (*GR* New Surveys No. 2, 2nd edn., Oxford 1978), ch. 5.
FORTENHAUGH, W. W., and STEINMETZ, P. (eds.), *Cicero's Knowledge of the Peripatos* (New Brunswick and London 1969).
GLUCKER, J. P., 'Cicero's Philosophical Affiliations', in J. Dillon and A. A. Long (eds.), *The Question of 'Eclecticism'* (Berkeley 1988), 34 ff.
GRIFFIN, M., 'Cicero and Roman Philosophy', *CAH* ix (2nd edn., Cambridge 1994), 721 ff.

HUNT, H. A. K., *The Humanism of Cicero* (Melbourne 1956).
MACKENDRICK, P., *The Philosophical Books of Cicero* (London 1989).
* POWELL, J. G. F. (ed.), *Cicero the Philosopher* (Oxford 1995).
REID, J. S., edition of *Academica* (London 1885), Introduction.

7. STOIC ETHICS

(Texts in *Long–Sedley, i. 344 ff., ii. 341 ff.)
BARNES, J., 'Antiochus of Ascalon', in Griffin and Barnes (below), 51 ff.
COLISH, M. L., *The Stoic Tradition from Antiquity to the Early Middle Ages*
    (London 1985).
GLUCKER, J., *Antiochus and the Late Academy* (Göttingen 1978).
* GRIFFIN, M., and BARNES, J. (eds.), *Philosophia Togata* (Oxford 1989).
LONG, A. A., *Hellenistic Philosophy* (London 1974), 179 ff.
—— *Stoic Studies* (Cambridge 1996).
RIST, J., *Stoic Philosophy* (Cambridge 1969).
—— (ed.), *The Stoics* (Berkeley 1978).
SANDBACH, F. H., *The Stoics* (London 1975), ch. 3.
SCHOFIELD, M., 'Two Stoic Approaches to Justice', in Laks and Schofield,
    Justice and Generosity (Cambridge 1995), 191 ff.

8. ROMAN CIVIL LAW

BAUMAN, R. A., *Lawyers in Roman Transitional Politics* (Munich 1985).
* CROOK, J. A., *Law and Life of Rome* (London 1967).
GREENIDGE, A. H. J., *The Legal Procedure of Cicero's Time* (Oxford 1901).
WATSON, A., *The Law of Obligations in the Later Roman Republic* (Oxford
    1965).
—— *Law-making in the Later Roman Republic* (Oxford 1974).

9. LATER INFLUENCE

BOLGAR, R. R., *The Classical Inheritance and its Beneficiaries* (Cambridge
    1954).
DYCK, A. R. *Commentary*, 39 ff.
MACKENDRICK, P. *The Philosophical Books of Cicero*, 258 ff.
NELSON, N. E., 'Cicero's *De officiis* in Christian Thought, 300–1300', in *Essays
    and Studies in English and Comparative Literature* (Ann Arbor 1933), 59 ff.

Chronology of Cicero the Philosopher

44	Assassination of Caesar. Increasing dominance of Mark Antony
Sept.–Oct. 44	*First* and *Second Philippics*. Cicero re-emerges into politics
Dec. 43	Proscribed and murdered at instigation of Mark Antony

Cicero

On Obligations

Book One

For a whole year now, Marcus my son, you have been a pupil of   1
Cratippus,* and you have been resident at Athens. So the supreme
authority of both teacher and city should ensure that you are well
grounded in the injunctions and principles of philosophy, for the
first can enrich you by his knowledge, and the second by her examples.* None the less, I think that you should emulate my invariable
practice of combining Latin studies with Greek, for this has served
me well not merely in the study of philosophy but also in the practice
of oratory. In this way you may become fluent equally in both lan-
guages. I think that I myself have rendered signal service to my countrymen in this respect, so that not merely those who are novices in
Greek but also men who are learned in it believe that they have made
some progress in both learning and discernment.*

So your apprenticeship to the outstanding philosopher of our day   2
will continue—yes, it will continue for as long as you so wish. That
desire should last as long as you remain satisfied with your progress.*
At the same time, in reading my works—my views do not differ
markedly from those of the Peripatetics, for both they and I aspire to
be followers of Socrates and Plato*—you must exercise your own
judgement on the content without pressure from me. But your
scrutiny of them will certainly enhance your knowledge of how to
express yourself in Latin. Please do not think that I am boasting
when I say this. I yield to many in knowledge of the practice of philosophy, but it is the particular province of the orator to speak with
relevance, clarity, and elegance, and since I have spent my life seeking to do this, any claim of mine on this score seems in some degree
justifiable.

This is why I strongly urge you, my dear Cicero,* to read with care   3
not only my speeches but also these philosophical works which now
number almost as many.* The speeches are admittedly more force-
fully expressed, but this level and restrained type of utterance
should also be cultivated. I note that no Greek has so far worked in

both fields and succeeded in developing to perfection both the genre of forensic utterance and the dispassionate mode of argumentation, unless perhaps Demetrius of Phalerum* can be so categorized. He is precise in argument, but lacks vigour as an orator; still, he is agreeable to listen to, so that you can identify him as a pupil of Theophrastus.* But it is up to others to pronounce on the extent of my success in both genres; at any rate I have tried my hand at both.

4   I certainly believe that if Plato had opted to practise forensic oratory, he could have spoken with the greatest dignity and fluency. Likewise had Demosthenes memorized and chosen to express the doctrines which he had learnt from Plato, he could have achieved this with polish and brilliance. I take a similar view of Aristotle and Isocrates;* each was absorbed in his own discipline, and despised the other.

Since I have decided to address a few words to you here and now, and more fully later on, I intend to begin with the subject most suited to both your years and my paternal authority. Philosophy embraces many weighty and profitable issues discussed by philosophers meticulously and at length, but the injunctions on obligations which they have passed on appear to have the widest application; for there is no aspect of life public or private, civic or domestic, which can be without its obligation, whether in our individual concerns or in relations with our neighbour. Honourable behaviour lies entirely in the performance of such obligations, and likewise base conduct lies in neglecting them.*

5   This issue is in fact the common concern of all philosophers. Would anyone presume to claim the title of philosopher if he failed to pass on any teachings on obligation? Yet several schools undermine obligation in general by their theories of the supreme good and the supreme evil.* The philosopher who claims that the highest good has no connection with virtue, and measures it by his own interests rather than by what is honourable, cannot cultivate friendship, justice, or generosity so long as he remains consistent in his views, and is not prevailed upon by his own better nature. And further, the person who pronounces pain to be the greatest evil cannot possibly be brave, and he that accounts pleasure the highest good cannot be self-controlled.*

6   These findings are so clear-cut that there is no need to press the case, though in fact I have argued them elsewhere.* So if such

schools were to claim consistency, they would have nothing to offer about obligation. Indeed, only those who maintain that right behaviour alone is worth seeking, or those who claim that it should be our chief aim for its own sake, can enunciate principles of obligation which are steady and unshifting and inherent in nature. So instruction on obligation is the prerogative of Stoics, Academics, and Peripatetics, since the views of Aristo, Pyrrho, and Erillus have for long been discredited.* None the less, they would have the right to discuss obligation from their own viewpoint if only they had left open some choice between things, thus allowing some means of identifying what obligation is. So at this particular time in my enquiry I follow the Stoics chiefly, not translating them, but following my usual procedure of drawing from their wells as much as, and in whatever way, my judgement and inclination dictate.*

So as my entire discussion is to be about obligation, I should like   7
to begin by first defining it; I am surprised that Panaetius* neglected to do this. For every rational approach to instruction on any subject ought to begin with a definition,* to ensure that people know what the topic under discussion is.

All investigation of obligation is twofold. At one level it refers to the highest aim among goods, and at another to the moral guidance which can shape our daily lives in all their aspects. Representative of the first enquiry are questions such as whether all obligations are absolute, whether one takes precedence over another, and the like. As for obligations for which principles of guidance are laid down, they are relevant to the highest aim among goods, but less obviously so, because they seem to apply rather to the way we regulate our mundane lives. I am to elaborate upon these in the books that follow.

Obligation can be subdivided in another way, into what we may   8
call 'intermediate' and 'absolute'. I think that we are to term absolute obligation as 'the right', for the Greeks call it *katorthoma*, whereas they use the word *meson* for ordinary obligation.* These terms they define as follows: 'absolute' obligation they define as what is right, whereas they use the expression 'intermediate' obligation for when a plausible reason can be given for undertaking some action.

Thus in Panaetius' view three questions arise when considering a   9
course of action. People are first exercised whether what they are contemplating is right or reprehensible, and often as they ponder this their minds are drawn to contrary opinions. Second, they

investigate or debate whether or not the course which they have in mind makes their lives beneficial or agreeable, enhances their control over possessions and augments their resources, and furthers the wealth or power by which they can advance themselves and their circle: this line of thought is entirely concerned with the useful. The third issue which gives them pause arises when what is apparently useful seems to conflict with what is right; for when the useful seems to pull them towards itself and rectitude seems to draw them back in its direction, the mind as it reflects is tugged in opposite directions, and this makes for troubled indecision.

10   In such classification of a topic,* the most grievous fault is to leave something out, and in Panaetius' discussion two points have been overlooked. We usually ask ourselves not only whether some action is honourable or base, but also, when there are two honourable courses of action, which is the more honourable; and again, if two useful courses lie open to us, which is the more useful. So what Panaetius considered to be a threefold enquiry we find we must separate into five parts. The first issue, then, concerns what is honourable, but it comprises two questions. Similarly the useful has two aspects. Finally, we must discuss the comparison between the honourable and the useful.

11   Our starting-point* is that all species of living creatures are endowed by nature with the capacity to protect their lives and their persons, to avoid things likely to harm them, and to seek out and procure all life's necessities such as food, hidden lairs, and the like. Again, all living creatures share the instinct to copulate for the procreation of offspring, and once these are begotten, they show a degree of concern to look after them. But between man and beast there is this crucial difference: the beast under sense-impulses applies itself only to what lies immediately before it, with quite minimal awareness of past and future, whereas man is endowed with reason, which enables him to visualize consequences, and to detect the causes of things.* He is not unaware of what precedes things, what we may call their antecedents. He compares parallel cases, and future events he attaches to and links with those of the present. Without effort he visualizes the course of his whole life, and prepares the necessities to live it out.

12   Nature also joins individuals together, enabling them by the power of reason to share a common language and life. She especially infuses

in them surpassing love for their offspring; she constrains men to aspire to gatherings and meetings, and to take part in them, and for these reasons to lay in adequate supplies of clothing and food, not merely for themselves but also for their wives, children, and the others dear to them whom they should protect. Such responsibility further kindles men's spirits, and develops them for the performance of tasks.

Especially unique to man is the search and scrutiny into truth.* This is why, when we are free from unavoidable business and concerns, we are eager to see, hear, and learn things. We reckon that the acquisition of knowledge of hidden or remarkable features is necessary for the happy life. This fact enables us to appreciate that what is true, simple, and genuine is what is most suited to man's nature. Associated with this eagerness for the vision of the truth is a kind of aspiration for leadership, so that the mind well fashioned by nature is willing to obey only a moral guide or teacher or commander who issues just and lawful orders for our benefit. From such an attitude greatness of soul develops, and indifference to purely human concerns. **13**

However, it is no trivial dispensation of nature and reason which makes man alone of living creatures aware of the nature of order and propriety and due measure in deeds and words. The result is that no other creature shares his awareness of the beauty, charm, and harmonious structure which lie before our eyes; and nature and reason, transferring this by analogy from eyes to mind, judge and ensure that such beauty, regularity, and order are to be maintained much more in our designs and actions. Their concern is to do nothing which is unsightly or degenerate, to do or to contemplate nothing capricious in all our actions and beliefs. **14**

These are the qualities which kindle and fashion that honourable conduct which we seek. Even if it were not accorded acclaim, it would still be honourable, for we rightly call it praiseworthy by nature even if no one praises it.

It is here, Marcus my son, that you discern the very shape and countenance, so to say, of the honourable. In Plato's words,* 'If wisdom could be seen with the eyes, it would arouse astonishing feelings of love for it.' All that is honourable emerges from one or other of four sources. It is found in the perception and intelligent awareness of what is true; or in safeguarding the community by assigning to each individual his due, and by keeping faith with compacts made; or in the greatness and strength of a lofty and unconquered spirit; or in **15** the order and due measure by which all words and deeds reflect an underlying moderation and self-control.

Though these four virtues are bound up and interconnected with each other, certain types of obligation arise from each of them individually. Thus the first of the four divisions, to which we allocate wisdom and prudence, embraces the search and scrutiny into the
16 truth, which is the peculiar function of that virtue; for the more clearly a person sees the essential truth of a situation, and the keener and swifter is his ability to grasp and explain its logic, the more prudent and wise he is commonly and justifiably regarded. So truth is, so to say, the matter which is the concern of this virtue, which is to handle it and be associated with it.

17 The task of providing and maintaining the essentials for living out our lives falls to the three remaining virtues. This is to ensure that the community and its cohesion are preserved, and that the high quality and nobility of spirit should be apparent both in building up resources and in promoting the interests of our families and ourselves, and much more important, in viewing these matters with indifference. An ordered existence, holding fast to principles, restrained behaviour, and such like are qualities demanding not merely mental application but some physical action as well, for by applying a certain measure and order to everyday activities we shall maintain decency and decorum.

18 Of the four heads under which we have divided the nature and significance of proper behaviour, the first, namely knowledge of the truth, comes closest to the essentials of human nature, for we are all impelled and attracted towards a desire for discovery and knowledge. We think it a fine thing to excel in this, whereas we regard it as wicked and shameful to relapse into error or ignorance or being duped. In this natural and honourable activity there are two faults which we must avoid. First, we must not regard as known things that are unknown, and give rash credence to them. The person who wishes to avoid this fault—and everyone should wish to avoid it—
19 will take time and trouble to reflect on such matters. There is a second fault to which some people fall victim: they devote too much energy and effort on matters which are not merely arcane and taxing, but also unnecessary.*

If these faults are avoided, trouble and care lavished on honourable subjects worth pursuing will rightly win praise. For example, I am told of Gaius Sulpicius' researches on astronomy, and I have personal acquaintance with Sextus Pompeius who works on geometry:* many people study dialectic, and more still devote themselves to civil law. These disciplines are all relevant to the search for the truth. But to be diverted from public service by enthusiasm for research is denial of one's duty.* This is because praise for moral excellence accrues entirely to the active life. However, a break from it often occurs, and many opportunities for a return to study present themselves. Moreover, the mind is never at rest, and its activity can preoccupy us with the thirst for knowledge even when we do not work at it. But all our thinking, all our mental activity will be directed either to plans for worthy projects relevant to the good and happy life, or to studies which advance our knowledge and learning. These, then, are my thoughts on the first source of obligation.

So far as the three remaining heads are concerned, the broadest 20 issue affecting them is the means by which the adhesion of members to the community, and what we may call their communal life, may be preserved. Two elements are involved in this: the first is justice, that brightest adornment of virtue, the means by which men gain the title of *boni*;* and the second is its close companion beneficence, which we may also label kindness or generosity.*

The primary function of justice is to ensure that no one harms his neighbour unless he has himself been unjustly attacked. Its second concern is that communal property should serve communal interests, and private property private interests.

Private property has been endowed not by nature, but by long- 21 standing occupancy in the case of those who settled long ago on empty land; or by victory in the case of those who gained it in war; or by law or bargain or contract or lot. As a result, the territory of Arpinum is said to belong to the Arpinates, and that of Tusculum to the Tusculans;* and the allocation of private possessions is of the same order. So since what was by nature common property has passed into the ownership of individuals, each should retain what has accrued to him, and if anyone else seeks any of it for himself, he will transgress the law of the community.

But as Plato so nobly put it,* we are not born for ourselves alone, 22 for our country claims a share in our origin, and our friends likewise; and again, as the Stoics have it,* all that the earth produces is created for men's use, and men have been begotten for men's sake to be of service to each other. Therefore we should follow nature as our guide in this sense of making available shared benefits by exchange of our obligations, by giving and receiving, and in this way binding the community and its individuals closely together by our skills, our efforts, and our talents.

23   The foundation of justice is good faith, in other words truthfully abiding by our words and agreements. So though some may find this rather difficult to accept, let us steel ourselves to imitate the Stoics in their zealous pursuit of etymologies, and accept that good faith (*fides*) is so called because what is promised becomes fact (*fiat*).*

So far as injustice goes, there are two kinds: the injustice of those who inflict it, and that done by those who do not protect victims from injury when they have the power to do so. When a person fired by anger or other violent feeling launches an unjust attack upon another, he is, it seems, laying hands on a fellow-member of the community; and the man who does not repel or oppose some wrong when he can do so, is as much at fault as if he were abandoning

24   parents, friends, or country. Observe that injuries purposefully inflicted to do harm often stem from fear, when a man who contemplates harming another fears that if he does not do so, he will suffer some disadvantage. But for the most part men who purpose to inflict injustice do so to obtain something which they are keen to have. Greed is the most widespread motive for this vice.

25   Men hanker after riches both to obtain life's necessities and to enjoy pleasures. But those who have keener ambitions channel their desire for money towards accumulating resources and dispensing favours. For example, not long ago Marcus Crassus observed* that for one seeking to be pre-eminent in the state, no amount of money was enough if the interest on it could not maintain an army. Sumptuous trappings and an elegant, costly lifestyle also attract. These are the factors which have caused longing for money to be insatiable. But accumulating property when it does harm to no one is not to be condemned. However, committing injustice thereby is always to be avoided.

26   But most men when fired by desire for military commands, high offices, or glory totally forget the claims of justice. Hence those words of Ennius:*

No sacrosanct alliance,
And no faith either, from a king upon his throne.

These lines have a wider application. Once you have a situation in which more than one person cannot be pre-eminent, such a power-struggle usually ensues that it becomes most difficult to maintain a 'sacrosanct alliance'. The shameless conduct of Gaius Caesar* recently illustrated this: he undermined all laws, divine and human, in order to establish that dominance which his erroneous belief had targeted for himself. What is distressing in this situation is that the ambition for civil office, military command, power and glory is usually nursed by men of the greatest and most outstanding talent.* So greater precautions must be taken to ensure that no wrong in such circumstances is committed.

In all cases of injustice, there is a world of difference between   27
wrong committed under emotional stress, usually short-lived and momentary, and that which is purposeful and carefully thought out. Incidents occurring as the result of some sudden emotion are less serious than plans carried through with careful thought and preparation.

So much for the type of injustice which is inflicted.

Often there is more than one reason for the failure to defend a   28
person in fulfilment of an obligation. People are reluctant to incur enmity or trouble or expense; and again, indifference, laziness, passivity, or concentration on some personal pursuits or activities is a hindrance, so that they allow persons whom they should protect to go without their support. We should ask ourselves whether Plato's remark* about philosophers—that they are just because they search for the truth, and despise and have no time for the burning ambitions which cause most men to battle it out with each other—is not actually adequate. True, they do practise the first type of justice in not harming anyone by inflicting injustice upon them, but they fall into the other trap, when their zeal for learning proves an obstacle, causing them to abandon the persons whom they should defend. So Plato's view is that philosophers will not even enter public life unless compelled to do so. It would, however, be more reasonable to undertake such service voluntarily; for right action such as this is just only if performed voluntarily.

There is another class of persons who through commitment to   29
family concerns or because of some repugnance for the human race claim that they are minding their own business, seemingly not harming anyone. Such people refrain from committing the first type of

injustice, but they are guilty of the second by becoming deserters from the life of the community, for they contribute none of their pursuits, efforts or skills to the common weal.

We have now defined the two types of injustice, and have appended to them the causes of each; and earlier we established the means by which justice is maintained. So now we shall be able readily to assess what our obligation is at any particular juncture, unless our self-absorption becomes excessive—for worrying about the

30   interests of others is laborious. It is true that Chremes, the character in Terence,* 'thinks that there is nothing human that does not concern him', but we keep our eyes and minds trained more closely on our own good and evil fortunes than on those of the rest of the world, which we view as though from a great distance. The result is that we judge other people's problems differently from our own. So the advice of those who counsel us to hold off when uncertain whether an action is right or wrong is sound. Fair dealing casts its own clear light, whereas uncertainty indicates thinking that you may do wrong.

31   But occasions often arise when acts which seem wholly worthy of the just person and the man we label 'good' change their character, and become just the opposite. Sometimes it becomes justifiable to sideline and not to proceed with the intention to restore a deposit,* or to keep a promise, or to do what truth and good faith demand. It is appropriate to hark back to those principles of justice which I laid down at the beginning; first, that no person should suffer harm, and second, observance of the common good. When these principles are affected by circumstances, our obligation is likewise affected, and

32   does not always stay the same. It can happen that some promise or agreement turns out to be prejudicial to the recipient of the promise, or to the person who offered it.

Take an example from one of the classic stories. If Neptune had not carried out the promise which he made to Theseus, the king would not have been bereaved of his son Hippolytus. The story goes that as the third of his three wishes,* Theseus in a fit of anger prayed for the death of Hippolytus, and when his wish was granted, he was plunged into overwhelming grief. So on the one hand, promises which are not advantageous to the recipients should not be kept; and on the other, if fulfilment of a promise which you have made is more harmful to you than advantageous to the recipient, you do not contravene your obligation if the greater good is preferred to the lesser. Take this example: if you have arranged to speak on some person's behalf in court on some pressing issue, and in the meantime your son falls seriously ill, it would not be a breach of obligation to fail to implement your promise. In fact, the recipient of the promise would be in breach of his obligation if he complained that you had let him down. Or again, it is obvious to everyone that promises need not be kept when the person making them has been intimidated, or has been misled by trickery. Usually such promises are annulled by the praetor's right of ruling, and occasionally by the laws.

In addition, injustices often occur through a species of trickery 33 which takes the form of an extremely clever but wilful interpretation of the law, and this has given rise to the hackneyed cliché, 'Give the law its head, and injustice rules instead.'* Many wrongs of this kind are committed also in the life of politics. A notorious case* was that of the general who made a thirty-day truce with enemies and then ravaged their territory by night, claiming that the truce covered the days but not the nights. And if the story is true (I have it only on hearsay), the behaviour of a fellow-Roman, Quintus Fabius Labeo* or whoever it was, cannot be sanctioned either. They say that he was appointed by the senate to act as arbitrator between the citizens of Nola and of Naples in a boundary dispute, and that after reaching the area, he discussed the matter separately with each side, urging them not to be greedy and grasping in their negotiations, and to agree to pull back rather than to push forward with their claims. Both sides did this, so that a fair-sized stretch of territory was left unoccupied between them. He accordingly laid down the boundaries of the dis-putants as they had stipulated, and the residue of the land between them he assigned to the Roman people. That in fact was chicanery, not adjudication, and therefore such sharp practice should be avoided whatever the circumstances.

Certain obligations must be met even when they are owed to persons who have wronged us, for revenge and punishment have their due limits. It is perhaps sufficient if the aggressor shows remorse for his wrongdoing, so that he refrains from acting similarly in future, and other people too then become less ready to commit such injustice.

At the level of state policy, rights in warfare must be scrupulously 34 observed. There are two types of military dispute, the one settled by negotiation and the other by force. Since the first is characteristic of human beings and the second of beasts, we must have recourse to the 35 second only if we cannot exploit the first. It therefore follows that wars should be undertaken for the one purpose of living peaceably without suffering injustice;* and once victory is won, those who have not indulged in cruel monstrosities in the war should be spared. In this spirit our ancestors went so far as to confer citizenship on the Tusculans, Aequi, Volsci, Sabines and Hernici, whereas they utterly destroyed Carthage and Numantia. I would not have sanctioned the destruction of Corinth,* but I believe that there was a particular reason for it, notably its favourable location and the danger that this might at some time be an incitement to war. My opinion, for what it is worth, is that we should always aim at a peace which does not contain the seeds of future treachery. If this policy of mine had been followed, we should still have some sort of republic, even if one far from ideal, whereas now we have none.*

Consideration should also be shown to those who have been subdued by force, and men who lay down their arms and seek the sanctuary of our generals' discretion should be granted access to them, even if a battering ram has shattered their city wall.* In this respect justice has been observed so scrupulously by fellow Romans that those very men who conquered cities or nations in war and then admitted them to their protective discretion, subsequently became their patrons in accordance with ancestral custom.*

36 The procedure for fair dealing in war has been most scrupulously committed to paper in the fetial code of the Roman people.* This code can help us understand that no war is just unless it is preceded by a demand for satisfaction, or unless due warning is given first, and war is formally declared.

[The commander Popilius was a provincial governor, and Cato's son was serving as a raw recruit in his army. Popilius decided to discharge one legion, and as Cato's son was serving in it, he was demobilized as well. But the boy was keen on fighting, and he remained with the army. So Cato wrote to Popilius stating that if he permitted his son to stay in the army, he should make him swear a second oath of allegiance, for he had forfeited his earlier rights, and could not join battle with the enemy. Such was the degree of punctiliousness observed in initiating warfare.]*

37 There is in existence a letter of Marcus Cato the elder to his son

Marcus,* in which he writes that he has heard that the boy had been discharged by the consul when serving as a soldier in Macedonia in the war with Perseus. He accordingly warns him to be sure not to engage in battle, stating that a non-soldier has no right to come to grips with the enemy.

A further point which comes to mind is that a man who strictly speaking was an enemy (*perduellis*) was earlier called a *hostis*. The sombre reality was thus softened by understatement, for our ancestors used the word *hostis* for the person whom we now call an alien (*peregrinus*). Phrases in the Twelve Tables* demonstrate this: 'on a day fixed for trial with an alien' (*cum hoste*), and again, 'In dispute with an alien (*aduersus hostem*), ownership is perpetual.' Can anything be milder than the use of so clement a term for an opponent in war? However, the course of time has now given the word *hostis* a harsher connotation; having lost the sense of alien, it remained specifically to describe an armed enemy.

When wars are fought for dominion to the bitter end, and glory 38 is sought in them, the same underlying motives ought to prevail which a little earlier I described as just causes of wars. But wars in which the glory sought is for empire* must be conducted with less harshness. Take this parallel: a conflict with a fellow-citizen is one thing if he is a personal enemy, but another if he is a rival for office, for in the second case the struggle is for office and distinction, but in the first for very life and reputation. War with the Celtiberi and with the Cimbri was the equivalent of conflict with personal enemies, and thus was fought not for supremacy but for survival, whereas we fought with Latins, Sabines, Samnites, Carthaginians and Pyrrhus for extension of empire. True, Carthaginians broke treaties, and Hannibal was cruel, but the others behaved more justly. So there is that celebrated speech of Pyrrhus* about the restoration of prisoners:

> No gold I ask for, no reward are you to give.
> Let each of us as warriors, not trafficers
> In war, with steel, not gold, determine life or death.
> Which one of us Dame Fortune destines for the crown,
> And what the end she brings, let us by valour seek.
> Hear too this word: those brave men whom war's fate has spared
> I too am minded both to spare and liberate.
> Take them; I give you them. The great gods will it so.

This is a truly regal utterance, one worthy of the race of the Aeacidae.*

39   Moreover, such pledges as individuals have made to the enemy under pressure of circumstances they must even then faithfully keep, as was the case in the First Punic War. Regulus* was captured by the Carthaginians, and when he was sent to Rome to negotiate an exchange of prisoners and had sworn to return, on his arrival he first proposed to the senate that prisoners should not be restored, and then, when relatives and friends sought to detain him, he preferred to return to face execution rather than to break his word which he had pledged to the enemy.

40   [In the Second Punic War, following the battle of Cannae Hannibal sent ten captives to Rome, having first exacted from them an oath that they would return if they did not succeed in ransoming his men who had been captured. Because they failed to abide by their oath, the censors reduced all of them to the rank of non-voting citizens for the rest of their lives. They punished similarly a man who had incurred guilt by crafty conformity with his oath. After Hannibal had given him leave to quit the camp, he returned a little later with the excuse that he had forgotten something. When he left the camp a second time, he believed that he was released from his oath, as indeed he was according to the letter, but not the spirit. What must always be kept in mind when honouring a pledge is the intention, not the form of words.

Our ancestors established a most important precedent of justice towards an enemy when a deserter from Pyrrhus promised the senate that he would kill the king by administering poison to him. The senate and Gaius Fabricius handed the deserter over to Pyrrhus. This was their way of refusing to approve the treacherous murder even of an enemy who was both powerful and an unprovoked aggressor.]*

41   Enough has now been said about obligations in war.

We must remember that justice is to be observed even to the lowliest in society. Slaves represent that lowliest condition and status. The advice of those who recommend that we treat them as hired hands is reasonable enough: make them work, but give them what is their due.*

There are two ways of inflicting injustice, by force or by deceit. Deceit is the way of the humble fox, force that of the lion. Both are utterly alien to human beings, but deceit is the more odious; of all kinds of injustice none is more pernicious than that shown by people who pose as good men at the moment of greatest perfidy. But enough has now been said about justice.

Our next topic as earlier proposed is to be munificence and gen- 42 erosity. Nothing more accords with human nature than this, but it has many pitfalls. We must ensure first that our benevolence does not prove deleterious either to recipients of what will seem to be a kindly gesture, or to any others; second, that such benevolence does not go beyond our means; and third, that it is apportioned to each recipient according to his worth.* Such qualifications are the basis of that just-ice which should be the touchstone of all such transactions. People who bestow favours which harm the individuals whom they are apparently eager to help are to be assessed as ruinous flatterers rather than men of kindness and generosity.

Again, persons who inflict damage on some in order to be gener-ous to others perpetrate the same injustice as if they were to make the property of others their own. There are many, especially if they 43 aspire to distinction and fame, who rob one set of persons in order to be generous to another. They imagine that they will seem to do their friends a good turn if they enrich them by fair means or foul. Such behaviour, however, is so far removed from rightful obligation that nothing can fly more in the face of it. We must therefore ensure that our generosity is such as benefits friends and does harm to no one. So when Lucius Sulla and Gaius Caesar took money from its rightful owners and gave it to outsiders,* such action must not be signalled as generosity, for nothing is generous if it is not also just.

Our second caveat was to ensure that our benevolence does not go 44 beyond our means.* Those who seek to be more generous than their resources allow are guilty in the first place of injustice towards their kin, by transferring to outsiders resources which would more justly have been both bestowed and bequeathed to their relatives. Such generosity often cloaks the desire to plunder and make off with resources unjustly, so as to command sufficient means to bestow largesse. Moreover, it is notable that many people are not so much open-handed by nature as motivated by a sense of vainglory, to appear to do out of kindness many things which seemingly arise out of exhibitionism rather than goodwill. Such pretence is closer to empty pride than to either generosity or honourable conduct.

45   The third condition laid down was that our munificence should take account of men's worth. Here we are to assess the character of the recipient of our kindness, his affection for us, our partnership and association in living, and the obligations which he has previously undertaken in our interest. It is much to be desired that all these qualities be concentrated in him; if all are not in evidence, the more of them there are and the greater their importance, the more weight they will carry with us.

46   Our lives, however, are spent not with men who are perfect and manifestly wise, but with people who at best embody some pale reflection of virtue. So we should acknowledge that no individual should be totally ignored, so long as some glimpse of virtue is perceptible in him. At the same time, we should especially cultivate the person who is notably endowed with the milder virtues of moderation, self-control, and justice; this last we have already discussed at length. I say 'milder' virtues, because if a man is not perfect or wise, a stout heart and a lofty spirit often make him too hot-blooded, whereas those other virtues apparently reside more especially in the good man. So much, then, for attention to character.

47   When persons show us goodwill, our main obligation is to be generous most of all to the one who feels greatest affection for us. Such goodwill, however, we must measure not as teenagers do by intensity of feeling, but rather by its steady and enduring nature.

    If we are in receipt of favours which cause us not to bestow kindness but to reciprocate it, we must take particular pains, for no obli-
48 gation is more pressing than the return of a favour. But if, as Hesiod bids us,* we must if possible repay in greater measure what we have received for our benefit, what are we to do when challenged by some act of kindness unsought? Should we not follow the example of fertile fields, which yield much more than they have received? If indeed we have no hesitation in discharging obligations towards those who we hope will benefit us, what should be our attitude to those who have already shown such kindness? There are two kinds of generosity: the first bestows a kindness, and the second repays it. It is up to ourselves whether we bestow a favour or not, but the failure to repay one is not an option for a good man, so long as he can reciprocate without injustice to anyone.

49   So far as kindnesses received are concerned, we must discriminate between them. Undoubtedly we owe the greatest debt for those that

are greatest. But we must in such cases attach particular weight to the affection, enthusiasm, and goodwill of the donor. Many people bestow any number of favours in a random and ill-considered way, prompted either by affection for the world at large* or by the gust of sudden impulse. Such kindnesses are not to be esteemed as highly as those which have been bestowed with judgement and prolonged thought.

In both granting a kindness and returning a favour, our greatest obligation, all else being equal, is to lend help above all to the person in greatest need. But many do just the opposite. They look to the interests particularly of the man from whom they have the greatest expectations, even if he has no need of their assistance. But the interests of the community and its coherence will best be served if our bounty is bestowed most of all on those most closely connected with us.

It seems necessary, however, to probe deeper into the fundamentals of community and human fellowship ordained by nature. First comes that which we see existing in the fellowship of the whole human race. The bond which unites them is the combination of reason and speech, which by teaching, learning, communicating, debating, and evaluating endears men to each other, and unites them in a kind of natural alliance. This more than anything separates us from the nature of the beasts. We often concede that animals such as horses and lions have courage, but lack justice, fairness, and goodness. This is because they lack reason and speech.*

This is human fellowship in its broadest sense, uniting all men with each other; within it the common ownership of all things which nature has brought forth for men's joint use must be preserved, in the sense that private possessions as designated by statutes and by civil law are to be retained as the laws themselves have ordained, while the rest is to be regarded, in the words of the Greek proverb, as 'all things shared by friends'.* These possessions common to all men are, it seems, of the kind which Ennius applies* to a single instance, but which can be extended to many:

> The friendly soul who shows one lost the way,
> Lights, as it were, another's lamp from his.
> Though he has lit another's, his own still shines.

This one example suffices to teach the lesson that what costs us

52 nothing to give should be bestowed even on a stranger. Arising out of
    this are the general maxims 'Do not prevent access to running
    water', 'Let all who want it take fire from your fire', 'Give honest
    advice to one in doubt'. Such gestures are useful to the recipients,
    and no trouble to the donor, so we should follow these precepts and
    always seek to contribute to the common good. Since, however, the
    resources of individuals are limited, whereas there is a numberless
    crowd of those in need of them, our generosity to one and all must be
    qualified by invoking that conclusion of Ennius, 'his own lamp still
    shines'.* This restriction will leave us with the means to be generous
    to our friends.

53   There is more than one level of human fellowship. Setting aside
    that shared by the entire human race without limit, there is the closer
    link between those of the same race, nation and tongue, which unites
    men intimately. Within this group lies the closer union of those from
    the same city-state,* for such citizens share many things in com-
    mon—a city-centre, shrines, colonnades, streets; their laws, rights,
    courts, and voting privileges; and beyond these, the circles of
    acquaintances and close friends, and the many who have connections
    with each other in public affairs and in business. Closer still is the
    social bond between kindred. Thus we start from the unrestricted
    fellowship of the whole human race, and arrive at this small and con-
    fined group.

54   For since all living creatures share by nature the urge to procreate,
    the primary bond of union lies in marriage, and the second liaison
    lies in children. Next comes the unity of the household, which shares
    all things in common. This is the foundation of the city structure, the
    seedbed so to say of the state. Next comes the link between brothers,
    followed by those between first and second cousins. Since these
    relatives cannot be accommodated in a single house, they migrate to
    other houses as though to colonies. Marriages and connections by
    marriage then develop, resulting in further kindred. From such pro-
55 creation and resultant offspring states have their beginnings.* This
    blood relationship binds men together in both goodwill and affec-
    tion, for possession of common memorials to forbears, shared reli-
    gious ritual, and family-tombs forges a strong link.
        Of all bonds of fellowship, however, none is more pre-eminent or
    enduring than the friendship forged between good men of like char-
    acter.* That integrity to which I often refer affects us even as we see

it present in another; it makes us friends of the person in whom we see it reside. True, every virtue attracts us towards it, and causes us to feel affection towards those in whom we observe it, but justice and generosity induce this response most of all. Nothing inspires greater affection or intimacy than decency of character which is shared. When two people have the same ideals and aspirations, they take the same pleasure in each other as in themselves. In this way Pythagoras' requirement for friendship is met,* that though more than one we become one.

Another important mode of fellowship is that which results from exchanging kindnesses. Provided these are reciprocal and welcomed, those who bestow and receive them are bound together in stable association.

But once you have surveyed this entire scene with reason and close attention, none of these affinities has more weight and induces more affection than the allegiance which we each have to the state. Our parents are dear to us, and so are our children and relatives and friends; but our native land alone subsumes all the affections which we entertain. What good man would hesitate to face death on her behalf if it would be of service to her? So the barbaric conduct of these contemporaries of ours* who have torn our land asunder with every criminal act, engaged as they are and have been in its utter destruction, is all the more heinous.

If, however, a kind of rivalry should arise and comparisons be made as to which of these we owe the greatest obligations, our country and our parents must take first place,* for the debts we owe to the benefits which they bestow are the greatest. Next come our children and our entire household, for we are their sole resource, and they can have no other refuge. After them come those relatives whom we find congenial and with whom our future prospects also are often shared. So provision of the basic necessities of life is owed most of all to these whom I have mentioned. But as for the life we lead, the daily contacts with each other, our projects, discussions, words of encouragement and consolation, even our occasional rebukes—all flourish best in friendships;* and the most satisfying friendship is that cemented by similarity of moral outlook.

As we dispense all these obligations, we must look to the particular needs of each individual, and note what each of them can or cannot achieve even without our help. We shall find that affinities and

56

57

58

59

circumstances both produce different levels of obligations, and that some obligations are owed to some people in preference to others. For example, you should be more ready to lend help to a neighbour when he gathers in his harvest* than to a brother or close relative; on the other hand, you should defend a relative or friend who is standing trial in court rather than a neighbour.* So in undertaking all obligations, these and similar factors must be taken into account, [and you must adopt this habit and practice] so that you become proficient at working out your obligations. By addition and subtraction you can see the amount you are left with, and this will enable you to decide how much is owed to each person.

60   We see, however, that doctors and army commanders and orators have absorbed the basic theories of their professions, but none the less cannot achieve results worthy of great praise without experience and practice, and it is the same with maintaining obligations. The principles are transmitted as I myself am transmitting them now, but this very important duty demands experience and practice as well. However, I have now explained reasonably fully how the honourable conduct from which obligation stems is derived from the principles of justice in human society.

61   We are to realize, however, that though we have established four qualities as sources of such integrity and obligation, the most glittering of them in men's eyes is that performed with a great and lofty spirit indifferent to human interests. Thus in framing insults, some such quotation as this springs most readily to mind:

> You young men show a woman's heart, that maid a man's,*

or one on these lines:

> O son of Salmacis, your spoils are won
> Without expenditure of sweat or blood.*

By contrast, when we praise exploits achieved with magnanimity, courage, and surpassing competence, our eulogies are uttered in some more eloquent strain. Because of this, the battles at Marathon, Salamis, Plataea, Thermopylae, and Leuctra* have become exercise-grounds for rhetoricians, and likewise our native heroes Horatius Cocles, the Decii, Gnaeus and Publius Scipio, Marcus Marcellus,* and countless others, and above all the Roman people itself are signalled as outstanding for greatness of spirit. Their zeal for glory in war is attested also by the fact that their statues we see usually clad in military dress.

But if this lofty spirit so conspicuous in dangers and toils is devoid 62 of justice, and if it battles not for the safety of all but for personal interests, it ranks as a vice. Not merely has it no part in virtue; rather, it is a species of barbarism which shrugs off all that is civilized. So courage is splendidly defined by the Stoics when they term it 'the virtue which champions the right'.* This is why no one who has won fame for courage has gained praise through treachery and under-hand behaviour; there can be no integrity where there is no justice. So Plato puts it very well:* 'Not merely is knowledge divorced from 63 justice to be called cunning rather than wisdom, but if the spirit geared to face danger is fired by personal motives rather than by the common good, it should bear the title of recklessness rather than courage.' So our requirement is that men of courage and greatness of spirit should also be good and guileless, friends of the truth and total strangers to deceit; for when we praise justice, such qualities lie at the heart of it.

But the distressing thing is that such lofty spirit and greatness of 64 mind very easily breed a defiant and excessive lust for supreme power. We read in Plato* that the Spartans were habitually fired by lust for victory; likewise individuals notably outstanding for great-ness of soul feel the most pressing urge to be preeminent among all, indeed to wield sole power.* Now when you aspire to rise higher than all others, it is hard to maintain that even-handedness which is absolutely integral to justice. The result is that such men do not allow themselves to be overruled by argument or by any political or lawful sanction; and frequently they exploit bribery and disruption in the state to gather the maximum resources and to elevate them-selves above others by force rather than achieve equality with others by justice. However, the greater the difficulties we encounter, the greater the glory; whatever the crisis, it must not witness the absence of justice.

So we must account as courageous and high-souled not those who 65 inflict injustice, but those who banish it. Now the greatness of mind which is genuine and wise regards the honourable conduct on which nature chiefly attends as resident in deeds and not in fame, and it prefers to take the lead in reality rather than merely appear to do so. Indeed, the man who is reliant on the false assumptions of the ignorant mob is not to be numbered among the great. Moreover, the loftier a man's spirit, the more easily in his desire for fame he is drawn to unjust deeds; this is a slippery slope on which he is poised, for it is hard to find one who has undertaken toils and confronted labours, and yet does not long for fame as reward for what he has achieved.*

66   A spirit which is utterly courageous and noble is conspicuous especially for two features. The first of these is disregard for external circumstances, springing from the conviction that a man ought to revere or aspire to or seek nothing except what is honourable and proper, and should not lie down before any man or emotional disturbance or twist of fortune.* The second is that once you have attained this cast of mind which I have mentioned, you should embark on activities which are of course important and highly useful, but are in addition extremely taxing, full of toils and dangers which threaten both life and the many strands that compose it.

67   All the glamour and distinction and, I may add, the material profit are found in the second of these, whereas the root cause and means of a man's becoming great lies in the first, for it is that which engenders the attitude which makes spirits rise high and become indifferent to human affairs. This attitude is manifest in two ways: first, by regarding as a good only what is honourable, and second, by being free of all mental disturbance, for we must consider it characteristic of the brave and noble spirit to think little of the things which most men reckon special and glorious, and to despise them with the steady and unflinching eye of reason. As for the apparently harsh experiences which on numerous and varied occasions affect the human condition throughout life, it is the mark of the mature spirit and the great resolution it shows to endure them in such a way as not to abandon either the life of nature or the dignity of the philosopher.

68   It is inconsistent for the man not undermined by fear to be undermined by greed, or for the man demonstrably unconquered by toil to be conquered by base pleasure. So these vices are to be avoided, and likewise we should eschew greed for money, for nothing is so characteristic of the narrow and petty spirit as love of riches, and nothing is more honourable and splendid than contempt for the money you do not possess, and the application towards benevolence and generosity of that which you have. You should also be chary of greed for glory,* as I said earlier, for it deprives men of that freedom which the high-

minded individual should strain every nerve to defend. Nor should you covet military commands; sometimes it is preferable to decline them, or else on occasion to relinquish them. You should clear your mind of all troubling emotions—desire and fear, anguish and excessive pleasure and anger—*so that you may acquire the mental tranquillity and freedom from anxiety which make for steadfastness of purpose and high dignity. 69

There are and have been many who in pursuit of the tranquillity I mentioned have renounced affairs of state and had recourse to a life of leisure.* Amongst them are philosophers of the greatest fame and eminence, and also a number of austere and serious men* unable to stomach the conduct of the people or its leaders; several of them have retired to the country, where they have found satisfaction in administering their family properties. These men have adopted the pattern 70 of life enjoyed by kings: they lack nothing, they are at the beck and call of no one, and they enjoy that freedom which in essence means living as you please.

This aspiration is thus shared between those eager for power and the men of leisure just mentioned. But the first group think that they can attain it by possessing great resources, and the second by being satisfied with their own modest means. The attitude of neither party is wholly contemptible. But the life of the man of leisure is easier and safer, and it bears less oppressively and tiresomely on other people, whereas the life of those who have devoted themselves to politics and to the conduct of important affairs brings more profit to humanity, and is more conducive to fame and distinction.

So we must perhaps allow abstention from public affairs both to 71 individuals of outstanding talent who have devoted themselves to learning, and to men hindered by ill-health* or some other cogent reason who have renounced politics and have yielded to others the power and praise of administering the state. But if those who have no such excuse were to state that they despise the military and civil offices which most men admire, I think that we should not merely withhold praise from them, but also impute it to them as a fault. It is difficult not to approve their stance in so far as they claim to despise fame as worthless, but they give the impression of fearing the toils and troubles, together with the apparent disgrace and dishonour of setbacks and rejections. Some people in fact do not behave consistently in the face of contrasting circumstances: while they despise pleasure most austerely, they are chicken-hearted in facing pain, and again, they are indifferent to fame but shattered by notoriety. Even in these attitudes they are not consistent.

72   But men whom nature has endowed with the resources for conducting public business should renounce all hesitation, seek entry to public office, and administer the state. In no other way can a city-state be governed, or greatness of spirit be made manifest. Statesmen no less than philosophers—perhaps I should say even more than philosophers—should display that greatness of spirit and that indifference to human considerations to which I repeatedly refer, and in addition mental tranquillity and freedom from anxiety, if they are to avoid the stresses and strains, and adopt a sober and unswerv-

73   ing course in life. It is easier for philosophers to do this, for in their lives there are fewer occasions which are exposed to the blows of fortune; they need fewer resources, and if they meet with some reverse the humiliation is not so harsh. So it is inevitable that public figures experience greater emotional upheavals, and show greater eagerness for achievement, than men in retirement, which is why it is more important for them to manifest a lofty spirit and an untroubled outlook.

The person who embarks on affairs of state must be sure to give thought not only to the honourable nature of the work, but also to whether he has the capacity to perform it. In undertaking it, he must be sure not to succumb to thoughtless despair through cowardice, nor to become overconfident through greed. Before undertaking any business whatsoever, careful preparations must be put in train.

74   There is a common assumption that military achievements are more important than civil ones, a belief which must be toned down;* for many have often had recourse to warfare out of desire for glory. This frequently happens with men of great spirit and talent, the more so if they have military competence and are eager to conduct campaigns. But if we are willing to make an honest assessment, there have been many civic issues of greater importance and celebrity than operations in war.

75   Though Themistocles wins deserved praise and his name is more famous than that of Solon,* and though Salamis is invoked to attest that the most glorious victory there is to rank higher than Solon's scheme for the foundation of the Council of the Areopagus, the achievement of Solon is to be accounted as no less impressive than

that of Themistocles. Why? Because that victory brought the state only momentary advantage, whereas Solon's reform will be of perennial benefit to it, for the laws of the Athenians and their ancestral traditions have been preserved by Solon's planning. And whereas Themistocles could not cite any contribution made to the Areopagus, the Council could justifiably argue that it had aided Themistocles, for the war was waged according to the strategy of that body which Solon established.

The same point can be made about Pausanias and Lysander. 76 Though the Spartan dominion is believed to have been won by their operations, these bear absolutely no comparison with Lycurgus' laws and system of training;* on the contrary, these reforms were the very reason why the armies of those generals were more disciplined and courageous. As I saw it during my boyhood, Marcus Scaurus did not seem inferior to Gaius Marius, nor during my political career did Quintus Catulus seem to rank below Gnaeus Pompeius;* for arms wielded abroad count for little unless there is counsel at home. A further example: Africanus, that unique personality both as man and as commander, did not bring more benefit to the state by demolishing Numantia than did Publius Nasica as private citizen when in that same era he assassinated Tiberius Gracchus.* Admittedly Nasica's action was not confined merely to the civil domain; it had also a military aspect, since it was achieved by a show of force. None the less, the deed was carried out by political action and without the aid of an army.

This viewpoint is expressed very well by the verse which I am told 77 is often derided by malicious and envious critics:

Let arms unto the toga yield, the laurel to men's praise.*

For not to mention others, did not arms yield to the toga when I was helmsman of the state? Never was the danger to the republic more grave; yet never was the peace more relaxed: so quickly, thanks to my strategy and watchfulness, did the arms fall from the hands of utterly reckless citizens and clatter to the ground. So what achievement in war was ever so great, or what triumph is comparable? To 78 you, Marcus my son, I can make this boast, for this fame of mine is your inheritance, and my deeds are for you to imitate. At any rate Gnaeus Pompeius, a man who gained lavish praises for his deeds in war, in the hearing of many paid me this tribute:* he said that his

return to Rome for his third triumph* would have been in vain if
he had not through my service to the state had a place in which to
celebrate it.

There are instances of courage, then, on the home front which are
on a par with bravery in war; indeed, they demand more application
and effort than those in war.

79   It is quite true that the integrity which we demand from a lofty
and high-souled spirit is the fruit of strength of mind rather than of
body, yet we must train and discipline the body to ensure that it can
obey counsel and reason in the performance of business and in the
endurance of hard work. But the integrity which we are investigating is attributable wholly to care and concentration exercised by the
mind; in this respect civilians who preside over the state perform a
role no less useful than those who wage war. So it is by their strategy
that on many occasions wars are either not undertaken or else carried
through to the end (and sometimes also initiated, as was the case with
the Third Punic War, begun at the behest of Marcus Cato,* whose
80   authority prevailed even after his death). So establishing the rationale for making war is more desirable than courage in battle, though
we must beware of formulating the arguments with the sole intention of avoiding war more than deciding on the beneficial course. But
recourse to war should be had with the intention of establishing
peace.*

It is the mark of a brave and resolute spirit not to get rattled in difficult circumstances, and when plunged into commotion not to be
knocked off one's balance, as the saying goes. Rather, we must maintain presence of mind, keep our counsel, and not depart from the
81   path of reason. Such conduct makes demands on the spirit. There
is a further demand which calls for considerable brain-power: this
is the anticipation of future events by studied reflection, working
out some time beforehand the possible outcome one way or
another, and the action to be taken against any eventuality. What we
do must not result in our having to say later 'I had not thought
of that'. This is how a person of great and lofty spirit operates. He
puts his trust in foresight and planning. On the other hand, random
activity in the battle-line and engaging the enemy is a barbaric,
quasi-bestial pursuit, though when the hour and the need demand it,
we must fight to the end, and death must be preferable to slavery and
disgrace.

[So far as the destruction and sacking of cities is concerned, pre-   82
cautions must be taken against licentious and cruel behaviour.]* In
times of disruption it is the mark of the great man to punish the
guilty, to spare the great majority, and in all circumstances to pursue
the right and honourable course. As I stated earlier, some people
rank war-activities higher than urban administration, and similarly
you can find many who consider hazardous, hot-headed projects to
be more glorious than unimpassioned policies carefully thought
through. We must at all costs never flee from danger so as to appear   83
craven and cowardly, but we must also refrain from exposing ourselves to dangers needlessly, for nothing could be more stupid. So in
confronting dangers we should model ourselves on the practice of
physicians: they provide gentle remedies for patients who are merely
off colour, but they are forced to apply hazardous and problematic
treatments to more serious illnesses. It is the mark of the madman to
long for bad weather when the sea is calm, but the role of the wise
man is to lend support by any means when a storm breaks, the more
so if the benefit gained from a successful outcome should outweigh
the disadvantage arising from hesitation.

The hazardous conduct of operations falls partly on those who
shoulder them, and partly on the state; and again, some men are
forced to endanger their lives, while others stand to lose their repu-
tations and the citizens' goodwill. Accordingly we must be readier to
confront dangers which affect ourselves rather than the community,
and to be more prepared to fight for our honour and glory than for
our other interests. We find that in the past many were ready to shed   84
not only their money but even their life-blood on behalf of their
native land, yet were unwilling to endure even the slightest loss of
personal glory although the state was demanding it. Callicratidas* is
one example: as a Spartan commander in the Peloponnesian War, he
had fought many engagements with distinction, but he finally
ruined everything entirely by refusing to accede to the advice of
those who thought that the fleet should be evacuated from Arginusae, and that battle with the Athenians should be avoided. His
retort to them was that if the fleet were lost, the Spartans could
assemble another, but that he could not flee without personal disgrace. However, this battle was no more than a modest reverse.* A
truly disastrous one was when Cleombrotus through fear of jealous
critics joined battle rashly with Epaminondas,* which led to the

collapse of Spartan power. How much better was the policy of
Quintus Maximus, of whom Ennius writes*

> One man by holding back restored our state.
> Rome's safety he preferred to common talk;
> Hence to this day his fame shines brighter yet.

The kind of fault I mentioned must be avoided also in the civil
domain. There are people who dare not say what they think, however outstanding their contribution would be, because they fear
ill-will.

85   At all events, those who are to take over administration of the state
must observe the two precepts which Plato lays down:* first, they
must protect the interests of the citizens in such a way that all they do
should be directed towards that end without thought of personal
advantage. Second, the whole body-politic should be their concern,
so that they do not protect one section at the expense of the rest.
Supervision of the state is comparable to the duty of a guardian: it
must be conducted for the benefit not of those in charge, but of those
entrusted to their care. People who consult the interests of one section of the citizens and show indifference to another, introduce a
most destructive element into the state, namely dissension and
disharmony. The outcome is that some are seen as 'men of the
people', others as followers of 'the best citizens',* and few as
supporters of the whole community.

86   The Athenians experienced great dissensions as a result of this,
and because of it our own state has witnessed not merely outbreaks
of strife but also baneful civil wars.* The sober and courageous citizen who merits leadership of the state will shun and loathe such
struggles. He will devote himself wholeheartedly to the state, will
seek no resources or power for himself, and will protect the whole in
such a way as to maintain the interests of the individual. He will not
level false charges against any person and thus expose him to hatred
or jealousy, and he will cleave so closely to justice and integrity that
so long as he preserves them, he will endure any setback however
daunting, and he will confront death rather than abandon those
virtues which I mentioned.

87   Canvassing and scrambling for offices is an utterly wretched business. Plato again provides a splendid commentary on this when he
says that those who struggle with each other for government of the

state behave like sailors vying with each other to see who will be the best helmsman. He further recommends* that we should regard as opponents those who take up arms against us, not those who seek to safeguard the state by following their personal judgement; the disagreement between Publius Africanus and Quintus Metellus* conducted without bitterness offers an example of this.

Further, we should not lend an ear to those who will have it that we 88 should show bitter anger towards adversaries, and who will pronounce that this is the right attitude for a man of proud spirit and courage. In fact, nothing is more praiseworthy or more worthy of a noble and exemplary man than to be conciliatory and forgiving. Indeed, those of us who live in free societies where there is equality before the law should make a habit of affability and what some call 'a high level of tolerance';* otherwise, if we explode when people buttonhole us at inconvenient moments or make shameless requests of us, we may develop a sour temper which is both fatuous and objectionable. Yet such gentleness and tolerance are praiseworthy only if we are stern when the state demands it, for otherwise city-government is impossible. But all punishment* and rebuke must be free of insult, and must look to the welfare of the state and not to the satisfaction of the man who punishes or rebukes an individual.

We must also ensure that punishment does not outweigh guilt, 89 and that when the same charges are laid some are not chastised while others are not even indicted. Punishment meted out under the impetus of anger should be totally outlawed, for if a person is in a fury when he pronounces punishment, he will never maintain that mean between too much and too little which the Peripatetics uphold*— and rightly uphold if only they would not praise irascibility, and say that this is a useful gift bestowed by nature, for irascibility is to be rejected in all circumstances. It is desirable that those who preside over the state should take their cue from the laws, which when imposing punishment are guided by fairness and not by anger.

Furthermore, when we are enjoying success and things are going 90 our way, we must make strenuous efforts to avoid arrogance, contempt, and disdain. It is a mark of instability to be intemperate in the face of success no less than in adversity. It is a splendid thing to remain level-headed in every condition of life, and to show the same demeanour and outlook at all times. We are told that Socrates and Gaius Laelius did this,* and I note that though Philip, king of the

Macedonians, was surpassed by his son in achievements and in fame, he was the more affable and considerate of the two.* So the father was always 'The Great', but the son was often as mean-minded as could be, which underlines the apparent truth of the advice of those who say that the more exalted we are, the more humble should be our behaviour. Panaetius indeed states that Africanus, his disciple and friend, was fond of making this comparison:* just as horses when fierce and frisky through frequent engagements in battle are often consigned to trainers to make them more amenable, so when men become unbridled through success and form too high an opinion of themselves, they should be hauled into the training-ring, so to say, of reason and learning to enable them to discern the frailty of human affairs and the instability of fortune.

91   Moreover, even in times of greatest success we must exploit the advice of friends to the full, and lend even greater weight than previously to their authority; and under those same favourable circumstances we must beware of lending an ear to sycophants, and of exposing ourselves to flattery, for it is easy to be deceived in that way once we believe that our standing merits such praise. This fallibility gives rise to countless lapses when individuals become puffed up because of what people tell them, and as they commit the most grievous errors, become a contemptible laughing-stock.

92   So much, then, for deportment in public life. On the earlier question,* our conclusion must be that the activities of greatest importance, and ones appropriate to the greatest spirit, are those performed by men who conduct public affairs, because the tasks they handle have the widest repercussions and affect the greatest number of people. On the other hand, we must say that there are and have been also many men of lofty spirit who live in retirement. Some of them have either researched or embarked upon important projects while confining themselves within the boundaries of the private domain. Others have adopted an intermediate role between the philosophers and the politicians: they have taken pleasure in their private wealth, not however exploiting every means to add to it; and have not debarred those of their circle from drawing upon it. Instead, they have shared it with their friends and with the state whenever there was need of it. Such possessions should first of all have been honestly acquired without sleazy or disreputable profit-making. Second, they should be made usefully available to as many

people as possible, so long as the recipients deserve it; and third, they should be increased by calculation, care, and thrift, and be devoted not to loose and wasteful living, but to generous acts of philanthropy. The man who observes these injunctions* can live a splendid, dignified, and vigorous life while simultaneously exhibiting simplicity, loyalty, and truth.

We must next discuss the sole remaining component of the honourable, in which we discern modesty, temperance (the jewel, so to say, which embellishes life), moderation, total cessation of mental disturbances, and due limit in all things. This subdivision includes what in Latin we may render as *decorum* ('the fitting'), for the Greek word is *prepon*. The effect is such that it is inseparable from the honourable,* for whatever is fitting comes into view only when the honourable precedes it. It is easier to grasp rather than define the nature of the difference between the honourable and the fitting. What is fitting emerges once it is preceded by the honourable, so what is fitting is discernible not only in this fourth subdivision of the honourable, which we are about to discuss, but also in the earlier three. Thus it is fitting to deploy reason and speech wisely, to perform any act with due reflection, to recognize and maintain the truth in all matters; contrariwise, to be misguided, to go off course, to fall into error, to be deceived—all these are as unfitting as are madness and mental illness. Again, all that is just is fitting, and on the other hand all that is unjust is loathsome and therefore unfitting. The relationship with courage is similar, for what is performed in a manly and lofty spirit is seen to be worthy of a man and to be fitting, whereas the opposite is unfitting because it is despicable.

So this element of the fitting which I am discussing is relevant to every aspect of the honourable; relevant, that is, as visualized not in some obscure way, but as a prominent feature. For there is an aspect of the fitting which is perceptible in every virtue, and can be detached from them more in theory than in practice. Just as physical attractiveness and beauty are inseparable from glowing health, so this element of the fitting of which we speak is wholly integrated with virtue, though distinguishable from it as a mental concept.

The definition of it is twofold, for we envisage the notion of the fitting first in general, as present in the honourable as a whole,* and secondly in the subordinate sense as being relevant to each subdivision of the honourable.* The first of these is usually defined in terms

93

94

95

96

such as this: the fitting is what is consistent with man's excellence in the respect in which his nature differs from all other living creatures. As for the subordinate sense of this general concept, those who define it would regard the fitting as according with nature in the exercise of restraint and self-control on the one hand, and the deportment of a free spirit on the other.

97   We can infer that this is how men regard the question from the concept of the fitting which the poets pursue, a topic often discussed more fully in a context different from this.* We maintain that the poets observe what is fitting when what is worthy of each character is reflected in both their actions and their words. For example, if Aeacus or Minos were to say

> Yes, let them hate, if only they feel fear as well,

or

> The father is himself his offspring's tomb,

that would seem unfitting, because tradition has it that these characters were just. But when Atreus utters the lines,* they evoke applause, because the words are in keeping with the character. However, whereas poets will assess what is fitting for each person according to his character, nature has herself invested us with a character of
98   supreme excellence, surpassing that of other living creatures. So poets who handle a wide range of characters will envisage what is appropriate and fitting even for villains, but nature has endowed us with the role of steadfastness, restraint, self-control, and modesty. And since nature also teaches us not to ignore our relations with other people, it becomes clear how widely relevant the fitting is both to the honourable in general and to its presence in each individual category of virtue. Just as physical beauty attracts the eye because of the apt harmony of the bodily parts, and our pleasure lies in the fact that all those parts are as one in sharing a native grace, so this notion of the fitting, which gleams so brightly in our daily lives, wins the applause of our contemporaries through the regularity, consistency, and control reflected in every word and action.

99   We should accordingly treat other people—not just the best of them, but also the rest—with a modicum of respect. Disregard for what others feel about you is a mark not merely of conceit but also of lack of integrity. Mind you, there is a difference between justice and

deference when taking stock of other people. It is the role of justice not to wrong them, but of deference to avoid bruising them; the impact of the fitting is especially notable here.

This explanation, then, makes clear, I think, the nature of what we call the fitting. The obligation which stems from this advances first   100 on the path which leads to harmony with nature and to the preservation of its laws. If we take nature as our guide, we shall never go astray; and we shall pursue both the sharpness and clarity of vision which nature promotes, and the quality which is designed to bind men together and, thirdly, that which is forceful and strong. But the greatest impact of the fitting lies in the subdivision which we are now discussing; not merely must we win approval by our physical movements which accord with nature, but much more with the movements of the spirit which are likewise consonant with nature.

The thrust and nature of the soul of man have two aspects. The   101 first lies in the appetite (in Greek, *horme*), which pulls a man in different directions; and the second is in the reason, which teaches and expounds what we are to do, and what to avoid. Accordingly the reason commands, and the appetite obeys.* Our every action must steer clear of rashness and carelessness, and must do nothing for which a praiseworthy motive cannot be adduced; indeed, this is virtually a description of obligation. We must ensure that our appetites obey   102 the reason, and neither run ahead of it nor shrink from it through laziness or cowardice. They must also be serene and clear of all mental disturbance, and this will ensure that steadfastness and self-restraint will emerge in all their glory. As for the appetites which roam too far, and in the exuberance, so to say, of greed or of evasion are insufficiently reined in by reason, they undoubtedly transgress all bounds and limits; for they renounce and reject obedience and do not submit to reason, to which they are subject by the law of nature. Not only men's spirits but even their bodies are thrown into turmoil by them. When people are livid with anger, or stirred by some lust or fear, or elated by excessive pleasure,* you can see it in their very faces; the features, voices, movements, demeanour of each and all of them are transformed.

All this makes us realize—to revert to our theme of obligation—   103 that all appetites are to be restrained and tranquillized, and our attention and care must be awakened, to ensure that we do nothing rash or at random, without due consideration and in an offhand way.

Nature has not fashioned us to behave as if we have been created for fun and games.* Rather, we are moulded for self-discipline and for more sober and important pursuits. Fun and games are indeed permissible, but they fall into the same category as sleep and relaxation in general, to be enjoyed once we have done justice to serious and weighty business. Moreover, such sportive behaviour should not be extravagant or licentious, but rather, wholesome and spiced with wit. Just as we grant boys no unlimited freedom in their recreation, but allow what is consonant with honourable activity, so even when we make sport, the beam of light cast by worth of character should shine out.

104   In general, the sportive element falls into two categories. The first is ill-bred, rude, scandalous, indecent, whereas the second is refined,* urbane, clever, and witty. This second type abounds not only in the plays of our poet Plautus and in old Attic comedy, but also in the books of Socratic philosophy; and besides these, many witticisms have been coined by many people, such as those gathered by old Cato which go under the title of *Apophthegms*.* So it is easy to distinguish between the joking which reflects good breeding, and that which is coarse; the one, if aired at an apposite moment of mental relaxation, is becoming in the most serious of men, whereas the other is unworthy of any free person, if the content is indecent or the expression obscene. Moreover, a certain limit must be imposed on such joking, to ensure that it all does not get out of hand, and to avoid our being so swept off our feet by pleasure as to relapse into base behaviour of some sort. Activities on our *campus Martius*, and fondness for hunting, offer respectable examples of sportive recreation.*

105   It is relevant to every aspect of obligation always to focus on the degree to which the nature of man transcends that of cattle and of other beasts. Whereas animals have no feeling except pleasure, and their every inclination is directed towards it, human minds are nurtured by learning and reflection; and enticed by delight in seeing and hearing, they are constantly investigating something or performing some action. Indeed, if a person is a little too prone to seek sensual gratifications—always assuming that he is not an animal (for certain men are human only in name, and not in practice), and that he stands rather more upright than the beasts—even if he is in the grip of base pleasure, he seeks to cloak and disguise his appetite for such pleas-

106   ure because he is ashamed of it. We infer from this that base pleasure

of the body is insufficiently worthy of man's superior status, and that it should be despised and rejected. But if an individual does lend countenance to such pleasure, he must be careful to observe a limit in its enjoyment. So the nurture and cultivation of our bodies should be directed towards health and strength rather than to pleasure. Moreover, if we are willing to reflect on the high worth and dignity of our nature, we shall realise how degrading it is to wallow in decadence and to live a soft and effeminate life, and how honourable is a life of thrift, self-control, austerity and sobriety.

We must also grasp that nature has endowed us with what we may 107 call a dual role in life. The first is that which all of us share by virtue of our participation in that reason and superiority by which we rise above the brute beasts; from this the honourable and fitting elements wholly derive, and from it too the way in which we assess our obligation. The other is that which is assigned uniquely to each individual, for just as there are great variations in physical attributes (for we see that some can run faster and others wrestle more strongly, or again, one has an imposing appearance, while another's features are graceful), so our mental make-up likewise displays variations greater still. So Lucius Crassus and Lucius Philippus had abundant wit, and 108 Gaius Caesar, Lucius' son,* had it in greater measure and applied it more deliberately, whereas their contemporaries Marcus Scaurus and the young Marcus Drusus* were notably serious. Gaius Laelius was the most genial of men, but his close friend Scipio nursed greater ambition, and his life was more austere.* Amongst the Greeks, so we are told, Socrates was an affable and witty man, amusing in conversation, exhibiting feigned ignorance in everything he said (what the Greeks indeed call an 'ironical' man), but by contrast Pythagoras and Pericles attained their supreme influence without recourse to gaiety.* Tradition has it that among Carthaginian generals Hannibal, and amongst our own Quintus Maximus,* were men of guile, adept at concealment, tight-lipped, dissemblers, laying traps, and forestalling the stratagems of the foe. The Greeks reckon Themistocles and Jason of Pherae as supreme examples in this category; and that trick of Solon* was especially crafty and clever, when he pretended to be insane so as to attain greater personal safety and to enhance his service to the state.

In stark contract to these, other men are candid and open, believing 109 that nothing should be hidden or underhand; they cherish the truth, and abhor deceit. Others again would stoop to anything and kowtow to anyone to achieve their ends, as we saw with Sulla and Marcus Crassus.* The most guileful and submissive Spartan of this type by all accounts was Lysander, whereas Callicratidas,* his successor as admiral of the fleet, was the very opposite. Again, we find that the most eminent of individuals makes himself out in social discourse to be one of the common run; we saw this in the cases of the Catuli, father and son, and of Quintus Mucius [Mancia].* I am told that the same was true in an earlier generation of Publius Scipio Nasica, whereas his father, the man who punished the heinous forays of Tiberius Gracchus, was never genial in conversation,* and this very trait lent him stature and celebrity. There are countless other variations in men's natures and habits which should not in the least be criticized.

110   We should each of us stick closely to the characteristics peculiar to us as long as they are not flawed; this is how we can more easily maintain that element of the fitting which we are investigating. We must follow this course so as not to resist the general sway of nature, and so as to follow our natural bent in conforming with this. Thus even if there are pursuits more important and better than ours, we can assess those which we ourselves follow by the criterion of our own nature. It is pointless to go to war with nature and to aim at something which cannot achieve. This is a truth which lends greater clarity to the nature of the fitting; for nothing is fitting if it flies in the face of Minerva,* as the saying goes, in other words if nature confronts and conflicts with it. If the concept of the fitting means anything at all, it is surely nothing more than keeping our whole life and all our activities on an even keel within it, and we cannot achieve this if we forsake our own nature by mimicking that of others. In conversation we should use the language familiar to us so as not to attract deserved derision by inserting Greek words, as some do;* similarly we should not contaminate our activities and our entire lifestyle with any incongruities.

112   Indeed, this variation between natural temperaments has such force that sometimes one individual is driven to suicide while another in the same circumstances is not. We can hardly say that Marcus Cato's situation* was different from that of the rest who surrendered to Caesar in Africa. Yet if those others had killed themselves, it would perhaps have been regarded as a fault because their manner of life was less exacting and their behaviour more easy-

going. But Cato had been endowed by nature with a seriousness of purpose beyond belief; he had reinforced this unfailing steadfastness, and remained always true to his principles and the policy which he adopted, and for this reason he had to die rather than meet the tyrant face to face.

Think of the many hardships which Ulysses endured* in his lengthy wanderings. Though he was at the beck and call of women (if 'women' is the right word for Circe and Calypso), he strove to be courteous and pleasant in all his dealings with everyone; and again, once he reached home he bore the insults even of slaves and maidservants in order finally to attain the goal which he sought. On the other hand, Ajax with that fabled temper of his* would have preferred to face death a thousand times rather than endure such treatment. As we reflect on these exemplars, we must each of us assess our own characteristics and regulate them, without seeking to experiment with how others' traits may suit us, for a person's most distinctive characteristics are what suit him best.

So we should each be aware of our own abilities, and show ourselves to be keen judges of our merits and failings. Otherwise actors on stage may appear to be more farsighted than we are. They do not opt for the best plays, but for those most suited to their talents. Those who pride themselves on their voices choose *Epigoni* and *Medus*; those who rely on gesture go for *Melanippa* and *Clytaemestra*; Rupilius by my own recollection always played in *Antiope*, while Aesopus did not often appear in *Ajax*.* So will the wise man in real life not grasp what the actor grasps on the stage?

We must therefore work hardest at the things for which we are best suited. But if at some time the need forcibly diverts us to undertake tasks unsuited to our talents, we must devote all our attention, thought, and concentration to be able to perform them if not fittingly, at least as little unfittingly as possible. Our effort should be directed not so much at attaining good results beyond our abilities as at avoiding pitfalls.

To the twin roles which I mentioned earlier,* a third is added when some chance or circumstance demands it; and there is also a fourth which we attach to ourselves by our own studied choice. Regal powers, kingships, military commands, noble birth, magistracies, riches, resources—and the opposites of these—are a matter of chance, depending on circumstances. On the other hand, the role

113

114

115

which we should like to play is prompted by our own choice. So some devote themselves to philosophy, others to civil law, and others again to eloquence; and even in the practice of the virtues different people
116 prefer different ones at which to excel. Men whose fathers or forbears achieved outstanding fame in some capacity are often eager to obtain celebrity in the same field; for example, Quintus Mucius, son of Publius, in civil law, and Africanus, son of Aemilius Paulus, in soldiering.* Some sons complement the distinctions taken over from their fathers with some additional glory of their own; for example, the same Africanus crowned his fame in war with eloquence. Timotheus, the son of Conon,* did the same; not only did he not fall below his father in military renown, but he reinforced that renown with the fame of his learning and intellect. But from time to time some sons forgo imitation of their forebears to strike out on a path of their own; men of high ambition whose ancestors are little known often work particularly hard at this.

117 So when investigating the notion of the fitting, we must mentally grasp and reflect on all these aspects. But above all we must establish who and what kind of person we wish to be, and what pattern of life we wish to adopt. This is the most difficult decision of all to reach, for it is when we are on the threshold of manhood, at a time when our powers of judgement are at their weakest, that we each opt for the kind of lifestyle which appeals to us most. So the individual becomes trapped in a fixed pattern and career in life before he is able to assess what is best.

118 According to Xenophon,* Prodicus states that when Hercules was reaching maturity, the time designated by nature for choosing one's future path in life, he retired into the wilderness, and sat there for a long time. He saw ahead two paths, one of Pleasure and one of Virtue, and he pondered long and hard which it was better to take. This could perhaps have been possible for Hercules, 'sprung from the seed of Jupiter' as he was, but it is not an option for us, for we each imitate those who take our fancy, and we are drawn towards their enthusiasms and practices. Very often we are steeped in the injunctions of our parents, and are propelled towards their routines and habits. Others are borne on the wind of popular opinion, and they aspire chiefly to what seems most attractive to the majority. But some by a kind of blessed fortune or innate virtue follow the right path of life without constraint from their parents.

One class of people is particularly rare—those endowed with 119
exceptional brain-power, or with outstanding learning and scholarship, or with both, and who in addition have had space to ponder the
course in life which they would particularly love to follow. But as
each individual reflects on this, his entire thinking must be drawn
back to his own natural bent; on the one hand in all that we do our
search for what is fitting is by reference to our native endowments, as
has been said before; and on the other hand, in ordering our whole
life, the greater part of our concern must be directed at being able to
be true to ourselves as long as we live, not faltering in the performance of any obligation.

Since in this process nature plays the greatest part, closely fol- 120
lowed by fortune,* we must certainly take account of both, but of
nature chiefly, in choosing our manner of life; for nature is much the
more steadfast and consistent, so that on occasion fortune seems to
grapple with nature like a mortal engaging with an immortal. Therefore the person who has harmonized his entire plan of life with the
sort of nature which is free of faults should hold a steadfast course,
for this is supremely fitting, unless perhaps he realizes that he has
made a mistake in his choice of a manner of life. If this happens, as it
can do, he should change his practices and procedures. If circumstances further the change, we shall achieve it more easily and more
conveniently; if not, we shall have to proceed gradually step by step,
just as men of sense deem it more fitting gradually to renounce
friendships which are less pleasing and praiseworthy, rather than to
sever them abruptly. But if we do change our pattern of life, we must
use every means to ensure that we are seen to have exercised good
judgement in doing so.

I stated a moment ago that we should imitate our forbears, but 121
there are exceptions to this rule. First, their faults should not be imi-
tated, and second, nature may not allow the possibility of imitating
some features. For example, the elder Africanus' son, who adopted
that son of Paulus just mentioned, was prevented by ill-health from
being able to match his father in the way that his father could do.* So
if a son cannot act as advocate for the defence, or make arresting
speeches to the citizen assembly, or wage wars, he will have to show
the qualities which lie within his power—justice, good faith, generosity, moderation, self-restraint—to prevent those which he does
not possess being demanded of him. The finest inheritance passed

down from fathers to sons is renown for virtue and for achievements, which excels any patrimony; to dishonour this must be accounted sacrilege and disgrace.

122   Since obligations laid on men of different ages are not identical, those shouldered by the young being different from those imposed on older men, we must add a word about this distinction.

A young man's obligation, then, is to respect his elders, and to choose from among them the best and most highly proved, on whose advice and authority to rely, for the ignorance of early manhood should be stabilized and governed by the wisdom of the old. That period of youth is to be shielded especially from lustful behaviour, and hardened by toil and endurance in mind and body, so that the young may apply themselves vigorously to their obligations in war and in civic affairs. Even when they wish to seek mental relaxation and to devote themselves to enjoyment, they must guard against lack of restraint, and never forget to be respectful. This will be easier if they do not object to older people participating even in activities of that kind.

123   As for the elderly, their physical exertions must obviously be restricted, but their mental activities actually increased. Indeed, they should ensure that they offer by sage advice the greatest possible help to their friends, to the youth, and above all to the state. What men in old age must avoid above all is surrendering to tiredness and idleness.* Again, over-indulgence, which is demeaning at every stage of life, is especially disreputable in the old. And if it is accompanied by lewd excesses, the result is doubly heinous, for on the one hand old age itself gains notoriety, and on the other it encourages more shameless misbehaviour in the young.

124   Also relevant to our discussion are the obligations of magistrates,* private individuals, citizens and foreigners. So the particular function of the magistrate is to be aware that as the personification of the state he must maintain its dignity and glory, preserve its laws, dispense its justice, and remember that these tasks have been entrusted to his good faith. As for the private individual, his life must be one in which he maintains just and equal rights with his fellow-citizens, without grovelling and servility on the one hand and without lordly posturing on the other; and he should want peaceful and honourable policies to prevail in the state. Our practice is both to regard and to

125   call such a man 'a good citizen'.* Foreigners and resident aliens*

have the sole obligation of conducting their own affairs without prying into those of other people, and without concerning themselves in the least with the business of a state not their own.

Some such obligations as these will emerge when the question is raised about what is fitting and appropriate to individuals, to circumstances, and to different ages. What is fitting above all is to remain consistent throughout in carrying out every act, and in adopting every plan.

This concept of the fitting is to be observed in every act and every 126 word, and also in every movement and posture of the body. It consists of three elements: beauty, due arrangement, and adornment as applied to action. These concepts are difficult to define, but it will be sufficient to understand what they are. The three take in also our concern to win the approval of those with whom and among whom we live. So a word must be said about these matters as well.

Nature at the outset* seems herself to have devoted much thought to our bodies, for she has lent prominence to our features and to the rest of our make-up which presents a decent appearance, whereas the bodily parts given over to nature's needs she cloaked and concealed, since they would be unsightly and ugly to look at. Our human 127 modesty has fallen in with this most careful design of nature, for all men of sound sense keep out of sight the parts which nature has hidden;* they take pains to answer the call of nature in as much privacy as they can. People do not use the precise terms either for the parts of the body which carry out these necessary functions, or for the functions themselves. There is no shame in performing these functions, so long as this is done in private, but to speak of them is unfitting. So neither performing such actions in public nor indecent discussion of them escapes the accusation of immodesty.

We are to ignore the Cynics or such Stoics as were virtually Cynics* 128 who scold and mock us because we consider it scandalous to use the terms for acts which are not shameful, and yet we call by their proper names those which are. Robbery with violence, swindling, adultery are all disgraceful when performed, but we speak of them without indecency, whereas the effort of begetting children is honourable but a filthy expression.* Those same philosophers offer further examples to the same effect to impugn our modesty. But we should follow nature, and avoid whatever our eyes and ears do not approve. Our stance and walk, our sitting and reclining, our facial expression and our eyes, and the movement of our hands should all preserve that element of propriety.

129   The two things in this connection which we must above all avoid are effeminate and unmanly conduct on the one hand, and boorish and uncouth behaviour on the other.* We must not agree with actors and orators that these are rules which apply to them but have nothing to do with us. True, it is customary for actors to show such modesty dictated by their long-standing profession that none of them ever mounts the stage without wearing a loin-cloth; their fear is that if certain parts of the body chance to be exposed, they may make an unfitting exhibition of themselves. Our own practice indeed dictates that sons on reaching puberty do not bathe with their fathers, nor sons-in-law with their fathers-in-law.* So modesty of this kind is to be maintained, especially as nature is our teacher and guide.

130   There are two kinds of beauty. Comeliness resides in the one, and dignity in the other. So we are to consider the first as suited to women, and the second to men. So any adornment unworthy of a man* should be isolated from his person, and he should be careful not to betray a similar effeminacy in his gestures and movements. The movements rehearsed on the exercise-ground, for example, are often rather offensive, and some gestures of actors are rather foppish. In both these cases what wins praise is the straightforward and wholesome.

A dignified appearance is to be maintained by the healthy complexion which is the outcome of physical exercise. In addition, we are to cultivate a neatness which is not objectionable through being too meticulous, but which is tidy enough to avoid boorish and uncivilized slovenliness. We must devote similar care to our dress; as in
131   most things, the ideal here is the golden mean. We must be careful also not to saunter along too mincingly, looking like the tray-bearers in public processions, nor again to hurry along at breakneck speed* so that we puff and blow, go red in the face, wear agonized expressions—all indicating clearly that we lack fixed purpose. But we must work even harder than this to make sure that our mental processes do not forsake nature's path. We shall achieve this if we are careful not
132   to fall into fits of agitation and panic, and if we concentrate on what is fitting. These mental processes are of two kinds, thought and impulse. Thought is concerned chiefly with investigating the truth, whereas impulse provokes us to action. So we must ensure that we

direct our thoughts to the best possible ends, and subject our impulses to reason.*

The power of speech is considerable, and has a twofold application, in argumentation and in conversation.* The first is to be employed in debate in the courts, in public assemblies, and in the senate; the second should have its place in social gatherings, philosophical discussions, meetings with friends, and it also has a place at dinner. The rhetoricians lay down rules for argumentation, but there are none for conversation, though perhaps there should be for this as well. Tutors are available to supervise the studies of pupils, but none of these students make conversation their chosen discipline, whereas the whole educational scene is mobbed with students crowding round the rhetoricians.* Yet their rules govern words and statements, and so they will be relevant to conversation as well.

Since we use the voice as the vehicle for speech, and since in deploying it we aim at the two purposes of clarity and euphony, we should of course look to nature to achieve both, but practice will improve the first, and imitation of those who speak concisely and smoothly will further the second. There was nothing about the Catuli* to make you think that they showed refined literary judgement, though they were educated men; but then, so were others, yet the Catuli were regarded as supreme in their use of the Latin language. Their timbre was euphonious, their articulation neither over-elaborate nor stifled, and thus they avoided being either affected or indistinct. Their delivery was not strained, and neither laboured nor shrill. Lucius Crassus* as public speaker was well-rounded and no less witty, yet the reputation of the Catuli for eloquence was just as high. Caesar, brother of the elder Catulus,* was so superior to one and all in wit and repartee that even in forensic speeches he prevailed over the arguments of other advocates by use of his conversational style. So in all these ways much effort is needed to attain what is fitting in all we do.

So this conversational mode, in which the disciples of Socrates are the supreme masters,* must be mild, wholly undogmatic, and witty. A spokesman should not act as if entering upon his birthright by silencing others; rather, in general conversation as in all else he should not resent others having their turn. He should especially give thought to the subjects which he is to discuss. If they are weighty, his contribution should be serious; if they are frivolous, he should be witty. He should particularly ensure that his conversation does not

133

134

expose some defect in his character, as chiefly tends to happen when people make a point of speaking maliciously and abusively, whether jokingly or in earnest, to disparage persons who are not present.

135 Very often exchanges centre on family affairs, or politics, or cultural pursuits and scholarship; we must therefore ensure that even if the conversation begins to roam on to other topics, it should be brought back to the original theme, as long as those present consent to this*—for we do not all take pleasure in discussing the same subjects all the time or in a similar way. We should also take note of how far the conversation is being enjoyed; just as there was an occasion for beginning it, so there should be a way of foreclosing it.

136 Just as throughout our daily lives the golden rule is to avoid mental disturbances when excessive emotions fail to obey the reason, in the same way our conversation ought to steer clear of such feelings. We should not allow anger to obtrude, nor any grasping or world-weariness or faint-heartedness or any such attitude to surface. Above all we should demonstrate our apparent respect and affection for those with whom we are to converse.

A further point. Occasions arise when reprimands are necessary, and in issuing them we must perhaps use a more argumentative tone and a harsher weight of words in such a way as to appear to do this in the flush of anger. But we should have recourse to this kind of rebuke as rarely and as reluctantly as physicians turn to cautery and the knife*—that is, only when the need arises and if no other remedy can be found. Even then anger should be kept at bay,* for under its
137 impulse no right or judicious action can be taken. On most occasions the rebuke we utter can be kindly but reinforced by gravity, so that there is an air of seriousness, but insult is avoided; and we must indicate that the very asperity implicit in the rebuke is directed at the good of the person being reproved. Even in the case of disputes which blow up with our bitterest enemies, and even if we are subjected to unworthy gibes, it is right to remain dignified and to suppress irritation; for exchanges made under a degree of stress cannot be conducted with steadiness, and they do not gain the approval of bystanders.

It is also degrading to boast about yourself, especially when what you claim is untrue, and to attract the derision of those listening by imitating 'the braggart soldier'.*

138 Since I am investigating all possibilities (for this at any rate is my

intention), I must also describe the kind of house desirable for a leading figure of repute. The end in view here is its use; the design of the building should be directed towards this, but thought should be given also to comfort and impressive appearance. The story goes that Gnaeus Octavius, the first of that family to be elected consul, gained prestige for having built a splendid, highly impressive house on the Palatine. All the world went to see it, and it was thought to have won votes for its owner, a 'new man', when he sought the consulship. Scaurus* pulled it down, and in its place he attached an annexe to his own residence. What followed was that Octavius was the first of his family to bestow the consulship on his house, whereas Scaurus, the son of an outstanding man of great renown, brought on his extended house not only electoral rejection but also shame and disaster.

The fact is that though a person's standing can be enhanced by a   139
house, it should not be sought wholly from it. An owner cannot be ennobled by his house, but a house can be ennobled by its owner. Just as in all other things one must take account not only of oneself but also of other people, the same is true with regard to the house of any notable; care must be taken to ensure plenty of room, because many guests have to be housed, and crowds of visitors of every description have to be admitted. But if a large house is always empty, it spells notoriety for its owner, especially if in earlier days it used to be crowded under another owner. It is shaming when passers-by remark

A fine old house! How different is your owner!*

a comment applicable to many houses today. You should be wary of   140
overstepping the mark in expense and grandeur, especially if you are building a house yourself; that kind of behaviour does a lot of harm by the very example which it sets. Many are keen to emulate the practice of prominent citizens in this way. Take the case of Lucius Lucullus,* that outstanding man. Does anyone aspire to his merits, yet how many ape the splendour of his villas? A limit should surely be set with regard to these, a reversion to a more modest standard, and the same moderation should likewise be shown in the enjoyment and splendour of life generally.

So much for that topic. In undertaking any action three prin-   141
ciples should be observed. First, impulse should obey reason; nothing is more relevant than this in maintaining obligations. Second, we

should assess the importance of a project we seek to achieve, to ensure that neither more nor less attention and labour is expended than the case justifies. Third, we must take pains to safeguard all that pertains to the image and standing of a gentleman. The ideal way to do this is to hold fast to that notion of the fitting which we discussed earlier, and not to overstep it. Of these three principles, the overriding one is that impulse should obey reason.

142   The next questions for us to discuss are the due ordering of things and the right moments to achieve this. These considerations fall under the branch of knowledge called by the Greeks *eutaxia*—not in the sense which we translate as *modestia* (moderation), a word which contains the notion of *modus* (limit), but that sense of *eutaxia* by which is understood maintenance of due order.* The Stoic definition of *modestia*, if the word is taken in this same sense, is 'knowledge of how to set everything to be done or said in its due place'. Thus the sense of 'due order' and of 'due place' will be the same; for the Stoics define order as the arrangement of things in their apposite and relevant places. This 'place for action' they say means the apposite moment. In Greek this apposite moment for action is called *eukairia*, and in Latin *occasio*. Thus *modestia*, interpreted in the sense which I have mentioned, is 'knowledge of the chance afforded by moments appropriate for action'. The same definition can stand for *prudentia*,
143   which we discussed at the outset of the treatise,* but at this stage we are investigating moderation, self-restraint, and their kindred virtues. So the aspects relevant to prudence have been treated in their due place; what must now concern us are those which relate to modesty and to the approval of our fellow-citizens.

144   We must, then, order our actions in such a way that all the aspects of our lives are consonant and in harmony with each other, like the themes of a well-integrated speech. It is demeaning and utterly wrong in the course of a serious discussion to introduce comments appropriate to a dinner-party or any risqué conversation. The response of Pericles* was admirable in this connection. He and the poet Sophocles were fellow-generals, and had met to discuss the duties which they shared. A handsome boy happened to walk past, and Sophocles remarked: 'I say, Pericles, what a comely boy!' Pericles replied: 'My dear Sophocles, a general should guard not only his hands but also his eyes.' Now if Sophocles had passed the same remark when athletes were being put through their paces, he would

not have incurred the rebuke which he merited. So vital is the bearing of the place and the time; for example, if an advocate when on a journey or taking a stroll were to commune with himself when preparing a case, or were to give closer thought to something else, no one would blame him; but if he behaved in the same way at a dinnerparty, he would be regarded as uncivilized, because he failed to acknowledge the nature of the occasion.

However, flagrant departures from civilized behaviour such as   145
singing in the forum* or similarly gross tomfoolery are easily recognized, and they require no special proviso or instruction. What we must be more careful to avoid are what seem to be mere peccadilloes which most people cannot detect. Supposing that harps or flutes are just slightly out of tune: the knowledgeable ear usually picks this up. In the same way we must ensure that nothing in our lives happens to be out of kilter; or rather, our care should be all the greater, according as harmony in our behaviour is more important than and superior to harmony in sounds.

Thus just as musicians' ears detect the slightest discord in harp-   146
playing, so if we are prepared to be keen and attentive in taking note of faults, we shall often draw major conclusions from slight evidences. A glance of the eyes, a raising or knitting of the eyebrows, a sad or a cheerful look, a smile, a remark or its suppression, the raising or lowering of the voice—these and the like will enable us readily to assess which of them is an apt reaction, and which of them is at odds with obligation and with nature. Such indications make it helpful for us to judge the nature of each of them from the reactions of other people, so that we may avoid anything unbecoming in them, for somehow or other failings in others seem more blatant to us than those in ourselves. This explains why in the learning process faults are more easily corrected when masters mimic them* for the purpose of correction.

When adopting courses of action in which there is an element of   147
doubt, it is not inappropriate to consult men of learning and also those of wide experience, and to enquire after their preferred option in each kind of obligation; for most of us are usually borne in the direction towards which nature herself guides us. In such consultation we should heed not only what each of them says but also their feelings,* and why they feel that way. Take the parallel of painters, sculptors, and indeed poets who one and all wish to have their

creations assessed by the public, so that a work can be corrected if it
is criticized by most people; they ask themselves and others where
the fault lies. In the same way there are numerous occasions when we
should follow the judgements of others in action, or in refraining
from action, or in changing or amending our policies.

148   We need offer no instruction on policies when they are dictated by
custom and by civic practice, for these are guidelines in themselves.
No one should be misled into thinking that because Socrates and
Aristippus acted or spoke against the established custom of the city,*
we can do the same. Those Greeks attained that discretion because
the great blessings they enjoyed were inspired by heaven. As for the
Cynics,* their entire philosophy is to be rejected, for it is inimical to
that sense of modesty without which nothing upright or honourable
can exist.

149   As for those whose lives have been well tried in honourable and
great achievements, those men of sound patriotism who in past or
present have deserved well of the citizens, we should honour and
respect them as having attained civil office or military command. We
should also show great deference to old age, give precedence to magistrates, distinguish between citizen and foreigner, and in the case of
foreigners distinguish between private and public visitors. To sum
up without going into further detail, we should respect, defend, and
preserve the bond of union and association between members of the
whole human race.

150   To turn now to professions and gainful occupations,* the tradition which we have inherited about which of them are to be regarded
as suitable for a free man, and which are demeaning, is on these lines.
First, those ways of money-making which inspire general loathing,
such as those of customs officials and moneylenders,* are regarded
as contemptible. The gainful occupations of all hired workmen,
whose manual labour is on hire rather than their skills, are servile
and mean; their very wages are a reward for their slaving. Also to be
accounted mean are those who purchase from merchants for immediate resale; if they did not tell downright lies they would make no
profits, and nothing is more despicable than such untruthfulness.
The trades practised by all artisans are also vulgar, for there can be
nothing in a workshop which befits a gentleman. Least praiseworthy
of all are the trades serving coarse pleasures—in Terence's words,*
'Fishmongers, butchers, cooks, poulterers, and fishermen'. And if

you like, you can count in perfumers, dancers, and the entire retinue of the low stage.

On the other hand, the professions which demand greater saga- 151
city, or bring no little benefit, such as medicine, architecture, and teaching worthy subjects, are honourable for those of the appropriate social class.* Petty trading is to be considered mean, but large-scale commerce, which transports many commodities from round the world and distributes them to a mass market without dishonesty, is not entirely worthy of censure; indeed, if such businessmen when sated, or better satisfied, by their gains progress from harbour to country estates as previously they often progressed from the open sea to harbour, it seems that there are very good grounds for winning possible praise.* But of all profit-making activities none is better, more fruitful, more enjoyable, more worthy of a free man than agriculture. However, I have discussed this quite fully in my *Cato Maior*,* so you can find there observations relevant to this topic.

I think that I have now sufficiently explained how obligations are 152
derived from the component parts of the honourable. But often conflict and comparison can arise between these very aspects of the honourable, raising the question: of two honourable courses, which is the more so? This is a topic which Panaetius has omitted.* Since all honourable conduct derives from the four components of knowledge, sense of community, greatness of soul, and temperance, it is vital to make frequent comparisons between these in deciding upon our obligation.

In my view, then, obligations which arise from sense of commu- 153
nity conform more with nature than do those which stem from knowledge.* This standpoint can be validated by the following proof. Suppose that a philosopher has lived a life with abundant provision of everything, and has enjoyed absolute leisure to study and ponder in solitude all that is worth knowing. Still, if his isolation was such that he could not set eyes on another human being, he would die.* Now chief of all the virtues is the wisdom (*sapientia*) which the Greeks call *sophia*; we mean something rather different by prudence (*prudentia*), which the Greeks call *phronesis*, namely, knowledge of things to be sought and things to be avoided. This wisdom which I have called the chief virtue is knowledge of things divine and human, and this embraces the sense of community between gods and men, and the relationship between man and man. So if wisdom is the

greatest virtue, as it undoubtedly is, then the obligation stemming from the sense of community must undoubtedly be the greatest. Indeed, knowledge and contemplation of the world of nature would be feeble and unfulfilled if no practical action were to flow from it. The action which does follow is seen to best advantage when it protects men's interests and is therefore concerned with the fellowship of the human race. It must accordingly be ranked higher than that from knowledge.*

154   Every citizen of merit echoes this judgement and exemplifies it in practice; for is anyone so eager to investigate and discover the nature of reality that if, as he pored over and pondered the most significant researches, he was suddenly informed of critical danger to his country and he could lend it help and support, he would not forsake and abandon all those researches even if he thought that he could calculate the number of the stars, or measure the dimensions of the universe? And he would do the very same in the interests or the danger

155   of a parent or a friend. These considerations make us realise that obligations of justice, involving as they do the welfare of mankind (and nothing should be more hallowed in our eyes), are to be given precedence over the pursuit of knowledge and its obligations.

Yet those whose pursuits and whose entire lives have been devoted to the acquisition of knowledge have not shrunk from furthering the benefits and interests of mankind. They have educated many to become better citizens, and to render more useful service to their communities. Take as examples the Pythagorean Lysis who taught Epaminondas of Thebes, and Plato who taught Dion of Syracuse.* Such teachers have been many, and many have benefited. My own services to the state, such as they were (if indeed there have been any), stemmed from my having entered public life schooled and

156   equipped by my teachers and their learning.* Not merely do these men educate and instruct those willing to learn during their lives among us; even after their deaths they achieve the same end by the writings which are their legacy. No issue concerning laws, ancestral customs, and political conduct has been passed over by them. Their political inactivity seems to have been devoted to promoting our activity. Thus those very scholars by their devotion to learning and wisdom are applying their intelligence and insight to the benefit of mankind above all. It is for this reason that copious utterance, if it is sagacious, is better than the most penetrating speculation which is

not communicated; for speculation turns in on itself, whereas eloquence embraces those with whom we are joined in community.

Bees do not swarm to fashion honeycombs; they fashion them 157
because they are sociable by nature. It is the same with humans,* but
much more so; only when nature has brought them together do they
apply their intelligence to action and reflection. It follows that if the
virtue whose role lies in the protection of society (in other words, in
the fellowship of the human race) were to have no connection with
the pursuit of knowledge, that knowledge would appear isolated and
barren; and again, greatness of soul, if detached from society and the
bonding between men, would be akin to bestiality and barbarism. So
human association and community take precedence over the thirst
for knowledge.

Some people advance the thesis that community and fellowship 158
among men have arisen from the needs of life, because we could not
achieve and perform what nature required without the help of
others; but this is untrue. If all that we need for food and clothing
were supplied to us by the magician's wand, as the saying goes,* then
everyone with outstanding brains would abandon all business activities, and spend their time in reflection and the pursuit of knowledge.
But such is not the case; a man like that would flee from his isolation
and look for a companion to share his study. Then he would be eager
to teach and learn, to listen and speak, turn and turn about. So every
obligation which effectively safeguards men's association and fellowship with each other is to be preferred to that which is inherent in
reflection and the search for knowledge.

The question should perhaps be raised whether the sense of com- 159
munity, which is especially linked to nature, is always to be ranked
above restraint and moderation as well. I do not believe so, for there
are activities, some so degrading and others so criminal, that no man
of wisdom would perform them, even to save his country. Posidonius
has listed many of these,* but some are so grisly and so indecent that
it seems demeaning even to mention them. So the wise man will not
undertake these on behalf of the state, and the state will not even
wish to have them undertaken on its behalf. But happily enough no
situation can arise when it is in the interest of the state that a wise
man should perform any such acts.

So we can consider it proved that when we have to choose between 160
different obligations, the kind that takes precedence is that

demanded by fellowship in society; for when action is the outcome of knowledge allied to prudence, it will be thought through. Thus considered action is of more value than prudent reflection.

So much, then, for this question. The topic has now been clarified so that it is not difficult, when we investigate what our obligation is, to see which should prevail over another. And when we consider the sense of community in itself, there are different levels of obligation, but it can be readily realised which of these takes precedence over others. The first duty is owed to the immortal gods, the second to our country, the third to our parents, and others to the rest on a descending scale.*

161   Our brief survey of this question allows us to realise that people are often in doubt not only whether some act is honourable or mean, but also which is the more honourable when two honourable courses lie before us. As I said earlier, this problem was passed over by Panaetius.* Let us now proceed to the rest of our discussion.

Book Two

I think, Marcus my son, that in the previous book I have sufficiently   1
explained how obligations derive from what is honourable, and from
each type of virtue. My next step is to analyse the kinds of obligation
which impinge upon our mode of living and on the availability of the
things which men put to use, their wealth and their resources. As I have
mentioned,* our investigation here concerns what is useful and what
is not, and beyond that, which of these useful things is the more and the
most useful. I shall begin discussion of these issues once I have said a
few words about my overall purpose and my method of approach.

Though these books of mine have roused a number of people with   2
eagerness not only to read but also to write, from time to time I fear
that mention of philosophy is abhorrent to some men of integrity,*
and that they are surprised that I devote so much attention and time
to it. My position is this: so long as the state was governed by those
to whom it had entrusted itself, all my concerns and thinking were
concentrated upon it. But once Rome was wholly in thrall to the
dominion of a single man,* and there was no scope whatever to offer
advice or authoritative guidance, and finally, once I had lost the men
of the highest calibre* as associates in the defence of the republic, I
refused to surrender either to feelings of anguish,* which would
have laid me low if I had not battled with them, or in turn to the low
pleasures which are unworthy of men of learning.

I only wish that the state had retained the form which it had of old,   3
and that it had not fallen into the hands of men who were eager not
so much to reform its politics as to subvert them. In the first place, I
should now be devoting more effort to public activity than to writing,
as was my routine when the republic still stood; and secondly, I
should be committing to writing not my present works but my
speeches, as I often did.* But once the republic, in which all my
attention, thought, and effort were centred, ceased wholly to exist,
inevitably those speeches delivered in court and in senate fell silent;
there were none to be written down.

4   But since my mind could not lie fallow, and since from my earliest days I had devoted myself to these studies, I decided that my troubles could be most honourably shrugged off if I turned back to philosophy. In my youth I had spent a great deal of time in educating myself in it, and once I began to shoulder the burden of offices and to commit myself wholly to politics, I gave such time to philosophy as I had left from that devoted to friends and to the state. But that time was spent entirely in reading,* for I did not have the leisure to write.

5   So though beset by the greatest misfortunes, I have, it seems, gained this blessing, of writing on topics with which my fellow-citizens were insufficiently acquainted, and which were supremely worth knowing; for in heaven's name, what is more desirable, more pre-eminent, better, and worthier of a human being than wisdom? Philosophers is the name given to those who seek it, and *philosophia*, should you wish to translate it, is nothing else but zeal for wisdom. As philosophers of old defined it,* wisdom is the knowledge of things divine and human, and of the causes that hold them together. Should anyone pour scorn on such study, I cannot possibly imagine

6   what such a person thinks worth praising. If on the one hand you seek intellectual pleasure and respite from your troubles, can there be any to compare with the pursuits of those who are for ever investigating all that looks to and promotes the good and happy life? If on the other hand what you have in mind is the means to steadfastness and virtue, this is the discipline* by which to attain them, or no such possibly exists. To claim that there is no branch of study which broaches the greatest questions when no subject however trivial is without one, is the mark of men who speak with insufficient reflection, and who go astray in matters of the greatest importance. But if some means of studying virtue does exist, where will you look for it if once you abandon this branch of learning?

When I recommend the study of philosophy, I usually argue this case more meticulously, as I have done in another book.* But at the present time it was incumbent on me merely to explain why I had recourse to this pursuit rather than to any other, once I was deprived of my functions in politics.

7   But objections are raised against me,* and this, mind you, by men of learning and education. They ask whether I seem to show consistency, for though I maintain that we can grasp nothing for certain, I am none the less in the habit of discoursing on other issues, and at

this very time I am pursuing the rules for obligation. I only wish that these critics were sufficiently aware of our position. We are not the sort of people whose minds are adrift in error, and who never have a guiding star to follow.* What sort of mentality, or rather, what sort of life would it be, if a rational basis not merely of argument but also of living were taken away? The other schools say that some things are certain and others uncertain;* we disagree with them, and say that some things are probable and others improbable. So what is there to prevent me from following what seem to me to be probabilities, and from repudiating improbabilities? And by avoiding the conceit of making dogmatic claims, from giving a wide berth to the rash judgement which is so greatly alien to true wisdom? Our school mounts arguments against every thesis, because what is actually probable could not emerge clearly unless there were the clash of arguments from the two sides. But I consider that I have explained this with sufficient care in my book the *Academica*.* I know that you, my dear Cicero, are installed in a most ancient and famous school of philosophy, with Cratippus as your spokesman;* he comes very close to matching the founders of your noble tradition. None the less, I did not wish you to remain ignorant of these tenets of ours which are akin to yours.*

Let us now embark upon our appointed topic.

For the performance of obligations I have advanced five approaches.* Two of them relate to what is fitting and honourable. A further two are concerned with advantages in life, namely resources, wealth, and talents. The fifth lies in making a studied choice should there appear to be conflict between those which I have mentioned. The part of our discussion dealing with the honourable is now completed, and I want you to be familiar with this above all.

The topic with which we are now concerned is termed 'the useful'. Usage with regard to this word has become corrupted and has lost its way. It has gradually declined to the point at which the honourable is detached from the useful, and it maintains that there is something honourable which is not useful, and something useful which is not honourable. Nothing more destructive than this can be imposed on human life.

Philosophers who wield the highest authority quite rigorously and conscientiously make a distinction in thought between these three intermingled concepts:* they argue that what is just is also useful, and again that what is honourable is also just. The conclusion from this is that whatever is honourable is also useful.* Those who fail to see this are people who often venerate only tricksters, and mistake perversity for wisdom. Their misguided thinking should be eradicated, and their views should be wholly converted to the expectation of coming to realize that they can achieve their aims by honourable designs and by just deeds, not by deceit and evildoing.

11   To proceed, then. Of the things which make for the maintenance of human life,* some are inanimate, like gold and silver, produce from the earth, and other things of the same kind. Others are animate, and possess their own instincts and appetites; some of them are devoid of reason, while others apply it. Creatures devoid of reason include horses, oxen, other kinds of cattle, and bees;* their labour makes a contribution to men's needs and lives. The use of reason is ascribed to two classes: first, to the gods, and second, to men. Devotion and integrity will appease the gods, and following close behind the gods, men can be of the greatest service to their fellow-men. The

12   same division can be made with regard to things which harm and impede us, but because the gods are not thought to inflict harm, they are excluded from consideration, and men are thought to be the greatest stumbling-block to their fellow-men.

The things which we have called inanimate are mostly produced by men's labours.* We would not possess them without the application of manual labour and skill, and we would not enjoy them if men did not administer them. Indeed, without human effort there could have been no health care, no sailing, no agriculture, and no harvest-

13   ing or storing of crops and other types of produce. Further, there would certainly be no exports of our surplus products, nor imports of the goods which we need, if men did not discharge these tasks. By the same token, stones would not be quarried from the earth for our use, and 'iron, copper, gold and silver, hidden deep within'* would not be mined without man's manual labour. As for houses for warding off the crippling cold and alleviating the oppressive heat, how could they have been made available to the human race in the first place, or once they collapsed through a violent storm or earthquake or in the course of time, how could they have been repaired* subsequently, if men sharing life in community* had not learnt to seek

14   help in those circumstances from their fellows? Think, too, of aqueducts, canals diverted from rivers, irrigation channels in the fields,

breakwaters, artificial harbours—from where could we obtain these without men's labour? These examples and many others make it clear that the produce and benefits extracted from inanimate things could in no way have been obtained without the work of men's hands.

Finally, what benefit or advantage could be gained from the brute beasts if men did not lend a hand? Whoever those pioneers were who devised the benefit which we could derive from individual beasts, they were certainly human; and even today, if human beings did not apply themselves, we could not feed or tame or protect those animals, nor obtain from them the products which they yield in due season. Moreover, men both slaughter beasts which inflict damage on us, and capture those which can be of service.

Why should I catalogue the numerous skills without which 15 human life could not even have existed? How could the sick be tended, what pleasure could those in rude health enjoy, what means of sustenance or cultivated life would we have if those numerous skills did not confer on us those things by which our refined human existence contrasts so greatly with the sustenance and way of life of the beasts? Further, if men had not congregated, cities would not have been built and populated. It was in consequence of this that laws and traditions were established, and these were followed by fair apportionment of justice and a fixed and ordered mode of living. As a result of these, men developed a peaceable outlook and a sense of restraint; human life thus became more secure, and by giving and receiving, by interchange and application of talents we came to want for nothing.

I have laboured this point more than is necessary, for is there any- 16 one to whom Panaetius' verbose observations* are not obvious— namely, that no war leader or civil magistrate could have performed such great and saving exploits without the enthusiastic cooperation of his fellow-men? He recounts the names of Themistocles, Pericles, Cyrus, Agesilaus, and Alexander,* stating that none of them could have performed such great achievements without men's assistance. On an issue which is beyond doubt, the witnesses he cites are superfluous.

On the other hand, just as we derive great advantages from the cooperation and approval of other men, there is likewise no plague so abominable that it is not visited by one man on another. Dicaearchus, that great and prolific Peripatetic,* wrote a work called *On the*

Extinction of Human Life. Having assembled the other causes—
floods, epidemics, ravages of nature, sudden invasions by hordes of
wild beasts, the onset of which he demonstrates has caused the
exstirpation of certain races—he then shows how many more men
by contrast have been wiped out by attacks made by other men in
wars or civil commotions, than by all other disasters.

17   So in this matter there can be no doubt that men are the source of
both the greatest help and the greatest hindrance to their fellow-
men. For this reason I regard it as the peculiar function of virtue to
win over men's minds, and to harness them to its purposes. So all
that is useful to our human lives in inanimate things and in the
exploitation and handling of the brute beasts is the province of manual skills, whereas the enthusiastic support of men, ready and willing
to further our interests, is awakened by the wisdom and virtue of outstanding individuals.

18   All virtue in fact centres for the most part on three things.* The
first lies in detecting what is true and genuine in any instance, what
is consistent with it, and what are its consequences, origins, and
causes. The second restrains those mental disturbances which the
Greeks call *pathe* ('emotions'), and it subjects impulses (the Greek
for which is *hormai*) to the control of reason. The third enables us to
treat our associates in a restrained and expert way, so that with their
support we may have our natural needs supplied in full and abundant measure. With their help too we may dispel any difficulty which
comes our way, wreak vengeance on those who have sought to harm
us, and inflict such punishment as justice and decency allow.

19   I shall presently describe the means by which we can acquire this
flair for grasping and maintaining men's affections, but first I must
mention a few preliminaries. Is anyone unaware that Fortune plays a
major role* in both success and failure? When we coast on her
favouring breeze, we are borne to the outcome which we desire, but
when she blows in our faces we are in deep trouble. It is Fortune herself who dispenses those more occasional mishaps which arise firstly
from inanimate causes—storms, hurricanes, shipwrecks, falling
buildings, fires—and secondly from the brute beasts, when they lash
out or bite or attack us. As I say, these mishaps are comparatively
20   rare. Contrast with them the destruction of armies (three most
recently,* but often a large number), the disastrous downfall of generals (most recently, that of an eminent and exceptional man),* and

in addition the odium of the mob which results in the exile, downfall, and hasty departure of citizens who are often well-deserving.* On the other hand are the successes—magistracies, military commands, victories. Though all these are the outcome of chance, they cannot be brought about for better or worse without the resources and support of other men. Once this factor is taken into account, we must explain how we can entice and arouse the support of people to serve our interests. If this discussion is rather long, we must compare it with the scale of its usefulness, and then it will perhaps even seem too short.

The fact is that any contribution by men to further an individual's   21
prospects and distinction is made for a variety of reasons. It is either a mark of goodwill, when for some reason they show him affection; or to honour him, if they respect a person's merits, and consider him worthy of outstanding distinction; or because they trust him, and think that he is promoting their welfare; or they fear the resources he brings to bear; or they anticipate benefits from people like him, as when kings or 'people-pleasers'* offer hand-outs; or finally they are swayed by payments or reward for their services. This last is the most despicable and disgusting of motives, both for those attracted by it, and for those who seek to exploit it; for things have come to a pretty   22
pass when money is used as the bait for what should be achieved by merit. Occasionally, however, resort to such support is necessary. I shall explain how it should be directed once I have discussed the measures more in keeping with merit.

[Further,* men subject themselves to the dominion and power of another for several reasons. They are attracted either by goodwill, or by generous benefits received, or by a person's imposing rank, or in the hope that it will prove advantageous to them, or through fear that they may be compelled by force to comply, or they may be enticed by the hope and promises of a hand-out, or finally, and this is frequently to be observed in this state of ours, they may be bribed.]

Of all these possibilities, none is more calculated to secure and to   23
retain influence than winning affection, and none is more repugnant than being feared. Ennius* expresses this second point well:

> Him whom they fear, they hate; and him whom all men hate
> They would see dead.

Realization has lately dawned, if it was not grasped before, that no amount of influence can withstand the hatred of the masses. The death of this tyrant of ours, whom our state when crushed by armed force endured, and whom it obeys more especially now that he is dead,* is not unique in testifying to the power of men's hatred to sow destruction; other tyrants too have met similar ends, and scarcely one of them has avoided a fate like his. Fear is a poor guarantor of a long life, whereas goodwill is a faithful one, and indeed endures forever.

24   Admittedly, those who by the power of office repress subjects who have been brought low by force must inevitably deal harshly with them, as masters do with their servants if these cannot be controlled in any other way. But men who set themselves up as objects of fear in a free society are the maddest of the mad, for even if the laws have been swamped by the resources of some individual, and even if freedom has been intimidated, sooner or later they surface again, whether in verdicts passed silently in court or in secret ballots for magistracies.* Freedom which has been discontinued has a fiercer bite than when it has been maintained. Let us therefore embrace the policy which extends most widely, and which is most efficacious in promoting not merely our safety, but also our resources and our power: fear must be banished, and affection must be preserved, for in this way we shall most easily fulfil our aspirations both in private and in public affairs.

25   Indeed, if men wish to be feared they must inevitably fear those by whom they will be feared. Take the elder Dionysius:* with what tortured fear do you imagine he was racked when through apprehension of the barber's knife he had his hair singed with a burning coal? As for Alexander of Pherae,* what mental strain do we reckon dominated his life? The version I have read has it that he loved his wife Thebe greatly, yet after feasting before joining her in the bedchamber he would order a barbarian (the written account has it, would you believe, that he was tattooed in the Thracian mode) to precede him with sword drawn, and he would send ahead members of his entourage to examine the lady's boxes and to search her clothing in case a weapon was hidden there. Poor fellow, imagining that a barbarian, and one tattooed at that, was more trustworthy than his wife! His fears were justified, for he was killed by her own hand because she suspected him of keeping a mistress.

Moreover, no high office wields power so great that it can continue

for long under the pressure of fear. Phalaris,* whose cruelty was   26
more notorious than that of any other, bears witness to this. He met
his death not in ambush like the Alexander I mentioned just now,
and not at the hands of a few like this tyrant of ours,* but in an attack
by the entire population of Agrigentum. Again, did not the Macedonians abandon Demetrius and as one transfer their support to
Pyrrhus?* A further example: when the Spartans wielded power
unjustly, did not virtually all their allies abandon them, and witness
their debacle at Leuctra* without raising a hand?

In such a matter as this, it is more pleasant for me to recall examples from abroad rather than those of our own. But for so long as
the empire of the Roman people was maintained in a spirit of service
rather than by injustices, wars were waged either on behalf of allies
or in the interests of empire; the outcome of those wars was dictated
either by clemency or by necessity. The senate was a haven and
refuge for kings, tribes, and nations.* Our magistrates and commanders were eager to win the greatest praise solely by endeavouring to
defend our provinces and allies with justice and fidelity. As a result,   27
'protectorate of the world' rather than 'empire' would have been a
truer title.

Even before Sulla won his victory,* we were already desisting
from this practice of disciplined behaviour, but after it we abandoned it entirely. All ill-treatment of our allies ceased to appear
unjust, once such monstrous cruelty towards citizens became conspicuous. Thus in Sulla's case an honourable cause was followed by
a dishonourable victory; for he erected the auction-spear in the
forum,* and in selling the possessions of men of principle and
wealth, and all of them at any rate his fellow-citizens, he had the gall
to claim that he was selling booty he had won. After him came the
man whose cause was sacrilegious, and whose victory was still more
despicable, for not only did he declare the possessions of individual
citizens public property, but he laid hands on whole provinces and
districts;* his sole code of conduct was to ruin them.

In consequence, foreign nations have been harassed and devas-   28
tated. We have witnessed the city of Massilia borne in triumph* to
exemplify the loss of empire, and a triumph celebrated over the city
without whose help our commanders never gained a triumph for
wars conducted beyond the Alps. I could recount many other
heinous wrongs against allies, if this had not been unique among all

the indignities on which the sun has looked down. So we are justly feeling the lash, for if we had not allowed the crimes of the many to go unpunished, such licence would never have passed to that one man. His estate has been inherited by the few,* but his acts of greed by numerous scoundrels.

29   The seed and root cause of civil wars will never disappear as long as unscrupulous men both recall and hope to see again that blood-stained spear. Publius Sulla had brandished it when his kinsman was dictator, and some thirty-five years later the same man did not shrink from grasping one still more crime-laden.* Yet another Publius Sulla,* who had been a clerk in that earlier dictatorship, was urban quaestor in this recent one, a fact which must make us realize that if such rewards are in prospect, there will never be absence of civil wars. So the walls of our city houses alone are up and standing, but even they now fear the final criminal assault; the republic we have lost utterly. And to return to the point at issue, we have plunged into this disaster through choosing to be feared rather than to be cherished as the object of affection. If such a fate could befall the Roman people through its unjust dominion, what attitude should individuals take?

So since it is obvious that the impact of goodwill is great, whereas that of fear is weak, it follows that we should now discuss the means by which we can most easily attain with honour and good faith the

30   affection which we desire. We do not all, however, have need of such affection to the same degree. We must adjust our thinking, according to the pattern of life we have each established, whether we require affection from the many, or whether that of a few is enough. What is certainly necessary as the first and most vital prerequisite is to have the faithful intimacy of friends* who love us and who admire our qualities. This is surely the one thing which eminent and undistinguished men alike have most in common; it is to be sought in almost

31   equal measure by both. It is perhaps true that all men do not need honour and glory and the goodwill of citizens to the same extent, but if these accrue to an individual, they are of considerable help both in general and in forging friendships in particular.

But I have discussed friendship in another book entitled *Laelius*. I must now speak of glory. Though there are two books of mine on this subject as well,* I must touch upon it here, since it is of the greatest help in dealing with matters of greater importance. Glory at its highest and most complete depends on these three factors: the affection of the commons, the trust they feel, and their belief mingled with admiration that recipients are worthy of honour. To put it plainly and briefly, these responses are evoked in the people at large in the same way as they are awakened in individuals. But there is another approach* as well to the people which enables us to gain access, so to say, to the minds of the whole community.

Of the three responses which have earlier been mentioned let us 32 look first at recommended means of obtaining goodwill. This is gained most of all by services rendered. Second, goodwill is awakened by the desire to perform these services, even if they fail to materialize. Then, too, what strongly rouses the affection of the masses is the actual report and reputation which a person has for generosity, kindness, justice, good faith, and all the virtues associated with civilized and affable manners. Indeed, because that very quality which we call the honourable and fitting is inherently pleasing to us, and since by its nature and beauty it awakens the approval of all as it reflects the brilliance of the virtues which I mentioned, we are compelled by nature herself to feel affection for those in whom we think these virtues reside. These, then, are the weightiest reasons why people feel affection; beyond these there can be others which are less substantial.

Trust reposed in us can be established by two qualities, that is, if 33 people come to believe that we have acquired prudence allied with justice. We put trust in those whom we regard as more perceptive than ourselves, who we believe can anticipate future events,* and who at a critical point in some action we think can cope with the situation by adopting a plan to meet the emergency—for this is the prudence which men account to be useful and genuine. As for men of justice, in other words, 'good men',* trust in them depends on their having no suspicion of deceit and injustice in their make-up. So these are the men to whom we believe our safety, our possessions, and our children are most justifiably entrusted. Of the two virtues, justice is 34 more influential in instilling trust, for it carries sufficient authority though unaccompanied by prudence; on the other hand, prudence without justice would be ineffective in inspiring trust, for should belief in a person's integrity be withdrawn, the more crafty and clever he is, the more loathsome and suspect he becomes. So justice when joined to good sense will possess all the desired resources to inspire trust. Justice without prudence will be highly effective, but prudence without justice will make no impact.

35   But all philosophers agree, as I too have often argued, that the man who possesses one virtue possesses them all.* I would not have anyone registering surprise that I now separate them from each other in this way, as if anyone who is not also prudent can be just. The fact is that truth itself when honed in argument is one thing, but quite another when all that we say is adapted to popular beliefs. So at this juncture I speak with the voice of the common folk when I say that some men are brave, others are good, and others still are prudent; for when discussing popular notions we must employ popular, everyday expressions. Panaetius adopted the same practice.*

36   We must now revert to the subject in hand. Of the three factors which we said contributed to glory, the third was that people should admire us and judge us worthy of honour. What this means is that men admire in general all great achievements which confound their expectations, and in particular if they observe in individuals certain good qualities of an unusual kind. So they look up to and lavish abundant praise on men in whom they think they see outstanding and unique merits, whereas they despise and hold cheap those who they believe lack excellence, spirit, and energy. So it is not that they despise all who meet with their disapproval. Men whom they regard as unprincipled, slanderous, deceitful, and disposed to commit injustice they certainly do not despise, but they have a poor opinion of them. So as I said before, the men whom they despise are those 'who profit neither themselves nor their neighbour',* as the saying goes, since they lack application, diligence, and responsibility.

37   By contrast, admiration is won by men believed to excel others in merit, to distance themselves from disgrace, and to withstand the vices which others find hard to resist: for on the one hand, pleasures, those captivating mistresses, prise the minds of the majority away from virtue, and on the other hand most men are terrified beyond measure when the flaming brands of physical pain are applied to them.* Issues of life and death, the prospect of riches or of poverty, are of great concern to them. When these contrasting challenges are viewed with disdain by men of lofty and proud spirit, especially when some momentous and worthwhile issue confronting them attracts and focuses universal attention upon them, who would not

38   admire the brilliance and beauty of such merit? Therefore this

disdain arouses great admiration; and justice above all, the single
virtue which bestows the accolade 'good' on men,* seems to the
rank-and-file to be something remarkable. And rightly so, for no
man can be just who fears death or pain or exile or poverty, or who
ranks the opposites of these before fair dealing. People admire most
of all the man who is indifferent to money; they consider that anyone
in whom this attitude is observed has been tried by fire.*

So justice fulfils all three prerequisites for gaining glory: goodwill,
because it seeks to benefit the greatest number; good faith, for the
same reason; and admiration, because it despises and ignores those
things which fire most men with greed, and possesses them.

My own opinion, for what it is worth, is that every ordered course 39
and direction of life needs the help of other men, especially those
with whom we can converse intimately, and this is hard to attain
unless you project the image of the good man. So a reputation for
justice is vital even for the isolated country-dweller, and it is all the
more important because if men do not have it, they will have no
defences to shield them, and they will become the target of many
injustices. Justice is vital also for those who buy and sell, for those 40
who hire and let, and in general for those involved in commercial
transactions. The impact of it is so great that even those whose bread
and butter is evildoing and crime cannot exist without some small
element of justice;* for if a man steals or extracts something from
one of his associates in brigandage, he forfeits his position even in the
ranks of banditry. As for the pirate-king so called, should he not allocate the booty fairly, he would be killed or abandoned by his com-
rades; indeed, it is said that bandits have their laws which they must
obey and keep. Hence it was because of their just allocation of booty
that Bardylis, the Illyrian brigand who appears in Theopompus'
pages, acquired considerable wealth, and Viriathus the Lusitanian*
gained much more. (It was this Viriathus who forced even Roman
armies and commanders to retreat. Gaius Laelius, who has the
sobriquet 'The Wise',* was the man who as praetor broke his resistance and cut him down to size, so restraining his aggression that he
bequeathed to his successors a war easy to win.)

So since justice makes such an impact that it strengthens and
increases the power even of bandits, how great do we assess its likely
effect to be in the realm of laws and courts and constitutional government? I believe that it was not merely among the Medes, as noted 41

by Herodotus,* but also among our own ancestors that in days of old men of good character were established as kings so that justice could be beneficial; for initially the common folk were oppressed by those with greater resources. They sought refuge with some individual outstanding in virtue; he shielded the more needy from injustice. By establishing fair dealing, he reined in highest and lowest together under the equality of justice. The establishment of laws had the same origin as that of kings; for rights made fair for all have always been sought, and they could exist in no other way. If the community obtained them from a single just and good man, they remained happy with him. When this failed to obtain, laws were devised* to speak with one and the same voice at all times and with all men.

42

So what emerges clearly is that men were regularly chosen to rule whose reputation for justice was high among the common folk. When in addition the same leaders were regarded as prudent as well, there was nothing which the citizens at large believed they could not achieve under their guidance. So justice must be cultivated and maintained by every means, both for its own sake (otherwise it would not be justice) and to enhance our honour and glory.

Just as there is a systematic way not only of making money, but also of investing it to meet our continuing expenses both for necessities and for generous giving, so glory must be systematically both acquired and invested. It is true, however, that Socrates nobly declared* that the nearest path to glory was by taking the short cut, so to say, of behaving in such a way as to be the kind of person you would like to be thought to be. If people imagine that they can obtain enduring glory by deceit and empty exhibitionism and hypocrisy in word and look, they are wildly off the mark. True glory drops roots and also spreads its branches wide, whereas all false claims swiftly wither like frail blossoms, for no pretence can be long-lasting. Numerous witnesses attest the good and the bad in this, but in the interests of brevity we will content ourselves with a single family. Tiberius Gracchus, son of Publius, will win praise for as long as remembrance of Roman history survives, whereas his sons in life failed to gain the approval of good men, and in death they are numbered among those who deserved to be slain.* So the man who wishes to win true glory must discharge the obligations of justice, as described in the previous book.*

43

44   Though there is the greatest force in the argument that we should

be as we wish to be regarded, certain rules must be laid down to ensure that we most readily appear to be what we are. If someone from his early years has some claim on fame and distinction, whether bequeathed by his father (as I think, dear Cicero, has happened in your case) or by some fluke or chance happening, the eyes of the world are directed upon him. People enquire about his activities and about the sort of life he is living. As if he were caught in a dazzling spotlight, no word, no deed of his can remain hidden.

By contrast, those whose early years are unknown to the world 45 because of their lowly origin and shadowy background, must on approaching manhood nurse great ambitions, and strive to achieve them by worthy pursuits. They will perform these with greater assurance because at that age not only do they not meet with envy, but they even win support. The first thing, then, which commends a young man for glory is if any of it can be gained in warfare. Many youths among our forbears attained prominence in this way, for wars were virtually always being waged. Your own youthful years coincided with the war in which one side showed excess of villainy, and the other failure to succeed. In that war Pompey appointed you to command a cavalry squadron,* and you won great praise from that most eminent man and from the army for your horsemanship, your skill with the javelin, and your endurance of all the toils of a soldier. That praise you won withered away just as the republic did. However, the discussion on which I have embarked is concerned not with you personally, but with the whole category of youths, so we must proceed to the issues which remain.

In other activities generally the roles played by the mind greatly 46 outweigh those of the body, and likewise the projects which we pursue by use of our brains and rational faculties are much more rewarding than those achieved by physical strength. Favourable notice, then, results initially from modesty, followed by devotion to parents and kindness to one's family-circle. But the easiest and most desirable way of gaining recognition is followed by young men who seek the company of the famous and wise who are devoted to the best interests of the state. If they often appear in the company of these men, they give folk the impression that they will turn out like those whom they have chosen as their models. The presence of Publius 47 Rutilius in the house of Publius Mucius* led public opinion to acknowledge the youth as a person of integrity with knowledge of the law. As for Lucius Crassus, even at a comparatively early age he did not borrow fame on credit from anyone else, but gained the greatest praise on his own account through that celebrated and famous speech* which he made for the prosecution. At the age when students usually win praise for school exercises, as we are told Demosthenes did,* Lucius Crassus revealed that he was already performing brilliantly in the courts with speeches which would have won him praise if they had been part of his studies at home.

48   There are two forms of discourse, the first conversation and the second argumentation.* There is no doubt at all that in pursuit of glory argumentation has the greater force, for this is the medium which we call eloquence; on the other hand, it is hard to say to what extent friendly and affable conversation captivates men's hearts. Letters have survived composed by three men who we are told were masters of practical wisdom: the first was sent by Philip to Alexander, the second by Antipater to Cassander, and the third by Antigonus to his son Philip.* Their advice in these letters is to win over the hearts of the common folk by graciously addressing them, and thus to gain their affection; and again, to soften the spirits of the soldiers by addressing them with honeyed words.

As for the argumentative type of speech made before a crowd, this is often a source of glory gained from all quarters, for there is great admiration for a person who speaks with fluency and wisdom, and his listeners believe that his understanding and intelligence transcend that of others. If indeed a speech combines sobriety with moderation, there can be no performance more admirable, the more so if these qualities are evinced in a young man.

49   There are several types of theme which call for eloquence, and in our state many young men have won praise by speaking before juries, and in the presence of the people, and in the senate. But the greatest admiration is reserved for speeches in lawsuits. These are of two kinds, speeches for the prosecution and speeches for the defence. Of the two, speeches for the defence are the more praiseworthy, but quite often speeches for the prosecution win approval. I mentioned the example of Crassus a moment ago, and Marcus Antonius did the same thing while still a young man. The eloquence of Publius Sulpicius also became celebrated by a speech for the prosecution, when he indicted that factious good-for-nothing of a citizen, Gaius Norbanus.*

But speeches for the prosecution should not often be undertaken,   50
and only ever for the good of the state, as was true in the cases of the
men I have mentioned, or as an act of revenge, as exemplified by
the two Luculli, or in the patron's role, like my action on behalf of the
Sicilians and that of Julius on behalf of the Sardinians.* The effort
put in by Lucius Fufius in indicting Manius Aquilius* has also been
recognized. So a prosecution should be undertaken only once, or at
any rate not often. If, however, someone has to prosecute more frequently, he should undertake the role on behalf of the state, for it is
not blameworthy to take vengeance on its enemies time and time
again. But there should be a limit to this activity, for it is seen as the
act of a heartless man, an act indeed bordering upon the inhuman, to
prosecute many people on capital charges. Putting yourself in the
situation of being called 'the prosecutor' is both hazardous to your
person and demeaning to your reputation. This is what happened to
Marcus Brutus,* a man of most distinguished family, and the son of
an outstanding expert in civil law.

There is this further stipulation which obligation demands   51
should be carefully observed: you must never indict an innocent
person on a capital charge, for in no circumstances can this be undertaken without doing grievous wrong. What deed is so unworthy of a
man as to prostitute that eloquence bestowed by nature for the safety
and preservation of our fellows, so as to achieve the ruin and destruction of good men? This must certainly be avoided; on the other hand,
one need have no scruple about defending a guilty man on occasion,
so long as he is not a sacrilegious scoundrel. The common folk consent to this; custom permits it; humanity tolerates it. In lawsuits it is
the duty of the juryman always to seek the truth, but sometimes the
advocate's task is to maintain the plausible, even if it is less than the
truth. I should not presume to write such words, especially in a treatise on philosophy, if Panaetius, that most earnest of Stoics, did not
approve the practice.*

But glory and popularity are gained above all by undertaking cases
for the defence, and the more so should it happen to be in support of
one who is apparently encompassed and harassed by the resources of
some powerful person. I myself did this on numerous occasions,
notably in defending Sextus Roscius of Ameria in the face of Lucius
Sulla's power when he was master of the state and I was still a young
man, That speech, as you know, still survives.*

52 Now that I have explained these obligations of young men which succeed in gaining glory, I must next discuss beneficence and generosity.* There are two ways of dispensing this: you can be generous to those in need with either active help or with money. The second is easier to provide, especially if you are wealthy, but the first is nobler, more impressive, and worthier of a courageous and eminent man: for though both types bespeak a generous willingness to show kindness, the one is a drain on your finances, but the other on your virtue. Moreover, to bestow money from family coffers means that you exhaust the very source of your generosity;* in this way kindness is eliminated by kindness, for the more people you have helped by drawing upon it, the fewer you will be able to help hereafter.

53 But if people demonstrate by their efforts kindness and generosity, that is, by their virtue and application, to begin with, the more people they benefit, the more helpers they will have in performing works of kindness. Second, the regular practice of showing kindness will make them readier and more practised, so to say, at gaining the gratitude of many.

That was a noteworthy rebuke of Philip's* to his son Alexander for seeking to win the goodwill of the Macedonians by gifts of money: 'What on earth were you thinking of, to hope that men whom you had bribed would be faithful to you? Is your aim to make the Macedonians hope that you will be not their king, but their servant and supplier?' That phrase 'servant and supplier' was splendid, because that role was demeaning for a king; better still was his description of gifts of money as bribery, for the person who receives them changes for the worse, and is readier to be always on the look-out for the same treatment. Philip made this point to his son, but we are to regard it as

54 advice for all. So there is absolutely no doubt that kindness which involves effort and application is the more honourable, extends more widely, and can benefit more people.

On occasion, however, gifts of money should be made, so this type of kindness is not to be wholly rejected. It should often be bestowed from the family coffers on suitable recipients in need, but with discretion and in modest amounts, for many people have squandered their inheritance by ill-considered gifts. What is more stupid than to act in such a way that you can no longer do what you enjoy doing? Moreover, profligate giving is followed by seizure from others,* for when men begin to run short through dispensing gifts, they are driven to lay hands on other people's possessions. The result is that though they wish to be benefactors in order to accumulate good-will, the support given by recipients is outweighed by the hatred of those who have suffered losses. So family finances are not to be battened 55 down so tightly that kindness cannot open them, nor yet made so accessible as to be exposed to all the world. Due limit must be observed, and must be related to our means. We should in all circumstances remember the phrase which is so often invoked by our countrymen that it has passed into proverbial usage: 'The pot of giving has no bottom.'* What limit can there be to it, when those who are regular recipients and others as well have their eyes trained on the same source?

In general, people who dispense money fall into two groups, the extravagant and the generous. The extravagant squander their money on civic feasts, distributions of meat,* gladiatorial shows, promotion of public games and wild-beast chases,* all outlays for which they will be remembered only briefly or not at all. Generous folk on the other hand apply their resources to redeeming captives from pirates,* relieving friends from the burden of debt, or helping them to provide dowries for their daughters, or aiding them in the acquisition or extension of property.

So I wonder whatever Theophrastus was thinking of in his book 56 *On Riches*,* in which among much that is admirable he makes a ridiculous suggestion. He waxes eloquent in praise of large-scale provision of shows for the people, and considers the reward of wealth to lie in providing the resources for such outlays. But in my view the fruits of generosity, as in the examples I have cited, seem much greater and surer. How much weightier and truer is Aristotle's rebuke, when he censures our failure to be astonished at such lavish expenditure of funds to appease the mob! He adds* that if defenders when blockaded by an enemy were compelled to pay a *mina* for a pint of water,* that would at first seem to us unbelievable and cause universal astonishment; but that if we reflect on it, necessity makes it pardonable. Yet we are not much surprised at that monstrous wastage and limitless outlay, even though it relieves no need, fails to enhance our worth, and affords delight to the mob for no more than a brief and passing moment: moreover, that delight is experienced by the most fickle of the citizens, whose recollection of the pleasure dies as soon as they are sated with it. Aristotle's conclusion is sound, that 57 these diversions amuse boys, giddy women, slaves, and free men with servile minds, but they can in no way be approved by the individual of serious bent who weighs events with steady judgement.

I do realize, however, that in the good old days of our state it had become customary to demand that prominent citizens should enhance their aedileships with public splendour. So it was that Publius Crassus, rich by surname (*Dives*) and rich in possessions, put on the most elaborate shows in his tenure of the aedileship, and a little later Lucius Crassus, aedile in the same year as that most modest of men Quintus Mucius, adorned the office* with the most spectacular display. After him Gaius Claudius, son of Appius, and many others subsequently—the Luculli, Hortensius, Silanus—did likewise.* But in the year of my consulship, Publius Lentulus outdid all his predecessors, and Scaurus followed suit; and my friend Pompeius* in his second consulship put on the most splendid shows. You know my views on all these performances.

58   Yet any suspicion of playing the miser is to be avoided. Mamercus, that richest of men, sidestepped the aedileship,* a move which caused him to be rejected for the consulship. So if such entertainment is demanded by the people, good men should provide it, if not enthusiastically at any rate with a good grace, so far as their means permit. This is what I myself did,* and what should be done if some more important and more useful purpose is served by distribution to the people. Orestes, for example, has recently won great prestige by providing street-dinners as religious tithe-offerings. People did not regard it as reprehensible, either, when Marcus Seius distributed corn to the populace at an *as* per peck, when the market price was high; he freed himself from considerable and long-standing odium by an outlay which was neither discreditable, since he was an aedile, nor expensive. But the greatest prestige of all was gained in recent years by my friend Milo,* for he purchased gladiators to defend the republic (for its cohesion was dependent on my safety), and thus he suppressed every fanatical onset of Publius Clodius.

59   So the justification for dispensing money is either necessity or expediency, and in these cases the rule of the golden mean is best. Mind you, that highly talented and outstandingly famous person Lucius Philippus, son of Quintus, used to boast that he had attained all the positions regarded as most distinguished without mounting any shows; Cotta and Curio made the same claim. I too can make the

same boast up to a point,* for the outlay in my aedileship was modest indeed when compared with the distinction of the magistracies which I obtained by the votes of all the tribes in the earliest year possible for me, a result which none of those men just mentioned managed to achieve.

There are also outlays of the better kind, spent on walls, dock 60
yards, harbours, aqueducts, and all works useful to the state. It is true that distributions pressed here and now into the hands, so to say, of recipients are more greatly appreciated, but the works I cited win more approval from a later age. Out of respect for Pompeius,* I am rather reluctant to criticize the building of theatres, colonnades, and new temples, but men of the greatest learning do not approve of these, including Panaetius, whom I have followed a great deal in these books though not word for word,* and Demetrius of Phalerum, who censures the Greek leader Pericles for wasting so much money on the famous Propylaea.* But I have discussed this whole category of expenditure with care in the books which I have written *On the Republic.**

To sum up, then, the practice of dispensing money on such a scale is flawed in kind, but on occasion is necessary. Even then it must be reconciled with our means, and be restricted to a moderate scale.

So far as the second mode of giving, that motivated by generos 61
ity,* is concerned, our attitude should not be one and the same when cases differ. The situation of the man hounded by disaster is different from that of the person who seeks greater prosperity but suffers no adversity. We should be more inclined to be indulgent to those 62
caught up in disaster, unless their plight happens to be deserved, but we should certainly not be at all niggardly to those seeking to better their status rather than to avoid disaster. But we are to apply judgement and care in selecting suitable recipients. As Ennius well says,*

Good deeds when ill-applied I count as evil deeds.

A gift bestowed on a man who is good and grateful gains its reward 63
both from the recipient and from everyone else; for so long as we forgo rash giving, generosity is highly popular, and most people praise it, because the kindness of eminent men is the common refuge of all. We must therefore ensure that we benefit as many people as possible with these kindly gestures, so that the recollection of them passes down to their children and to later generations, so that they

cannot show lack of gratitude; for the whole world detests one who forgets a kindness, and counts such conduct as injustice inflicted on themselves, because it discourages generous giving; and they regard the perpetrator as an enemy to all the needier members of society.

However, when captives are ransomed from slavery, and those in greater need are enriched, such kindness is a boon also to the community at large. In a detailed passage of a published speech of Crassus,* we see that this was a widespread custom of our senatorial order. This practice of good-heartedness I rank far above lavish outlay on public shows, for the first is characteristic of men of dignity and greatness, while the second is the practice of those who toady to the people by titillating the shallow minds of the mob with base pleasures.

64　　　　Fitting behaviour will include both generosity in giving and forbearance in exacting dues, and in the transaction of all business—buying and selling, hiring and letting, disputes with neighbours and boundary demarcations—being fair and affable, conceding to many people much that is rightfully yours, refraining from going to law in so far as a situation allows, and perhaps holding back a little more than that; for on occasion it is not only generous to forfeit a modicum of one's rights, but there are times when it is even profitable. We must, however, have regard for family possessions (for it is disgraceful to allow them to be frittered away), yet in such a way as to avoid suspicion of stinginess and miserliness. Undoubtedly the greatest boon of wealth is to be able to show generosity without plundering one's inheritance.

There is also the issue of hospitality, which is rightly praised by Theophrastus.* My view is that it is most appropriate that the houses of eminent men should lie open to eminent guests, and the fact that foreigners do not forgo this kind of generosity when in our city confers distinction on our state.* Moreover, for those who wish to exercise considerable power in an honourable way, it is emphatically useful to deploy resources and influence by way of such guests to make one's presence felt amongst nations abroad. Theophrastus notes that Cimon at Athens offered hospitality even to the Laciads,* the citizens of his own deme. This was the arrangement he had made and the orders he had transmitted to his stewards, that any Laciads who had made the detour to his country house should be accorded every facility.

The kindnesses bestowed by personal effort rather than by con- 65
ferment of money are a boon both to the state at large and to individual citizens; for safeguarding the interests of individuals at law,*
assisting them with advice, and offering help with this kind of knowledge to as many people as possible plays an important part in increasing both our resources and our influence. This was one of many
outstanding achievements of our ancestors, that the knowledge and
interpretation of the impressive foundations of our civil law were
always held in the highest honour. Leading figures kept this expertise in their own hands until the chaos of our own times, but now, in
common with magistracies and all positions of dignity, the glory of
this knowledge has been extinguished. This decline is the more
deplorable for having occurred in the lifetime of the man who has
easily surpassed his predecessors in knowledge of the law,* as he has
matched them in distinction. This kind of assistance, then, finds
favour with many, and serves to put people under an obligation
because of the kindnesses shown to them.

Closely related to this legal expertise is skill in public speaking, 66
which carries greater weight, is more favourably received, and is more
decorative; for what accomplishment can excel eloquence in winning
the admiration of an audience, in raising the hopes of the needy, or in
gaining the gratitude of clients defended in court? This was why our
ancestors made eloquence the most honoured of civil accomplish-
ments. So if a man is articulate and takes readily to hard work, and
undertakes the defence of many clients without reluctance and without payment,* as was the practice amongst our forbears, the opportunities for bestowing kindnesses and offering advocacy are legion.

If only I did not fear to be complaining on my own account, this 67
topic would prompt me to lament the cessation—I hesitate to use the
word extinction—of eloquence.* Even so, we are aware of the orators who have perished, of how few show promise, and how fewer
still have ability—and how many display effrontery.

Not all, and indeed not many, can be expert in the law or in public
speaking. Nevertheless, a person can benefit many by his efforts in
seeking advantages for them, by speaking on their behalf before
jurymen and magistrates, by keeping an eye on a neighbour's
interests, or by invoking the help of legal advisers or advocates for the
defence. Those who render these services obtain the greatest favour,
and report of their efforts leaks out to a wide public.

68   There is no need to offer the obvious advice to be careful not to
offend some people while seeking to help others; for it often happens
that people affront those who should not be affronted, or those
whom it is unwise to affront. Men who do this unthinkingly are
guilty of carelessness; if they do it knowingly, of rashness. If you
annoy certain persons unwittingly, you must offer an excuse as best
you can to explain why what you did was necessary, and why you
could not have acted otherwise; and you must atone for what will
appear to be offensive by other efforts and observances.

69   Though in lending aid to individuals the tendency is to assess
their character or their status, the temptation is to assert, and people
accordingly commonly say, that in bestowing kindnesses their criterion is men's characters and not their status. It is an honourable
claim to make,* but is there anyone, I ask you, who in offering support would not opt for the favour of a man of substance and influence, rather than the cause of an excellent person without resources?
The fact is that our preference usually inclines more to the man from
whom there is the likelihood of a readier and swifter return. But we
should pay more attention to the nature of the case. Surely the point
is that if the needy person is a good man, he will certainly be grateful
even if he cannot return the favour. Someone put it well* when he
said that the person who keeps his money has not repaid it, and he
who has repaid it does not keep it; but the man who repays gratitude
keeps it, and in keeping it has repaid it.

        On the other hand, those who consider themselves to be well-
endowed, highly regarded, and fortunate, do not wish even to be
beholden to a kindness. They imagine that they have even conferred
a favour by accepting a gift, however great; moreover, they suspect
that something is being demanded or anticipated from them. As for
accepting patronage or being greeted as 'clients',* they consider that
70   a sentence of death. By contrast, the needy person believes that any
service offered is a tribute to his person and not to his status, and
accordingly he is eager to show gratitude not only to the person who
has merited it, but also to those from whom he anticipates future
help, for he is in need of many things. And not only does he refrain
from any exaggeration about any service he happens to perform, but
he even understates it. A further point to note is that if you defend a
man of wealth and high position, continuing gratitude is confined to
the recipient himself or perhaps also to his children. But if you

defend a man of slender means who is honest and unassuming, all the underprivileged who are not rascals (and they constitute a large proportion of the citizens) visualize you as a ready-made means of protection.

For this reason I believe that kindnesses are better bestowed on 71 men of integrity rather than on men well-endowed. We must in general ensure that we can oblige every class, but should dispute arise, we must surely invoke Themistocles as our authority.* When someone asked him whether he should espouse his daughter to a poor man of integrity or to a rich man of doubtful morals, 'My choice' he said 'is for a man without money rather than for money without a man.' But our morals have been poisoned and debased by admiration for riches. Yet what relevance has the size of a man's wealth to each one of us? It is perhaps an advantage to the one who possesses it, though that is not always the case. But assume that it is. He may have more money to spend, but how does that make him more honourable? However, if he is not merely rich but also a good man, his riches should not be an obstacle to our aiding him, so long as his money is not a factor. All decisions should rest not on the degree of wealth, but on the character of each person.

The final rule to be observed in bestowing kindnesses and personal effort is to mount no obstacle in the way of fairness, and to promote no injustice, for justice is the foundation of enduring praise and good repute, and without it nothing can merit approval.

Since we have now dealt with the category of kindnesses appro- 72 priate for individuals, we must next discuss those which relate to the citizen-body and the state. Some of them are of the type affecting the citizens as a whole, while others which receive a warmer welcome attach to individuals. Consideration should certainly be given, if possible, to both; the interests of individuals should certainly not be regarded as of lesser account, but such benefits should be for the good of the state, or at any rate not work to its detriment. Gaius Gracchus distributed corn on a large scale, and in consequence he emptied the treasury; by contrast the distribution by Marcus Octavius was modest,* and was both easily borne by the state and a vital provision to the common folk. In that sense it promoted the well-being of both the citizens and the state.

The chief preoccupation of the state-administrator must be to 73 ensure that the individual keeps what is his; there should be no

public confiscation of the possessions of private persons. The proposal of an agrarian law by Philippus* in his tribunate was a destructive measure, though when it was rejected he accepted the outcome
readily, and in so doing exhibited notable moderation. But many of
the claims in his speech were those of the demagogue, and especially
reprehensible was the statement that less than two thousand persons
in the state owned property. This was a pernicious speech, promoting as it did the equalization of property; what could be more baneful than that? Why, the chief motivation behind the establishment of
states and city structures was to ensure the maintenance of private
property; for though nature guided men to form communities, it was
in the hope of guarding their possessions* that they sought protection in cities.

74   A further precaution which we should take is to avoid the imposition of a property tax.* Measures must be taken long in advance to
avoid this, which our ancestors often imposed* because the treasury
was depleted and wars were being continually waged. But if the need
for this burden confronts any state (I prefer to speak in these terms
rather than to presage it for our own, since I am discussing states in
general, and not specifically our own), care must be taken to ensure
that all citizens realize that if they wish to survive, they must bow to
the inevitable. Moreover, all who guide the ship of state will have to
ensure an abundance of life's necessities. There is no need to explain
here how provision for these is usually made, and should be
made, for the solution is obvious;* mere reference to the matter was
necessary.

75   In all supervision of business and public service, what is para-
mount is that even the merest suspicion of greed be banished. It was
Gaius Pontius the Samnite* who remarked: 'If only Fortune had
preserved me and my birth until the Romans began to accept gifts! I
would not have allowed their dominion to survive for longer.' He
would surely have had to wait for many generations,* for it was only
recently that this plague has infected the state. So I am quite relieved
that Pontius lived then and not now, since he was such a forceful
character! It is less than a hundred and ten years since Lucius Piso
pioneered a law on extortion,* for previously there had been none.
But since then there have been so many laws, each one more stringent than the last, so many men on trial, so many condemned, so
fierce a war* caused through fear of prosecutions, such widespread

fleecing and plundering of allies while the laws and lawsuits were abrogated, that our welfare is dependent on the weakness of others rather than on our own strength.

Panaetius praises Africanus for his incorruptibility,* and rightly so. But he had other greater qualities, and praise for incorruptibility is owed not only to the man but also to his times. Paulus acquired all the massive treasures of the Macedonians,* and lodged so much money in the Roman treasury that this booty of a single general signalled the end of property taxes, yet he bestowed nothing on his own household except the enduring recollection of his fame. Africanus followed the example of his father,* becoming no richer after the overthrow of Carthage. Again, his fellow-censor Lucius Mummius was not a penny richer* for utterly destroying the richest of cities; he preferred to embellish Italy rather than his own house, yet in my view his house was embellished the more by the embellishment of Italy. 76

Therefore, to revert to the point from which my discussion digressed, there is no vice more squalid than greed, especially when evinced by leaders and rulers of the state; for to exploit the state for gain is not merely base but also criminal and wicked. So the oracular utterance of Pythian Apollo,* that Sparta was doomed to die through greed and nothing else, seems to have been prophetic not only for the Spartans, but also for all wealthy nations. There is no easier way for men who administer the state to gain the goodwill of the common folk than by incorruptibility and restraint. 77

So those who seek to pose as 'people-pleasers',* and with this in mind raise the agrarian issue to have owners shifted from their properties, or think that money owed by debtors should be remitted, are undermining the foundations of the state, which depends first and foremost on the harmony between classes (and this cannot continue to exist when some citizens are robbed of their money and others have their debts remitted), and secondly on fair dealing, which is totally abrogated if the individual cannot keep what belongs to him. For, as I remarked earlier,* the distinguishing feature of the community and the city is that every individual should maintain free and undisturbed control of his possessions. Moreover, when such men undermine the body-politic in this way, they do not even gain the favour which they anticipate, for the person who is robbed of his property becomes an enemy, and the man who is given it goes so far 78

79

as to pretend that he did not want it; above all, he hides delight at the
remission of his debts in case it appears that he was unable to meet
them. As for the man who has sustained the injustice, he both
remembers and makes known his resentment, and even if those who
have dishonestly acquired the money outnumber those from whom
it has been unjustly taken, they are not on that account also more
influential. It is not numbers that count in these situations, but the
weight that men bring to bear. And what fairness is there when a man
without property gains possession of land which has been in a
family for many years or even generations, and when the man who
has owned it loses it?

80   This type of injustice led to the expulsion of the ephor Lysander
by the Spartans, who then put king Agis to death;* such an act was
unprecedented at Sparta. From that time onward,* such dissensions
followed that tyrants took over, the nobility were exiled, and a state
with the most admirable of constitutions fell apart. Not merely did
Sparta itself collapse, but it also dislocated the rest of Greece
through the contagion of evils which originated with the Spartans
and spread more widely. Again, did not agrarian disputes bring
down the Gracchi here at home,* though they were sons of that
greatest of men Tiberius Gracchus, and grandsons of Africanus?

81   On the other hand, Aratus of Sicyon* wins deserved praise. His
city had been occupied by tyrants for fifty years. He set out from
Argos to Sicyon, entered the city secretly, and gained possession of
it. Once he had brought down the tyrant Nicocles by an unexpected
attack, he restored six hundred exiles who were formerly the wealthiest burghers of the city, and by his arrival brought freedom to the
state. But then he took note of the severe problem posed by the
ownership of properties. On the one hand, he considered it wholly
unjust that the exiles whom he himself had restored, and whose
possessions others had seized, should be deprived of them, but on
the other, he thought it hardly reasonable to dispossess those
whose ownership was of fifty years' standing, for after that lengthy
period many properties were possessed innocently by inheritance
or by purchase or by dowries. He accordingly decided that these
occupants should not be deprived of them, but that the previous
owners should be paid compensation.

82   Having decided that the problem was to be solved by awards of
money, he announced that he intended to go to Alexandria, and he

gave instructions that the dispute should be left on the table until his return. He then swiftly travelled to join his host Ptolemy, the second king at Alexandria following its foundation. When he explained to the king his desire to free his native city, and his reason for doing this, that outstanding man readily obtained a huge subvention of money from the wealthy king.* On bringing it back to Sicyon, he called in fifteen leading citizens to advise him, and with them he reviewed the cases of those who were occupying properties not their own, and those who had lost theirs. He put valuations on the properties, and was able to persuade some to accept money and to abandon their occupancy, and others to regard it as more convenient to be paid the value of their properties rather than to have them restored to them. Harmony thus prevailed; all went off without complaint. What a 83 great man he was, worthy of having been born a Roman! His is the right way to negotiate with citizens rather than the spectacle we have seen on two occasions,* the spear erected in the forum and the citizens' possessions subjected to the auctioneer's cry for bids. That celebrated Greek decided, like the wise and eminent man he was, that he must consult the interests of all. This is the supreme demonstration of reason and wisdom as manifested by a good citizen, not prising apart the interests of citizens, but marshalling all under the same banner of equity.

'Let them dwell in the property of another without payment.'* Why should that be? So that after I have bought and built my property, maintaining it and sinking money in it, you can enjoy living there against my will? What else is that but robbing some of their possessions, and awarding to others what is not their own? What 84 basis has cancellation of debts other than allowing you to buy a farm with my money, and to own it, while I become penniless? We must therefore ensure that debts incurred do not damage the state. There are many possible ways of taking precautions, so that if debts are incurred, the wealthy do not lose their possessions, and debtors do not acquire those of other people. There is no more powerful means of bonding together the state than good faith, but this cannot exist at all unless payment of debts is enforced. At no time was pressure for the remission of these stronger than in my consulship,* when men of all persuasions and classes tried to force it through by recourse to arms and encampments, but my opposition to them was so powerful that this evil was totally eradicated from the state. Never were debts greater, but never were they more satisfactorily or more readily discharged, for once the hope of dishonest dealing was dashed, the need to settle followed. But though our present-day victor was defeated then,* when his plans were devised in his own interest, he carried them through when they were no longer of personal profit to him. Such was his lust for wrongdoing that sinning itself was his pleasure, even if he got no profit from it.

85 Our conclusion is that those charged with the defence of the state will dissociate themselves from the kind of lavish distribution which robs Peter to pay Paul. Their primary concern will be to ensure that the individual keeps his possessions through the just processes of law and the courts; that those in greater need are not victimized because of their lowly status, and that the wealthy do not incur envy in retaining or recovering their property; moreover they themselves are to employ all possible means both in war and at home to enhance the power, territories, and revenues of the state. These are tasks for great men, these were regularly achieved in the days of our forbears; obligations like these will obtain great favour and glory for those who carry them through, and they will be of the utmost advantage to the state.

86 The Stoic philosopher Antipater of Tyre,* who died recently at Athens, argues that Panaetius has omitted two topics, regard for health and for money, from these precepts for things that are useful. I suspect that the eminent philosopher omitted them because they are straightforward, but they are certainly useful. Good health is maintained by keeping a watchful eye on our bodies, by observing what usually benefits or harms them, by restraint in our general diet and style of living, by forgoing physical pleasures in the interests of our bodies' well-being, and finally by the skill of those whose expertise lies in this field of health.

87 As for our domestic finances, they are to be acquired by pursuits which are not repulsive. They are maintained by care and thrift, and augmented by these same qualities. Xenophon, the disciple of Socrates, has analysed these topics conveniently in his book *Oeconomicus*,* which I translated from Greek into Latin when I was about the age which you are now. But the whole genre of making and investing money (and, I should like to add, putting it to use) is more appropriately discussed by certain excellent men who sit at the central gate of Janus,* rather than by any philosophers of any school.

Still, we are to gain knowledge of these matters, for they are relevant to what is useful, which is the theme of this book.

But it is often necessary—this is my fourth main topic, which 88 Panaetius left out*—to make comparisons between different kinds of usefulness. Physical advantages are often contrasted with external ones, and vice versa; and again, physical assets are often compared with each other, as are external ones. Comparison made between physical advantages and external ones suggests that you would rather be healthy than rich. External advantages compared with those of the body are on the lines that it is preferable to be rich rather than outstandingly strong. Comparison between physical advantages is made to argue that good health is preferable to pleasure, or that strength ranks above speed. Comparison between externals is made to argue that glory is preferable to riches, or that urban revenues are better than returns from the country.

The celebrated *mot* of old Cato* exemplifies this last type of com- 89 parison. When asked what was the most useful item of domestic property, he replied: 'Good grazing.' And what was the next best? 'Adequate grazing.' And the third best? 'Poor grazing.' And the fourth? 'Ploughing.' When the questioner asked 'How about money-lending?',* Cato answered: 'How about murdering some-one?' These and many other examples should make it clear that com-parisons are often made between different kinds of useful things, and that this fourth category should rightly be added to our investiga-tions of obligations.

We shall now pass to the rest of our discussion.

Book Three

1 Marcus my son,

The Publius Scipio who was first hailed as Africanus was fond of saying—as his contemporary Cato noted*—that he was never less at leisure than in his leisure-time, and was never less lonely than when he was on his own. What an impressive remark, so worthy of a great and wise man, intimating as it does that even when he was at leisure he bent his mind to business, and when he was alone he would commune with himself, so that he was never idle, and did not occasionally feel the need for conversation with someone else. Thus the two situations which induce depression in others, leisure and solitude, would stimulate him.

I only wish that I could truthfully say the same thing of myself. But if I am unable to match such mental excellence by imitation, I certainly approximate to it in aspiration; for now that I am debarred from politics and from pleading in the courts by the force of sacrilegious arms, I pursue a life of leisure, and accordingly I abandon

2 Rome and am often alone as I roam the countryside.* But this leisure of mine is not comparable with that of Africanus, and again, my solitude is not to be ranked with his; for whereas he occasionally enjoyed leisure when relaxing from his most glorious services to the state, and from time to time he quitted the crowded throng of citizens to retire into the haven of solitude, my leisure has been imposed on me from want of things to do rather than through zeal for relaxation. For now that the senate has been snuffed out and lawsuits have been abolished,* what can I find worth doing in the senate-house or the

3 forum? So though my former life was lived attended by huge throngs before the eyes of the citizens, I now shrink from the gaze of the criminals who fill the whole city to overflowing. I hide myself away as much as I can, and am often alone.

However, men of learning instruct us on the need not only to choose the least of evils,* but also even from these to extract whatever good lies in them. So I am putting this peace and quiet to good advantage, though it is not the kind which is appropriate for one who in earlier days won peace and quiet for the state; and I am not allowing the solitary life imposed on me by necessity rather than by choice to stagnate. Yet as I see it, Africanus has merited the greater 4 praise, for no written records of his talents survive, nor any product of his leisure or fruit of his solitude.* From this we are to infer that he was never at a loose end or lonely, because his mind was restlessly investigating problems which he solved by concentrated thought. I myself on the other hand am not strong enough to find relief from loneliness in silent reflection, and therefore I have concentrated all my energies and attention on the activity of writing. As a result, in the short time since the republic was overthrown I have written more* than in the many years during which it remained intact.

All philosophy, my dear Cicero, is fecund and fruitful, and no part 5 of it is wasteland and barren; but no topic within it is more fertile and productive than that of obligations, for from them are derived the principles of consistent and honourable living. So though I am sure that you are being continually informed and instructed about these by my friend Cratippus,* the outstanding philosopher in our recollection, I none the less think it appropriate that your ears should ring with such precepts from every quarter, and that if possible they should be exposed to no other message. Every person who purposes 6 to embark upon an honourable life should undergo this, and you perhaps above all others. If you are to emulate my capacity for work,* the burden of expectation on you is not light; to attain the offices I have held, it is heavy; perhaps there is some expectation that you may match my fame. Moreover, your presence at Athens with Cratippus puts a heavy responsibility on you, for you have made your way there to enter the market, so to say, of cultural pursuits, and to return empty-handed would be thoroughly disgraceful, bringing shame on the reputation of the city and your master. So be sure to achieve all you can by mental effort and by hard work, if indeed the learning process is hard work, and not pleasure; and do not give the impression of having let yourself down when I have made provision for all your needs.

But enough of this, for I have exhorted you by letter at length and often. Now let us get back to the remaining section of the work before us.

Panaetius, then, discussed obligations in the most scrupulous 7

manner without provoking disagreement, and I have followed him
very closely* though with some amendments. He suggested three
headings* under which men usually ponder and discuss the question of obligation: first, uncertainty whether an action under discussion is honourable or base; second, whether it is useful or useless;
and third, if an action apparently honourable conflicts with what
appears useful, how a decision should be made between them. He
expounded the first two topics in three books, and wrote that he
would next discuss the third, but he did not carry out his promise.

8   This surprises me all the more because his pupil Posidonius wrote
that Panaetius lived for thirty years longer* after publishing the earlier books. I find it astonishing that Posidonius in certain treatises of
his touched so briefly on this subject,* especially as he writes that no
topic in the whole of philosophy is as vital as this.

9   I am in total disagreement with those who state that Panaetius did
not overlook this topic, but that he deliberately left it out,* there
being no need to discuss it at all because the useful could never be in
conflict with the honourable. On the second question, whether the
third of Panaetius' headings should have been appended or omitted
altogether, there can be some dispute. But on the first, there can be
no doubt that Panaetius raised the issue but then abandoned it. If
someone divides a topic into three parts and deals with two of them,
inevitably the third part remains for him to discuss; moreover, at the
10   close of his third book he promises to handle this aspect next. Then
too Posidonius provides abundant evidence on this matter. In a
letter, he makes the further observation that Publius Rutilius Rufus,
a former pupil of Panaetius,* used to make the following comparison: just as no artist had been found to fill in that part of the painting
of *The Venus of Cos* which Apelles had left unfinished* (for the
beauty of her features made it hopeless to think of matching it with
the rest of her body), so no one had completed what Panaetius had
left out, because of the consummate excellence of the parts which he
had finished.

11   So there can be no doubt about Panaetius' attitude to this matter,
though there can perhaps be debate on whether he was right or
wrong in his researches on obligation to append this third consideration. For whether, as the Stoics maintain, the honourable is the
only good, or whether the honourable is the highest good as you
Peripatetics argue, since both views lead to the conclusion that all

else when put on the opposing scale would scarcely register the slightest weight, there can be no doubt that the useful can never conflict with the honourable. This is why Socrates, so we are told,* used to curse those whose views first prised apart these concepts which nature joins together. The Stoics agreed with him, arguing that whatever is honourable is useful, and that nothing is useful which is not honourable.

Now if Panaetius had been the sort of man to claim that we must 12 practise virtue because it achieves what is useful (this is the view of those who assess the honourable by the criterion of pleasure or absence of pain),* he could have argued that the useful does on occasion conflict with the honourable. But since he was the type of philosopher who regarded the honourable as the only good, and believed that our lives are neither improved by the addition, nor worsened by the subtraction, of things which are apparently useful* but conflict with the honourable, it seems that he ought not to have initiated the sort of debate which compares the apparently useful with the honourable. The Stoics define the highest good as 'being in 13 conformity with nature', and what I think this means is that we must always align ourselves with virtue, and choose all else which accords with nature so long as it does not militate against virtue. In view of this, some people think that it was wrong to enter the comparison* into the discussion, and that no instruction at all should have been offered under this heading.

However, the honourable in its strict and true sense is the property solely of sages,* and can never be detached from virtue, whereas those who have not attained perfect wisdom cannot possess the honourable in its perfection at all, but grasp a mere semblance of it. Now 14 these obligations discussed in these books of mine are described by Stoics as 'intermediate'.* They are shared by all, and are widespread. Many people embrace them through the quality of their intellects and their progress in learning. But that obligation which Stoics call 'the right' is perfect and total; in the Stoic terminology, it 'fulfils all the numbers',* and cannot accrue to anyone except the sage. But an action in which 'intermediate' obligations make their 15 appearance seems to be totally perfect because the common herd does not usually grasp how it falls short of perfection, and in so far as they do understand it, they imagine that there is nothing in it which has been overlooked. It is often the same with poems, pictures, and a number of other things; those lacking experience of them take delight in objects undeserving of praise, and they shower compliments on them, the reason being, I believe, that the works possess something of value which attracts the ignorant who cannot identify the faults endemic in each and all of them. So once they get instruction from experts they readily abandon their previous opinion.

So the obligations discussed by me in these books the Stoics term 'honourable at a secondary level'. They are not confined merely to

16 the sages, but shared by the human race as a whole. So all persons with a penchant for virtue are influenced by them. When the two Decii or the two Scipios are cited as men of courage, or when Fabricius or Aristides is named 'The Just',* it is not that they are invoked as exemplars of courage and of justice respectively in the way a sage would be hailed, for none of these was a sage in the sense in which we would have the word understood. Nor were Marcus Cato and Gaius Laelius, who were regarded and named as 'The Wise', actually sages, nor indeed were the famous Seven.* But because they undertook 'intermediate' obligations, they bore the resemblance and appearance of sages.

17 For this reason it is not right to compare the truly honourable with any useful which militates against it; and again, what we in general designate as the honourable, which is cultivated by those who wish to be accounted good men, must never be balanced against financial profit.* We must observe and maintain our conception of the honourable as scrupulously as the sages observe it in its true sense. Otherwise any progress towards virtue which we have made cannot be preserved.

This advice is relevant to those who by fulfilling their obligations

18 are considered good men. As for those who assess everything by financial benefits and advantages, refusing to allow these to be outweighed by the honourable, often in their thinking they compare the honourable with what they conceive as the useful. But good men do not habitually do this. So my view is that when Panaetius stated that men are often hesitant about making this comparison, he meant precisely what he said, that 'they are often' hesitant, not that 'they should be';* for it is absolutely disgraceful not merely to rate the apparently useful higher than the honourable, but even to compare the two and to hesitate between them.

So what factor tends to raise doubts, and seems to demand careful thought? I think it is when doubt arises about the nature of the action under scrutiny; for there are occasions when an action which we 19 often tend to consider base turns out not to be base at all. Let us take an example which has wider significance. What crime can be greater than murdering not just any individual but a close friend? But if a man murders a tyrant, even if he is a friend, has he thereby implicated himself in a criminal act? The Roman people in fact do not think so, for they regard this as the most noble of illustrious deeds.* So in this instance has the useful prevailed over the honourable? On the contrary, the honourable has attended on the useful.

We must therefore lay down some general rule to enable us to make a choice without going astray, in cases where what we call the useful seems to be at odds with what we consider to be the honourable. If we follow this rule when we make comparisons between courses of action, we shall never forsake our obligation. Such a rule 20 will be entirely consonant with the system and doctrine of the Stoics, to which in these books I subscribe for this reason: though the Old Academy and your Peripatetic school (which at one time was identical with the Academy) rate honourable actions above those which are apparently useful, these issues will be more nobly expounded by those who regard all that is honourable as useful, and nothing as useful which is not honourable, than by those who believe that there is something honourable which is not useful, and something useful which is not honourable. My own position is that the Academy, to which I belong, gives me considerable freedom; it permits me to be within my rights in defending whatever position seems most probable.* But I come back to the rule to be laid down.

If a person deprives his neighbour of something, and furthers his 21 own advantage by another's loss, such behaviour flies in the face of nature more than death or poverty or pain or anything which can affect our persons or our external possessions; for first and foremost it undermines the fellowship and alliance between members of the human race.* Should the spirit move us to plunder or to assault our neighbour for our own profit, that fellowship between the human race which so closely accords with nature must inevitably be dismantled. Take this parallel:* if each of our bodily limbs took the 22 notion that it could flourish by appropriating the strength of the adjacent limb, then the whole of our body would inevitably be weakened, and would die. In the same way, if we each laid hold of the possessions of others, and seized from them all we could for our own profit, human fellowship and community would inevitably be overthrown, For though nature does not object to our opting to obtain for ourselves individually rather than for another what is needed for life's necessities, she does not permit us to increase our own resources, wealth, and possessions by plundering those of other people.

23   This principle, that it is wrong to harm a neighbour for one's own profit, is laid down not only by nature as reflected in international law, but also by the decrees of nations, which uphold the public interest in individual states. This is the aim and purpose of laws, to keep intact the unifying bonds between citizens. Those who seek to sunder them are restrained by sentence of death, or exile, or imprisonment, or fine. This principle is established much more effectively by the rationale of nature itself, which is the law laid down by gods and men.* The person who seeks to comply with it (and all who wish to accord with nature will comply with it) will never decide to lay hands on another's property, or to obtain for himself the possessions of

24   which he has deprived his neighbour. The truth is that a lofty and noble spirit, and attitudes of courtesy, justice, and generosity, are much more in harmony with nature than are pleasure, mere living,* and riches. It is the mark of that noble and lofty spirit to despise these last, and to account them as nothing compared with the common good. By contrast, to lay hands on another's goods for personal gain is more unnatural than death or pain or other hardships of that kind.

25   Again, it is more in conformity with nature (should it lie within our power to emulate the fabled Hercules, whom popular report as a tribute to his benefits has exalted to the council of the gods)* to undergo the greatest toils and privations so as to save or aid each and every nation, rather than to live apart from men, enjoying not only freedom from all troubles but also the greatest pleasures, rich in every resource and preeminent in looks and strength. So every man endowed with the noblest and most illustrious cast of mind accounts the life of toil to be far superior to the life of ease; and the logical outcome of this is that he who conforms with nature can inflict no harm on his fellow-man.

26   A further point. The man who wrongs his neighbour to attain some personal advantage either imagines that he is doing nothing unnatural, or he decides that death, poverty, pain, and the loss of

children, relatives, and friends are more to be avoided than doing someone an injustice. If on the one hand he sees nothing unnatural in harming people, what point is there in arguing with him, since he is stripping humanity of all that is human? If on the other hand he thinks that we should avoid such aggression, but that death, poverty, and pain are far worse evils, he is mistaken in his belief that any impairment to the body or to possessions is more serious than impairments to the soul.

Accordingly we must all adhere to the principle that what is use-   27
ful to the individual is identical with what is useful to the community. If we each appropriate such an advantage for selfish purposes, it
will spell the end of all human fellowship.

Further, if nature dictates that we should seek to consult the interests of any person whatsoever simply because he is a man, it necessarily follows that it is also in keeping with nature that what is useful
to each and all of us is possessed in common. If this is true, we are all
constrained by one and the same law of nature; and if this in turn is
true, the law of nature undoubtedly forbids us to do harm to another.
Since the premise is true, so likewise is the conclusion.*

As for the argument advanced by some that they will take nothing   28
for their own profit from a parent or a brother, but that the rest of the
citizen-body is a different matter, that is quite absurd. Such men are
claiming that there is no law or compact which they share for the
common welfare with their fellow-citizens. Such an attitude is
destructive of all fellowship in the body-politic. As for those who
argue that we must take sympathetic account of fellow-citizens but
not of outsiders, they are destroying the fellowship common to the
human race, and once this is removed, kindness, generosity, goodness and justice are wholly excluded. Those who dispose of these
virtues are to be convicted further of sacrilege against the immortal
gods, for they abrogate the alliance between men which the gods
have established. The bond which cements that alliance most intimately is the belief that it is more unnatural for someone to rob his
neighbour for his own profit than to undergo any loss of his property
or his person or even his soul, so long as such loss does not involve
injustice;* for justice is the single virtue which is mistress and queen
of all the virtues.

But perhaps someone may argue: 'Suppose that a wise man was   29
dying of hunger. He would surely take the bread away from a person

who was no use for anything. [Certainly not; for my life is not more useful than the cast of mind which commits me to do no harm to anyone for my own profit.]* Or again, if a good man could avoid dying of cold by robbing that cruel and monstrous tyrant Phalaris* of his clothing, surely he would do it?'

30   These examples are very easy to adjudge. If on the one hand you were to rob a wholly useless person to benefit yourself, your action would be less than human, and would conflict with natural law. If on the other hand you are the sort of person who can greatly benefit the state and society in general by remaining alive, and if with this motive in mind you deprive your neighbour of something, your deed is not blameworthy.* But if the circumstances differ from this, we should each and all bear with disadvantages rather than rob another of his advantages. So illness, poverty, and the like do not fly in the face of nature more than laying hold of or coveting another's possession, whereas to desert the path of communal benefit is opposed to nature, because it is unjust.

31   So the law of nature itself, which preserves and protects the interests of human beings, certainly ordains that what is vital for life should be diverted from one who is idle and useless to one who is wise and good and brave, for the death of the wise man will be a great loss to the common good; always supposing, that is, that self-regard and love of self do not exploit this ordinance as a pretext for committing injustice. In this way the good man will always fulfil his obligation by taking account of the interests of society and the fellowship of the human race which I so often emphasize.

32   Judgement in the case of Phalaris presents no difficulty, for we do not share fellowship with tyrants. On the contrary, there is the widest cleavage between them and us, and should it lie within your power, nature does not forbid you to rob the person whom it is honourable to kill. Indeed, the whole of that noxious, sacrilegious breed should be banished from human society. Just as certain parts of the body are amputated once they begin to be drained of blood, and in their virtually lifeless condition affect other parts, so once the savagery and brutality of the beast takes human shape,* it must be excised, so to say, from the body of humanity which we all share. All problems of this type need to be assessed according to the particular circumstances.

33   I imagine that Panaetius would have taken up these topics* if

some accident or pressure of work had not frustrated his intention. There is a host of recommendations in the previous books on these very issues, enabling us to visualize clearly what we must avoid because it is shameful, and what need not be avoided because it is not shameful at all. But now that I am putting the finishing touches, so to say, to this work which has been launched but is not quite complete, I model myself on those geometricians who tend not to demonstrate everything but ask us to allow them to take certain things for granted so that they may more readily explain the points which they wish to put across. In the same way, if you approve, my dear Cicero, I am asking you to allow me to claim that nothing is worth seeking on its own account except the honourable. If Cratippus does not permit you to accept this,* you can at any rate concede that the honourable is what is chiefly worth seeking on its own account. I am content with either formulation; sometimes the one, and sometimes the other appears more probable,* and nothing beyond these appears to have such probability.

I must here begin to mount a defence of Panaetius, for what he   34
stated was not that truly useful things could on occasion be in conflict with honourable ones (for he would have regarded that as impious), but only things which were apparently useful. He often attests that there is nothing useful which is not also honourable, and that there is nothing honourable which is not also useful; and he claims that no greater poison has ever infected human lives than the belief of those who have prised the two apart.* He therefore included in his work the conflict between them which was merely apparent and not real. His purpose was not to enable us to prefer on occasion things useful to things honourable, but to enable us to distinguish between them, should such situations occur, without falling into error.

So now I shall complete the remaining part of this work with no props to lean on, battling it out by myself, as the saying goes;* for since Panaetius there has been no treatment of this topic—at any rate, not one which met my approval from my scrutiny of the works which have come into my hands.

To resume, then. When something which appears to be useful   35
comes to your notice, you are bound to show interest, but if after considering it you observe something shameful attached to what is apparently useful, this must not cause you to abandon the search for the useful. Rather, you must realize that the useful cannot be present

in the company of the shameful. If indeed there is nothing so opposed to nature as the shameful (for nature demands things that are upright, appropriate, and consistent, and it despises things opposite to these), and if nothing is so much in keeping with nature as the useful, it is clear that the useful and the shameful cannot co-exist in the same action. Then again, if we are born to embrace the honourable, and this must either be our sole pursuit (as Zeno thought) or at any rate must be accounted to have immeasurably greater weight than all else (as Aristotle argues),* then the necessary conclusion is that the honourable is either the sole or the highest good. Now what is good is certainly useful, and so whatever is honourable is useful.

36   Now when men without moral standards mistakenly seize upon something which is apparently useful, they at once detach it from the honourable. So daggers, poisons, and forged wills come into play; so too do thefts, embezzlement of public funds, and the pillaging and plundering of allies and of citizens; and likewise greed for excessive wealth, intolerable power, and finally regal status,* even in states that are free; and nothing can be envisaged more grisly and foul than these things. Such men with erroneous judgement have their eyes fixed on the rewards which attend on their actions, but not on the penalty which they pay. I refer not to punishment under the laws, which they repeatedly violate, but to that imposed by their own base conduct,* punishment which is the bitterest possible.

37   So we must expel from our midst the kind of men whose thinking runs on those lines, for each and all of them are criminal and ungodly, pondering as they do whether to follow the course which they see to be honourable, or whether knowingly to defile themselves with crime. For their very hesitation has an element of wickedness, even if they do not proceed to the act of wickedness itself. So we must refrain totally from considering courses of action when the very contemplation of them is shameful.

Furthermore, we must exclude from all our deliberations the prospect or intention of secrecy or concealment, for provided that we have made some progress in philosophy, we must be thoroughly convinced that even if we could conceal our actions from all gods and men, we must do nothing redolent of greed or injustice or lust or

38   intemperance. To underline this obligation, Plato introduces into his work the celebrated figure of Gyges.* In the course of heavy storms, a fissure appeared in the earth, and Gyges descended into

the chasm. There, as the stories have it, he came upon a bronze horse with a door in its flank, and upon opening it he saw the corpse of a man of unprecedented size wearing a gold ring on his finger. He removed it, and placed it on his own finger; and later (he was a shepherd of the king) he attended a shepherds' gathering. Whenever he turned the bezel of the ring inward to the palm of his hand, no man there could see him, whereas he could survey all that was going on. When he turned the ring back the normal way round, he became visible again. So he exploited the opportunity afforded by the ring to indulge in sexual intercourse with the queen, and with her complicity he killed his master the king, and disposed of all the people who he thought stood in his way. No one could lay eyes on him when he committed these crimes, and thus thanks to the ring he suddenly emerged as the king of Lydia.*

Supposing, then, that a wise man got hold of this very ring. He would not believe that he had any more right to do wrong than if he did not possess it, for good men aspire to honourable deeds and not to secret intrigues.

In discussion of this episode, some philosophers who are quite   39
well intentioned but not very perceptive say that Plato has reported a fictitious, lying tale—as if he were claiming that the incident had or could have actually happened! But the point of the ring and what it illustrates is this: supposing that no one had knowledge or the slightest suspicion, when you performed some action to obtain riches or influence or dominion or sexual pleasure, and that your action remained permanently unknown to gods and men, would you do it? These philosophers respond that it could never happen. True, it could never happen,* but my question is: if what they claim is impossible were possible, what would they do? They press their argument like clodhoppers: they say that it cannot happen, and they refuse to budge, unable to see the drift of that word 'supposing'. When I enquire of them what they would do if they could conceal the deed, I am not asking whether such concealment is possible. What I am doing is turning the screw, so to say, so that if they reply that with the guarantee of impunity they would further their interests, they would be confessing that they were evildoers, whereas if they were to say that they would not, they would be conceding that all actions which are inherently shameful must be avoided.

Let us now return, however, to the question before us.

40   Many situations frequently arise to perplex our minds, because they have the appearance of being useful to us. The difficulty in contemplating these is not whether we should forsake the honourable because the benefit is so great (that would be despicable), but whether the apparently useful can be embraced without incurring dishonour. When Brutus deposed his colleague Collatinus from the consular power,* it might appear that he was acting unjustly, since Collatinus had been his ally and henchman in the expulsion of the kings. But since the leading citizens had decided that the family connections of Superbus, the name of the Tarquins, and all recollection of the kingship should be expunged, the useful element, namely the interests of the fatherland, was so honourable that it must have won the approval of Collatinus himself. In this case the useful was justified because it was honourable, for if it had not been, it could not have been useful either.

41   The same is not true, however, of the king who had founded the city, since it was the apparently useful which motivated him. For when he thought that it would be more advantageous to wield the kingship alone than to share it with another, he slew his brother.* By so doing he abandoned the obligations of kinship and humanity to attain what seemed to be useful but in reality was not, yet he made the city wall his pretext to give it an appearance of the honourable which was neither persuasive nor indeed appropriate. So with due respect to Quirinus, or if you prefer, Romulus,* what he did was wrong.

42   We are not, however, obliged to forgo our own interests and to allot them to others when we need them ourselves. Each of us should safeguard any personal interest which does not cause injustice to another. Chrysippus as usual put it neatly* when he said: 'A runner on the racetrack must strain and compete with all his might to come first, but on no account must he trip or hand off a fellow-competitor; and likewise in life, there is nothing wrong in an individual's seeking what is in his own interest, but it is unjust to deprive another.'

43   Obligations in the case of friendships—failing to discharge them when it is right to carry them out, and fulfilling them when it is not right to do so, are both breaches of duty—are particularly complex. But advice in all such situations is succinct and straightforward. Things which seem to be useful—public offices, riches, sensual pleasures, and the like—must never take precedence over

friendships.* But the good man will never promote a friend's interests to the detriment of the state or in defiance of his oath or pledged
word,* even if he is sitting in court over him, for he then quits the
role of friend to undertake that of judge. The only concession which
he will make to friendship will be to approve a friend's case because
it is the just one, and in so far as the laws permit, to arrange a date for
pleading the case* to suit his friend's convenience. Indeed, when he   44
has to deliver judgement under oath, he must remember that he is
calling God to witness, and this means, I think, his own conscience;
God himself has bestowed nothing more divine on man than that. So
the custom which we have inherited from our ancestors is a noble
one if we can maintain it, for it requests the judge TO DO ALL HE CAN
WITH INTEGRITY OF FAITH.* This request is germane to the honourable concessions which I mentioned a moment ago as licit for a
judge to make to a friend; for if all requests from friends were to be
met, we should have to regard such relationships as conspiracies
rather than friendships.* I am speaking here of common or garden   45
friendships, for no such situation can arise where sages who have
attained perfection are concerned.

The story goes that Damon and Phintias* had such affection for
each other that when the tyrant Dionysius named the day for the
execution of one of them, and the one who had been condemned to
death requested a few days' grace in order to commend his family to
the care of friends, the other stood surety for his appearance, accepting that he himself would have to die if his friend had not returned.
When the condemned man did return on the day appointed, the
tyrant was so edified by the faith they manifested to each other that
he begged them to enrol himself as a third partner in their friendship.

So when in the realm of friendship we compare the seemingly use-   46
ful with the honourable, what passes for the useful should count for
nothing, and the honourable should prevail; and when in the course of
such a friendship dishonourable demands are made, religious scruple
and good faith must claim precedence over friendship. This rule of
thumb will enable us to make the choice of obligation which we seek.

Wrongs are very often committed in the public sphere through
choice of what is ostensibly useful, as when we perpetrated the
destruction of Corinth.* Even harsher was the decree of the Athenians* that the Aeginetans, whose strength lay in their navy, should
have their thumbs cut off. This seemed to be a useful move, for

Aegina posed too dangerous a threat because it lay close to the Piraeus. But no action which is cruel is useful, for cruelty above all else is the foe of human nature, with which we must conform.

47　　　Also wrong is the disbarment of foreigners from residence in our cities, and their exclusion by such as Pennus in our fathers' time, and Papius* in recent years. It is reasonable, of course, that non-citizens should not have citizen-rights, and this was embodied in the law of Crassus and Scaevola,* wisest of consuls. But it is utterly inhuman to debar foreigners from the enjoyment of city life.

By contrast there are notable occasions when the illusory public benefit is spurned in favour of the honourable. The history of our state abounds with examples both on numerous other occasions and especially in the Second Punic War. When Rome sustained the disaster at Cannae,* she showed greater spirit than she ever did in times of success. There was no sign of fear, no suggestion of seeking peace. So great is the impact of the honourable that it overshadows the illusion of utility.

48　　　When the Athenians had no prospect whatever of withstanding the onslaught of the Persians, they decided to abandon the city, to evacuate their wives and children to Troezen, to take to their ships, and to defend the freedom of Greece with their fleet. When a certain Cyrsilus urged them to remain in the city and to admit Xerxes,* they stoned him to death. He seemed to be pursuing the expedient course, but this counted for nothing when confronted with the prin-

49　　　ciple of honour. After the victory in the war with the Persians, Themistocles announced in the assembly that he had a plan for the safety of the state,* but he said that it was vital that it should not become known. So he asked the people to nominate a person to whom to impart it. Aristides was the man appointed. Themistocles told him that the Spartan fleet drawn up at Gytheum could be secretly set ablaze, with the inevitable consequence the destruction of Spartan power. After hearing the proposal, Aristides entered the assembly to a buzz of expectation. He said that the project outlined to him by Themistocles was a highly useful one, but wholly dishonourable. The Athenians' reaction accordingly was that since it was not honourable, it could not be useful either, and on Aristides' proposal they rejected the entire plan without even having heard it. Those Athenians behaved better than we do; we tax our allies while allowing the pirates to pay nothing.*

The abiding rule, then, must be that the dishonourable is never useful, even when you lay hands on what you think is useful, for the very act of thinking that something dishonourable is useful is itself disastrous.

But as I remarked earlier, situations often arise when the useful 50 seems to conflict with the honourable, so that we must then investigate whether indeed it is in conflict, or whether the two can be reconciled. As an example* of situations of this kind, let us assume that a good man has shipped a large cargo of corn from Alexandria to Rhodes at a time when the Rhodians were suffering shortage and hunger, and grain was extremely expensive. Assume too that he knew that several merchants had put out from Alexandria, and that he saw their ships laden with corn on course making for Rhodes. Should he report this to the Rhodians, or without divulging the fact sell his own cargo at the highest possible price? I am assuming that he is wise and honest; the question I pose concerns the debate and discussion he has with himself, for he would not conceal the news from the Rhodians if he thought this dishonest, but he would be uncertain whether it was dishonest or not.

In such cases as this Diogenes of Babylon, that eminent and austere Stoic, takes a different line from that of his pupil Antipater,* a most incisive thinker. Antipater believes that all the facts should be divulged, so that the buyer is kept unaware of absolutely nothing which is known to the seller. Diogenes on the other hand believes that the seller is obliged to report any defects in his goods, in so far as the civil law prescribes, and to conduct the transaction otherwise without chicanery, but since he has goods to sell, he should sell at the best possible price. 'I have shipped them, and I have set out my stall; I charge no more for my goods than anyone else does. My price may even be lower when stocks are more plentiful. Who is getting a bad deal?' Antipater mounts the opposing argument. 'Are you serious? 52 Your duty is to have the interest of men at heart, and to promote human fellowship. From birth you were bound by the law of nature and you inherit her principles which you are to obey and observe. They prescribe that your interest is the interest of the community, and conversely, the interest of the community is yours. So will you conceal from your fellow men the availability and abundance which they have at hand?' Diogenes will perhaps respond: 'Concealment is one thing, and silence another. At this moment I do not conceal anything from you by failing to inform you of the nature of the gods or the highest good,* knowledge of which would be of greater value to you than wheat at a low price. I am under no obligation to tell

53   you what it is in your interest to hear.' 'On the contrary', Antipater will say, 'you are under an obligation, for you recall that nature has joined all men in alliance.' 'I do recall that', Diogenes will reply, 'but the alliance you mention is surely not the kind that forbids a man to possess anything of his own?* If it does so forbid, then nothing should be put up for sale at all; everything should be given away.'

In this entire discussion you notice the absence of the statement, 'Though this is dishonourable, I will do it because it is in my interest.' Rather, the one side argues that the action is advantageous without being dishonourable, and the other that it should not be performed because it is dishonourable.

54   Suppose that a good man is selling his house because of certain defects in it known to him but to no one else. Though considered healthy, it actually harbours disease. People do not know that snakes are found in every bedroom. The timber has rotted and is on the verge of collapse. But no one except the owner knows this. My question is: if the vendor did not inform buyers of these facts, and he sold the house for considerably more than the price which he anticipated, was his action unjust or despicable?

'It certainly was,' says Antipater. 'If allowing a buyer to go bald-headed for purchase, and thus inadvertently to sustain a serious loss, is not of the same order as failing to direct a lost traveller on the right way, a lapse which at Athens incurs a public curse,* I fail to know what is. Indeed, it is even worse than failing to point out the way, for it deliberately leads another person astray.'

55   Diogenes counters: 'So did the vendor force you to buy when he did not even recommend purchase? He put up for sale something which he did not like, and you bought something which you did like. If people who advertise a mansion as "good and well-built" are not regarded as tricksters if it is not good or soundly built, much less should vendors who did not praise the property. When a buyer is free to exercise his judgement,* how can the seller be guilty of deceit? Now if claims made for a property need not all be substantiated, do you think that failure to make claims should be brought to account? What, I ask you, is more stupid than for the vendor to report the

defects in what he is selling? What is so lunatic as for an owner to tell the auctioneer to announce: "Sale of a plague-ridden house"?

So these are certain doubtful cases, in which one side mounts a 56 defence of the honourable, and the other argues on behalf of the useful that it is not merely honourable to do what seems useful, but even dishonourable not to do so. This is the disagreement which seems often to arise between things useful and things honourable. An adjudication must be made between the two sides, for I have outlined the cases not to pose the questions but to unfold the answers.

The answer, then, seems to be* that the grain-dealer should not 57 have concealed the facts from the Rhodians, and the vendor of the house should not have concealed its defects from the purchasers. Concealment is not just reticence, for by it you seek to further your own interests by ensuring that your knowledge remains hidden from those who would benefit from it. Is there anyone who does not see the nature of this kind of concealment, and of the sort of man who practises it? He is certainly not an open or straightforward person, decent, or just, or honest; on the contrary, he is crafty, devious, sharp, deceitful, malicious, cunning, wily, and artful. It is hardly useful, is it, to hear ourselves stigmatized by all these and many other terms descriptive of our faults?

Yet if those who fail to speak out are to be censured, what view 58 must we take of those who tell lies? Gaius Canius, a Roman knight not devoid of native wit* and quite well-read, took himself off to Syracuse not on business, but as he liked to put it, to be 'business-free'. While there he kept mentioning that he was keen to buy a small estate to which he could invite friends and enjoy himself without people bothering him. When his wish was bandied about, one Pythius, a banker at Syracuse, told him that he owned an estate which was not for sale, but that Canius if he wanted could have the use of it as if it were his own. At the same time he invited him to dinner at the estate on the following day. When Canius accepted the invitation, Pythius, who boasted the sort of influence which bankers have with all classes, called in a gathering of fishermen, and asked them to fish in front of his small estate on the following day, and told them what he wanted them to do. Canius turned up for dinner at the appointed hour; Pythius had laid on a lavish spread. Before their eyes were dozens of fishing-boats. Each of the fishermen brought forward his catch and threw the fish at Pythius' feet. Thereupon 59

Canius said: 'Tell me, Pythius, what is going on? Why all these fish and all these boats?' 'That's no surprise', replied Pythius. 'Syracuse gets all its fish and its fresh water from here. The locals can't get along without this residence of mine.' Canius was fired with greed, and pressed Pythius to sell it to him. At first the banker played hard to get. Need I say more? Canius got his way. The greedy man had plenty of money, and bought the estate at the price Pythius asked, together with all the furniture. Pythius entered the details in a ledger, and completed the transaction.*

Next day Canius invited his friends. He turned up early himself, but there was not so much as a rowlock in sight. He asked his next-door neighbour if it was a fishermen's holiday, because there were none of them in sight. 'Not so far as I know', the other replied, 'but none of them usually fish here. So I was quite surprised yesterday at what happened.' Canius was furious, but what could he do?

60   Gaius Aquilius,* my colleague in the praetorship and my friend, had not yet published his provisions for fraud. When he was asked what in those provisions constituted fraud, his answer was: 'When the pretence differs from the actuality'—an excellent formulation indeed, as one would expect from an expert at definitions. So Pythius, and all who do one thing while pretending to do another, are treacherous, wicked, and wilful; so no action of theirs can be useful,

61   because all that they do is disfigured by so many vices. If in fact Aquilius' definition holds good, pretence and dissembling are to be entirely excluded from our lives. Thus the good man will not indulge in pretence or dissimulation to gain a better bargain in buying or selling.

In fact *dolus malus* (malicious fraud) which we have been considering has been punishable both by the laws (as, for example, in the matter of trusteeships by the Twelve Tables, and in defrauding minors by the Laetorian law), and by judgements unsupported by law where the phrase AS GOOD FAITH DEMANDS* is appended. In the other types of case, these phrases are especially noteworthy: in judgements on a wife's property, FAIRER AND BETTER; in the transfer of property in trust, HONEST NEGOTIATION AS BETWEEN HONEST PARTIES.* So can there be any scope for fraud when FAIRER AND BETTER prevails? Or when the formula HONEST NEGOTIATION AS BETWEEN HONEST PARTIES is pronounced, can there be any crafty or malevolent behaviour? Malicious fraud, as Aquilius states, lies in pretence. So all falsehood must be excluded from business transactions. A seller must not introduce a bogus bidder, nor a buyer someone who bids low against him. If it comes to naming a price, each side must state his terms only once.

Remarkably enough, when Quintus Scaevola,* son of Publius, 62 had stipulated that the price for a farm which he was buying should be declared once and for all, and the vendor complied, Scaevola then said that he valued it higher, and added 100,000 sesterces to the sum demanded. No one can deny that this was the behaviour of an honest man, but people say that it was not the gesture of a wise man; it was like selling for less than he could have got. So this is the pernicious tendency to categorize honest men as different from the wise, a view which led Ennius to say* that a wise man's wisdom is vain if he cannot do himself a good turn. This is true enough, if only Ennius and I could agree on what constitutes 'a good turn'.

I note that Hecato of Rhodes,* the pupil of Panaetius, says in his 63 books *On Obligation* addressed to Quintus Tubero that it is the mark of a wise man to have regard for family assets, though without transgressing the laws, customs, and traditions of the state—his argument being that we seek wealth not for ourselves alone, but also for our children, relatives, friends, and above all, the state; for the resources and wealth of individuals are the riches of the state. That gesture of Scaevola which I mentioned a moment ago cannot in any sense meet with his approval, for he states that absolutely the only thing which he will not do to line his own pocket is to flout the law. He is not to be accorded great praise or gratitude.

However, if both pretence and dissimulation constitute *dolus* 64 *malus*, there are very few occasions on which such malicious fraud does not raise its head. And if the honest man is the sort who assists those whom he can and who harms no one, it is sure that we do not readily encounter an honest man who fills the bill.*

The conclusion we reach is that it is never useful to do wrong, because it is always dishonourable; and honesty in a man is always useful, because it is always honourable.

So far as the law governing properties is concerned, our civil le- 65 gislation stipulates that when they are sold, any defects known to the vendor must be declared. For whereas the Twelve Tables ruled it as sufficient that defects specified by word of mouth* should be made good, and that if a vendor denied their existence the penalty incurred should be doubled,* our legal experts have further established a penalty for failure to declare them; for they have specified that any defect in an estate, if known to the vendor and not expressly stated, must be made good.*

66   An example* of this is afforded by what happened when the augurs proposed to observe an augury from the citadel. They ordered Titus Claudius Centumalus, who had a residence on the Caelian hill, to demolish those parts of the building whose height obstructed observation of the birds. Claudius advertised the block for sale, and Publius Calpurnius Lanarius purchased it. The same notice was then served on him by the augurs. So Calpurnius dismantled it, and having ascertained that Claudius had advertised the building for sale after having received the order for demolition from the augurs, he summoned Centumalus before the arbitrator for a decision on WHAT RESTITUTION HE SHOULD MAKE TO HIM ON THE BASIS OF GOOD FAITH.

The arbitrator who pronounced the verdict was Marcus Cato, father of our contemporary Cato* (we cite the names of other men as sons of their fathers, but since he was the parent of the light of our age, he must be identified by reference to his son). As presiding judge he declared that since Claudius when selling had known the circumstances and failed to report them, he must make good the loss

67   to the buyer. So his decision was that a defect known to the vendor should be made known to the purchaser as a mark of good faith. If his decision was correct, the grain-merchant I mentioned and the vendor of the plague-ridden house were in the wrong in not revealing the facts.

The civil law cannot, however, embrace all such suppressions of defects, but those which it can deal with are scrupulously followed through. Marcus Marius Gratidianus, a kinsman of mine, had sold to Gaius Sergius Orata* a house which he had purchased from him a few years previously. Other parties had rights on the estate, but Marius had not declared this at the time of the sale. The case came to court. Crassus acted for Orata, and Antonius defended Gratidianus.* Crassus pressed the letter of the law: the vendor ought to make good, he said, the defect of which he was aware and which he had failed to declare. Antonius pleaded fair play: he stated that since the defect had not been news to Sergius (for he had sold the property earlier), there had been no need to declare it; Sergius had not been misled, because he could remember the legal rights on the property which he had bought.

Why do I recount these cases? To make it clear to you that our forbears disapproved of tricksters.

But the laws deal with such acts of trickery in one way, and 68 philosophers in another, the laws by restraining them by force as much as possible, and philosophers as best they can by reason and intelligence. So reason demands that nothing underhand be done by pretence or deceit. So is it underhand to set snares, even if you do not intend to bring your quarry out into the open and drive him into your net? Wild beasts often fall into a trap when no hunter is pursuing them. So can you likewise advertise a house, erect a notice of sale as a sort of snare,* and allow someone who is off his guard to stumble into it?

I quite see that because of our degenerate practice it is not con- 69 sidered shameful to do this, nor is it vetoed by statute or by civil law; none the less, it is forbidden by nature's law. I have often made the point earlier,* but it must be repeated again and again: there is a bond of fellowship which in its widest sense exists between all members of the entire human race, an inner link between those of the same nation, and a still closer connection between those of the same state. This is why our ancestors distinguished between international law and civil law.* Civil law need not necessarily be international law, but international law must also be civil law. We do not, however, possess a substantial, fully-fashioned model of true law and genuine justice; we make do with its outline and hazy appearances.* I only wish that we could be true even to these, drawn as they are from the best examples provided by nature and by truth.

For how valuable is that formula, THAT I MAY NOT BE TRICKED AND 70 DECEIVED BY YOU AND YOUR PLEDGE OF GOOD FAITH. And how golden are those words AS BETWEEN HONEST MEN, DEALING MUST BE HONOURABLE AND WITHOUT DECEIT. But a big question is raised by who are the honest men and what is honourable dealing. True, Quintus Scaevola the chief priest* used to say that there was supreme force in all judgements to which were appended the words IN GOOD FAITH. He believed that the expression 'good faith' had the widest terms of reference, being applicable to cases of guardianships, partnerships, trusts, commissions, buying and selling, hiring and letting—activities which form the structure of our communal life. Such issues, he said, required a competent judge to lay down what one party should make good to the other, especially as in many of them opposing assessments were voiced.

71   So sharp practice should be discountenanced, and likewise ill-will posturing as sound sense, though it is removed at a vast distance from it; for whereas sound sense lies in choosing between good things and bad, ill-will (since all that is demeaning is bad) prefers bad things to good.

It is not merely in property transactions that the civil law, which derives from nature, punishes such ill-will and deceit. In the sale of slaves too all deceit on the vendor's part is barred. By edict of the aediles,* a vendor who should have had knowledge of a slave's health, record of escapes, and thefts makes that information available.

72   (Heirs who have inherited a slave are in a different category.)* This makes us aware that since nature is the basis of law, it accords with nature that no one should so act as to prey upon another's ignorance. No greater bane in life can be found than ill-will posing as rational thought;* this is how those countless occasions arise when the useful seems to conflict with the honourable. How few will there be to be found who can refrain from injustice, if impunity and general unawareness are assured!

73   We can test this out, if you agree, with further examples, in which the common run of people believes that no wrong is done. Here we are not to discuss cut-throats, poisoners, forgers of wills, thieves, and embezzlers of public funds, for they are to be suppressed by chains and imprisonment rather than by the words and arguments of philosophers. Let us consider instead the behaviour of those regarded as honest men.

Certain people brought from Greece to Rome a forged will of Lucius Minucius Basilus, a rich man. To enable it to pass muster more easily, they enrolled as heirs in addition to themselves Marcus Crassus and Quintus Hortensius, the most influential men of the day.* The two of them suspected that the will was a forgery, but since they themselves were not implicated in any wrongdoing, they did not spurn the paltry proceeds of the crimes of others. So is it good enough to appear not to have committed an offence? I do not myself think so, though I had great affection for one of them during his life, and I feel no repugnance for the other* now that he is dead.

74   Basilus had wanted his sister's son Marcus Satrius* to take his

name, and he had made him his heir (this Satrius, incidentally, is the patron of the Picene and Sabine territories; what a shameful stain on our times!). So it was not right that those leading citizens should obtain his estate, while Satrius got nothing but his name. If indeed, as I argued in the first book,* a person acts unjustly by failing to reject injustice or to repel it from his kin, how are we to categorize one who not only does not banish injustice, but even furthers it? In my view even legitimate legacies are dishonourable if sought by flattery with evil intent,* and by performing obligations in a hypocritical rather than sincere spirit.

In such cases what is useful tends from time to time to appear to differ from what is honourable. This impression misleads, for the guidelines for the useful are the same as for the honourable. The 75 person who does not appreciate this will regard no deceit or wrongdoing as alien to him, for if he reasons with himself 'the honourable lies here, but the advantageous lies there', he will have the effrontery to prise apart the things which nature has united, an error from which all acts of deceit, wrongdoing, and crime take their source. So if an honest man by clicking his fingers had it in his power to have his name wheedle its way as beneficiary into rich men's wills, he should not exercise that power, not even if he had ascertained that no-one would ever entertain the slightest suspicion of him. But if you had given Marcus Crassus this same possibility of being enrolled as heir by a click of his fingers when he was not a genuine heir at all, believe me, he would have danced a jig in the forum.*

The just man, however, one whom we feel to be honest, will not rob any person whatsoever to line his own pocket. The person who shows surprise at this must confess his ignorance of what constitutes an honest man. But anyone who wishes to tease out the notion of the 76 good man which lies enveloped in his mind* must first instruct himself that the good man is one who benefits all those whom he can, and who harms none unless he has been the victim of injustice.* So what is the implication of this? Would not such harm be inflicted by one who was able by casting some magic spell to dislodge genuine heirs and to usurp their position? Someone will remark 'So should he not do what is useful and advantageous?' The answer is no. He should realize that nothing is advantageous or useful if it is unjust. The person who has not learnt this lesson cannot become a good man.

When I was a boy I used to hear my father's story of the former 77

consul Gaius Fimbria.* He had acted as judge in the case of Marcus
Lutatius Pinthia, a highly honourable Roman knight, who had
deposited a sum in court to be forfeited IF HE WERE NOT A GOOD MAN.
Fimbria had thereupon told him that he would never adjudicate in
such a case, as he did not wish either to rob such a worthy man of his
reputation by ruling against him, or on the other hand to be seen as
having pronounced anyone to be a good man, when claim to that title
depended on countless deeds of service and praiseworthy achievement. Such a vision of the good man as recognized not merely by
Socrates but also by Fimbria* can in no way envisage anything as
useful which is not honourable. So such a man will not presume to
consider, let alone practise, any action which he would hesitate to
praise.

Is it not shameful for philosophers to have doubts about this,
when even plain country folk would have no doubts? It was from
country folk that the now hoary proverb took its origin. In praising
someone's trustworthiness and goodness, they say of him that 'He is
honest enough to play "How many fingers have I up?" with him in the
dark'.* The implication of this is surely that nothing is advantageous
which is not fitting, even if you can gain such an advantage without
78   rebuke. That proverb, as you must see, grants no pardon to Gyges,
nor to that hypothetical person I cited* a moment ago who can sweep
the board of everyone's legacies at a snap of the fingers; for just as
base conduct however much concealed cannot in any way become
honourable, so what is not honourable cannot be useful, since nature
opposes and wars against it.

79   But, you will object, when the rewards are high there is excuse for
sinning. Gaius Marius' hopes of attaining the consulship were
remote.* Six years after his praetorship he was still rejected, and it
seemed that he would never be a candidate for the consulship. Then
when he was legate to Quintus Metellus, that outstanding man and
outstanding citizen, he was dispatched to Rome by his commander.
There Marius before the people charged Metellus with prolonging
the war, and he promised that if they made him consul, in next to no
time he would make Jugurtha dead or alive submit to the power of the
Roman people. As a result he was indeed elected consul, but at the
cost of good faith and justice, for by his spurious accusation he caused
that outstanding and most dignified citizen, whose legate he was and
by whom he had been sent to Rome, to incur the odium of the public.

Even my kinsman Gratidianus* when he was praetor failed to 80 carry out the obligation of a just man. The plebeian tribunes had summoned the college of praetors to a meeting so that they could reach common agreement about the currency, for at that time it was so volatile that no one could establish the value of his holdings. Together they drafted an edict which included a penalty and an indictment of anyone who transgressed it, and they decided that they would all mount the rostrum together after midday. But when the rest went their various ways, Marius proceeded directly from the benches to the rostrum, and unaccompanied announced the decision which had been jointly drafted. That proclamation, you may care to know, gained him great glory—statues of him in all the streets, incense and candles burning before them. I need not elaborate; no one was ever the greater darling of the common folk.

Cases like these sometimes give us pause as we ponder them, 81 when the actual occasion on which fair play is outraged is scarcely notable, but its outcome is seen to loom large. In this case of Marius, it did not seem such a mean trick to forestall his fellow-praetors and the plebeian tribunes in winning popular favour, but his election by that means to the consulship,* which was the end he had in view, proved extremely useful. But there is a single rule for all such cases, and I am keen that you become thoroughly familiar with it: what seems useful must not be dishonourable, or if it is dishonourable it must not appear useful. So what do we infer from this? Can we regard either the famous Marius or Marius my kinsman as a good man? Open up and scrutinize your understanding, to examine the shape and notion* of the good man you find there. So does it accord with that vision of the good man to tell lies for his own profit, to make accusations, to steal a march on others, or to deceive them? Emphatically not.

So is there anything of such great value, or any advantage so much 82 worth winning, as to cause you to lose the lustre and repute of a good man? What can this so-called benefit confer which is commensurate with what it takes away, if it robs you of the title of good man, and deprives you of good faith and justice? [For what difference is there between a man transformed into a beast and one who retains human shape but exhibits the monstrous behaviour of the beast?]*

Moreover, do not men who disregard all that is right and honourable, as long as they can gain power, follow the example of the

man who even sought to obtain as his father-in-law one whose reckless behaviour would confer power on himself?* He thought it
advantageous to gain sovereign power while the odium descended
on another, and he failed to realise how unjust this was to his native
land, and how dishonourable. Mind you, that father-in-law himself
was constantly quoting the Greek lines from *The Phoenician Women**
which I shall render as best I can, perhaps crudely, but to make the
message clear:

> If justice must be set aside, to win the throne
> Let it be set aside; fear God in other things.

Eteocles, or rather Euripides, deserved to die for making an excep-
83 tion of the one thing which was most criminal of all. So why do we
assemble those petty charges—forged legacies, sharp practice in
trading and in selling? I present to you the man who lusted to become
king of the Roman people* and lord of all the world—and who
achieved his aim! Anyone who says that this ambition is honourable
is a lunatic; it justifies the extinction of laws and liberty, and regards
the squalid and accursed subjugation of them as magnificent. If anyone admits that it is dishonourable to become king in a state which
was free and which ought to be free, yet claims that it is useful for the
person who can achieve it, what rebuke, or rather, what censure can
I utter to try to detach him from so monstrous an error? Ye gods who
live for ever, can that most foul and squalid parricide of our native
land be useful to anyone, even though the man who has involved
himself in it is given the title of Father* by the citizens whom he has
ground down? The useful is therefore to be aligned with the honourable, and in such a way indeed that though the two may appear
different in words, they sound as one in actuality.

84   On the criterion of popular belief, I cannot cite anything which
brings greater benefit than being a king. But when I begin to direct
my rational thought back to the truth, I find by contrast that nothing
is more useless to the man who has attained that eminence unjustly;
for can worries, anxieties, fears by day and night, a life fraught with
ambushes and hazards be useful to anyone? As Accius puts it,*

> Kingship breeds many foes and faithless friends,
> Well-wishers all too few.

But to which kingship was he referring? Why, that bequeathed by

Tantalus and Pelops, a kingdom held by right. How many more such foes and friends, then, do you imagine confronted the king who exploited the Roman people's army to subjugate the Roman people itself, and forced the state which was not only free but also the ruler of the world to become his slave? What blemish, what scars do you 85 think he had on his conscience? Can anyone's life appear useful in his own eyes, when its status is such that the man who deprives him of it* will be held in the greatest gratitude and esteem? Thus if the things which seem most useful of all are not in fact useful, because they are steeped in shame and disgrace, that should be enough for us to believe that nothing is useful which is not honourable.

Such a judgement, mind you, has been made on many other occa- 86 sions, but especially by Gaius Fabricius* in his second consulship, supported by the Roman senate, during the war against Pyrrhus. When king Pyrrhus declared war unprovoked on the Roman people, and a struggle for dominion ensued with that spirited and powerful king, a defector came over from him into Fabricius' camp. He promised that if Fabricius offered him a reward, he would make his way back into Pyrrhus' camp as secretly as he had come, and would end the king's life by poison. Fabricius had the deserter escorted back to Pyrrhus, an action which was praised by the senate. Yet if we are seeking an apparent example and the popular conception of what is useful, here was this lone deserter who would have brought that great war and that oppressive foe of our empire to an end. But it would have been a sore disgrace and a scandal to have overcome by wickedness and not by courage the man with whom we had engaged in a contest for glory.

So would it have been more useful for Fabricius, the counterpart 87 in this city of Aristides at Athens,* or for our senate, which never isolated utility from true worth, to engage the enemy with arms or with phials of poison? If we are to seek dominion to win glory, there must be no place for crime, for glory cannot reside in it. But if power itself is sought by all possible means, it cannot possibly be useful since notoriety attends it. This is why the well-known proposal of Lucius Philippus,* son of Quintus, was not a useful one. Lucius Sulla in accordance with a senatorial decree had given certain communities tax-free status on receipt of a sum of money from them. Philippus proposed that they should resume paying taxes, and that we should not restore to them the money which they had paid for the exemption. The senate approved the measure. What a blot on our empire! The plighted word of pirates is more trustworthy* than that of the senate. 'But since the tax-revenues were increased, surely it was a useful measure?' For how long will our citizens have the

88   effrontery to call anything which is dishonourable useful? Can incurring hatred and notoriety be useful for any regime which should rely on its high esteem and on the goodwill of its allies?

I often disagreed even with my good friend Cato* on this. I considered him too rigid in his defence of the treasury and the tax revenues, and in his rejection of all requests made by the tax collectors, and the many made by our allies. We ought to have treated our allies generously, and to have dealt with the tax collectors as we customarily did with our tenants, the more so as harmony between the social classes was important for the welfare of the republic. Curio too was ill-advised; though he was fond of saying that the cause of the Transpadanes* was just, he invariably added: 'But the useful must prevail!' It would have been better for him to say that their cause was not just because it was not useful to the republic than to claim that it was fair while denying that it was useful.

89   The sixth book of Hecato's work *On Obligations** is full of questions like these: is it right for a good man to fail to feed his retinue of slaves when the price of corn goes sky-high? Hecato presents the arguments on both sides, but he concludes by aligning our obligation with what he regards as the useful rather than with humane conduct.

Again he asks: if a loss had to be sustained at sea, would it be preferable to lose an expensive horse or a lowly slave? In this case the owner is drawn one way by family property, and another by feelings of humanity.

If a fool lays hold of a plank in a shipwreck, should a wise man grab it from him if he can? Hecato says no, on the grounds that it would be unjust.* 'Very well, but should a ship's owner seize the plank that is rightfully his?' 'No, he has no more right to do that than to throw a passenger overboard in mid-ocean, merely because he owns the ship: for until the ship reaches the destination for which it was chartered, it belongs to the passengers, and not to the owner.'

90   Another question: assuming that there is one plank and two shipwrecked passengers, both of them wise men, should each try to grab it for himself, or should one yield to the other? 'One should give way, yielding to the one whose life is more important whether

intrinsically or to the state.' 'But supposing the balance is equal on both sides?' 'Then there will be no contest. One will yield to the other as if in a lottery or a game of chance.'*

'Another problem. Supposing a father plunders some shrines, or he tunnels his way into the treasury. Should his son delate him for this to the magistrates?' 'No, that would be impious;* he should even defend his father, if he is accused.' 'So does the fatherland not take precedence over all other obligations?' 'Indeed it does, but the fatherland itself benefits from having citizens who are devoted to their parents.' 'Well then, if the father seeks to shackle the state with tyranny, or to betray his fatherland, should the son keep his counsel?' 'No indeed; he will beg his father not to do such a deed. If he does not persuade him, he must accuse him, or even threaten him. As a last resort, if the destruction of the state is in the offing, he must put his country's safety before that of his father.'

A further question Hecato raises is this. Supposing a wise man 91 inadvertently obtains counterfeit coins instead of genuine ones. When he becomes aware of this, should he pass them off as genuine in payment to a creditor? Diogenes says yes, but Antipater says no,* and I agree rather with him.

If a man is selling wine and realizes that it has gone off, ought he to admit it? Diogenes does not believe that it is necessary, whereas Antipater thinks that an honest man would do so. The Stoics discuss such issues as if they were disputed points of law.

Should you when selling a slave detail his faults? The faults at issue here are not those which if unmentioned result in the return of the slave as required by civil law,* but his being a liar or a gambler or a thief or a drunkard. One Stoic thinks that such faults should be specified, whereas another thinks they need not be.

Suppose a person imagines that he is selling brass when it is actu- 92 ally gold.* Should an honest man inform him that it is gold, or should he buy for a denarius something worth a thousand? My own view, and the dispute between the philosophers whom I have mentioned, are both now clear.

Should agreements and promises, which in the regular formula of the praetors HAVE BEEN MADE WITHOUT COMPULSION OR MALICIOUS DECEIT,* be always kept? Suppose one man has given another a drug to cure his dropsy, and he stipulates that if it restores him to health, he should never use it again. The drug does restore the sick man to health. A few years later he falls victim to the same disease, and he fails to obtain permission to use the drug again from the person with whom he had made the agreement. Since the owner of the drug is barbaric in refusing permission and it does him no harm, the patient should put the interests of his life and health first.

93   Another case. Suppose that someone makes a wise man his heir, and proposes to leave him a hundred million sesterces, but stipulates that the recipient before claiming the inheritance should dance openly and in daylight in the forum.* The wise man promises to do this, because otherwise the donor would not enrol him as his heir. Should he keep his promise, or not? In my view he should not have made the promise, and that I think would have been the dignified thing to do. But since he has made the promise, if he thinks it degrading to dance in the forum, the more honourable way of reneging on his promise will be to take nothing from the inheritance rather than to accept it. Alternatively he could perhaps donate the money to the state to meet some major crisis, in which case it would not be demeaning even to dance a jig, since it would be in the interests of the fatherland.

94   Again, promises need not be kept if they are not useful to the people who exacted them. We can instance this as earlier from popular stories. The Sun assured his son Phaethon that he would fall in with whatever the boy wished. Phaethon asked to be taken up in his father's chariot.* He was taken up, and before he could disembark he was burnt to a cinder by a bolt of lightning. How much better it would have been if in this instance the father's promise had not been kept! Or again, take the promise which Theseus exacted from Neptune.* Neptune gave him three wishes, and he requested the death of his son Hippolytus, for the father suspected goings-on between his son and the stepmother. But when his wish was granted,
95   Theseus was overwhelmed with grief. A further example: Agamemnon solemnly vowed to Diana the most beautiful creature born that year in his kingdom. He sacrificed Iphigenia,* because no more beautiful creature was born that year. It would have been better not to keep his promise than to perpetrate such a grisly deed.

So promises on occasion should not be kept, and deposits should not always be returned. If a person left a sword with you when he was of sound mind, and asked for it back when he had gone mad, it would be a sin to give it back,* and your obligation would be not to do so.

Again, if a man who had left money with you were to make war on his native land, should you return what he had entrusted to you?* I believe not, for you would be acting against the interests of the state, which ought to be dearer to you than all else. Thus there are many actions which appear honourable by nature, but which cease to be honourable in certain contingencies. Keeping promises, observing agreements, returning deposits may become dishonourable if they cease to be useful.

I think that enough has now been said about actions which seem to be useful when disguised as sound sense, but which are actually 96 unjust. But since in Book One I derived obligations from the four sources of honourable conduct, we can concentrate our discussion upon them when we demonstrate how things which are actually not useful, though they seem to be, are opposed to virtue. We have already discussed prudence, and how ill-will seeks to imitate it; and again, we have discussed justice* as being invariably useful. There remain two dimensions of the honourable, the first of which is seen in the greatness and pre-eminence of an outstanding spirit, and the second in its being shaped and disciplined by self-control and restraint.

Ulysses thought it a useful ploy* (this at any rate is how the tragic 97 poets have recorded it; no such suspicion of Ulysses is voiced in Homer, that best of authors, but this is what the tragedies allege) to seek to avoid military service by pretending to be mad. Someone will perhaps maintain that it was a useful though dishonourable scheme to continue as king, living at leisure on Ithaca with his parents and wife and son. Do you think (so the argument runs) that any distinction won in daily toils and dangers can be compared with that untroubled existence? I myself think that such a life is to be spurned and rejected, for I believe that if it is not honourable it cannot be useful either. What notoriety do you think would have attended Ulysses 98 if he had maintained that pretence of madness? For in spite of his outstanding achievements in the war, this was the dressing-down he received from Ajax:*

> He was the first of us to swear this oath,
> As you all know. Alone he broke his word,
> To avoid the draft feigned madness cogently.
> Had not Palamedes' penetrating mind
> Seen through his ill-disposed effrontery,
> The law of pledged faith he'd for ever spurned.

99   It would have been better for him to engage not only with the foe but also with the waves* (as in fact he did) than to abandon Greece when she was at one in waging war on the barbarians.

But let us lay aside these popular tales and foreign concerns, and turn to actual events in our own history. Marcus Atilius Regulus* when consul for the second time was ambushed and captured by the enemy leader, the Spartan Xanthippus, at the time when Hamilcar, father of Hannibal,* was the Carthaginian supremo. Regulus was dispatched to the senate, having sworn an oath that if certain noble prisoners were not restored to the Carthaginians, he himself would return to Carthage. When he reached Rome, he knew full well what seemed to be the advantageous course, but he regarded it as not truly so, as the outcome makes clear. That course was to stay in his native land, to remain at home with his wife and son, to regard the disaster which he had sustained in battle as one common to many in the hazards of war, and to maintain the dignity of his consular standing. Who is there to deny that this was the useful course? Could you name anyone? But greatness of soul and courage do deny it, and you surely do not look for spokesmen more reliable than these.

100   It is the nature of these virtues to stand in fear of nothing, to despise all human fortunes, to consider as unbearable nothing which can befall a man. So what did Regulus do? He entered the senate and recounted his instructions, but refused to vote on them himself, maintaining that as long as he was bound by oath to the enemy, he was not a senator. But he went further—'What a fool', someone will remark, 'for opposing his own interests!'—and said that it was not the useful course for the captives to be returned, for whereas they were young and the stuff of good leaders, he himself was now spent with age. His authority prevailed in the senate; the prisoners were held at Rome, and Regulus himself returned to Carthage. Love neither of country nor of kin kept him back. At that moment he was well aware that he was setting out to confront the most cruel of foes and their refined torture, but he believed that he must be true to his oath. So even then, I maintain, when deprived of sleep and thus slowly killed,* he was better off than if he had remained at home as an aged prisoner of war, a consular who had forsworn his oath.

101   'But how foolish of him for not merely failing to vote to restore the prisoners, but even speaking against it!' But was it foolish? What,

even though it served the interests of the state? Can any action be useful to any of the citizens if it is not useful to the state?*

When men detach the useful from the honourable, they undermine the very foundations of nature. We all seek the useful, and are drawn to it; we cannot in any way do otherwise. What man is there who avoids useful things, or rather, does not pursue them most eagerly? But because we can find those useful things nowhere but in what is praiseworthy, seemly, and honourable, we regard these as our primary and highest aims, and we consider the term 'useful' as not so much illustrious as necessary.

'So what point is there' someone will ask 'in swearing an oath? We 102 surely do not fear the wrath of Jupiter? All philosophers, not merely those who say that God experiences no trouble himself and imposes it on no other, but also those who have it that God is always busy in activity and toil, share the view that God is never angry* and never causes harm. In any case, what greater harm could an angry Jupiter have caused than that which Regulus inflicted on himself? So religious scruple had no impact such as could undermine the effect of what was beneficial to him.

'Was the oath taken, then, so that he would not act basely? The first objection to this is the proverbial "Take the least of evils".* So did this base behaviour involve as much evil as the torture he suffered? Secondly, there is also the objection as voiced by Accius:*

[Thyestes]   Did you break your faith?
[Atreus]   No faithless man received it then, nor hears it now.

Though this response is spoken by an impious king, the sentiment is splendid.'

These critics add that just as I say that some things seem useful 103 but are not, so certain things seem honourable but are not. So, for example, Regulus' return to face torture in order to keep his oath seems honourable but proves not to be so, because the compulsion of enemy violence ought not to have been sanctioned.* The critics make the further point that what is especially useful becomes honourable, even if previously it did not seem so.

These are in essence the criticisms made of Regulus. Let us examine the first of them.

'He should not have feared that Jupiter in anger would harm him, 104 for it is not the way of the god to be angry or to inflict harm.' This argument is no more valid against Regulus than against oath-taking in general. So far as oaths are concerned, what we must grasp is not the fear they induce, but their impact, for swearing an oath is a scrupulous affirmation; you must keep the pledge which you made solemnly as though God were witnessing it. What is at issue here is not the anger of the gods, which is non-existent, but justice and good faith. As Ennius so splendidly says,*

> O winged Faith with kindly eye, and Oath witnessed by Jupiter!

105 So the man who renounces his sworn oath renounces the goddess Faith, whom our ancestors decided to set next to Jupiter Best and Greatest on the Capitol, as a speech of Cato attests.* 'But not even an angry Jupiter would have harmed Regulus more than Regulus harmed himself.' That would certainly be true if pain were the only evil; in fact, philosophers with the greatest standing maintain that pain is not merely not the greatest evil, but is not an evil at all.* Regulus is no mean witness to this; he is perhaps the most inspiring witness of all, so please don't criticize him; for what more reliable witness do we seek than that leader of the Roman people who endured torture voluntarily in order to fulfil his obligation?

Critics quote the proverbial 'Take the least of evils', in other words, prefer dishonour to disaster; but is there any evil greater than dishonour? If there is something repulsive about physical disfigurement, how monstrous must the deformity and foulness of a soul
106 steeped in dishonour appear! This is why philosophers of more intense views make bold to say that the dishonourable is the only evil, and even those who are less stringent* do not hesitate to call it the greatest evil.

As for the citation 'No faithless man received it then, nor hears it now', the poet was right to use it because in dealing with Atreus, he had to adhere closely to the character.* But if the critics intend to adopt for their own use the argument that a pledge given to a faithless person counts for nothing, they should be careful that they are not affording perjury a place in which to hide.

107 Even warfare has its code of law;* fidelity must often be observed in swearing oaths with the enemy, for an oath which is sworn with the intention to discharge it must be kept, though if there is no such intention, there is no perjury if it is not carried out. For example, if you fail to pay a ransom on your life when you have agreed it with

pirates, that does not constitute deception, even if before you failed
to pay you had sworn an oath; for a pirate is not specified as belong-
ing to the ranks of combatants, but is a foe in all men's eyes, and no
pledge or oath should be taken with him. To swear a false oath is   108
in itself not perjury, but to fail to carry out what you have sworn
WITH SINCERE INTENT,* as our custom phrases it, is indeed perjury.
Euripides expresses this well:*

> My tongue has sworn; my mind as yet remains unsworn.

As for Regulus, he had no right to undermine the terms and agreements made with the enemy in war. Conflict was joined justly and
lawfully with the foe; towards an enemy such as this, we deploy our
entire fetial law* and the many rights which both sides share. If this
had not been so, the senate would never have surrendered eminent
men in chains to the enemy.

Yet this was what happened with Titus Veturius and Spurius   109
Postumius.* In their second consulship they fought diastrously at
Caudium; our legions were sent beneath the yoke, and the consuls
concluded peace with the Samnites. They were then handed over to
the enemy, for they had acted without instructions from the people
and the senate. At the same time Tiberius Minucius and Quintus
Maelius,* who were plebeian tribunes in that year, were surrendered
so that the peace with the Samnites could be repudiated, for it had
been concluded on their authority. The man who advocated and proposed this surrender of the four officials was the very Postumius who
was himself handed over.

The same thing happened many years later. Gaius Mancinus had
made a treaty with the Numantines without senatorial authority.*
He spoke in support of the proposal that he be surrendered to the
Numantines, which was presented by Lucius Furius and Sextus
Atilius in accordance with a senatorial decree. The bill was passed,
and he was handed over to the enemy. Mancinus behaved more honourably than Quintus Pompeius* in the same situation, for Pompeius spoke against that bill, and the measure was not passed. In this
last case the apparently useful prevsiled over the honourable,
whereas in the earlier ones the false semblance of the useful was
overcome by the authority of the honourable.

'But what had been imposed by force ought not to have been bind-   110
ing.' As if force could be brought to bear on a brave man! 'So why did

he embark on that journey to the senate, particularly as he intended to argue against the release of the prisoners?' You critics here censure what is noblest about him. He did not rely on his own judgement, but initiated the case so that the senate should decide it. Yet if he himself had not made the proposal, the prisoners would certainly have been restored* to the Carthaginians, with the result that Regulus would have remained in his native land unharmed. But because he thought that this would not be beneficial to his country, he believed that it was the honourable course for him both to propose what he did and to suffer for it.

As to the critics' claim that what is especially useful becomes honourable, the more correct formulation would be to say that what is honourable becomes especially useful, or rather *is*, not becomes, especially useful. For nothing is useful which is not also honourable; and it is not honourable because it is useful, but useful because it is honourable. So of many remarkable examples, it would be by no means easy to cite one more praiseworthy or more outstanding than this.

111   But in this entire encomium of Regulus, the one thing uniquely worthy of admiration is his proposal that the prisoners should be detained at Rome. The fact that he himself returned seems remarkable to us nowadays, but in that era he could not have acted otherwise. So this tribute is not to the man, but his times, for it was the will of our ancestors that nothing should make a pledge more closely binding than swearing an oath. This is shown by the laws of the Twelve Tables, by the 'sacred' laws, by treaties in which good faith is binding even when they are struck with enemies, and by the inquiries and penalties imposed by the censors,* whose decisions relating to sworn oaths were more scrupulous than any others.

112   After Lucius Manlius, the son of Aulus, had held the dictatorship, he was indicted by the plebeian tribune Pomponius* for having extended the tenure of the office for a few days too long. Pomponius also charged him with having banished his son Titus, later called Torquatus, from the community, bidding him live in the country. The story goes that when the youthful son heard that his father was being harried, he hastened to Rome and arrived on Pomponius' doorstep at dawn. When his arrival was announced to the tribune, Pomponius imagined that the youth in resentment would lay some allegation before him against his father. So he got out of bed, and having dismissed any witnesses he ordered the boy to join him. The

young man on entering drew his sword, and swore that he would kill
the tribune there and then unless he swore to him that he would
quash the indictment of his father. Fear compelled Pomponius to
swear an oath; he then laid the matter before the people, informed
them why he had to abandon the suit, and acquitted Manlius. Such
was the importance attached to an oath in those days. (Notice that
this Titus Manlius was the man who acquired his surname at the
river Anio.* When he was challenged by a Gaul, he killed him, and
removed the collar (*torques*) from his neck. In his third consulship
the Latins were scattered and put to flight at the Veseris. An outstandingly great man, he showed great kindness to his father, but
was bitterly harsh towards his son.)

Whereas Regulus deserves praise for keeping his sworn word, the   113
ten Romans sent by Hannibal to the senate after the battle of Cannae
deserve rebuke,* if indeed they failed to return; for they had sworn
to go back to the camp occupied by the Carthaginians if they did not
succeed in getting Roman prisoners ransomed. However, all authorities do not concur in this account; for Polybius, an outstandingly
good source, states that when the senate did not grant this request,
nine of the ten high-born nobles sent at that time did return, but that
the tenth, who shortly after leaving the enemy camp had returned to
it on the pretext of having forgotten something, remained at Rome.
He claimed that by returning to the camp he had been released from
the oath which he had sworn. But that was no justification, for deceit
intensifies the perjury rather than nullifies it. Such guile, then, was
stupid in its wrong-headed caricature of prudence. The outcome
was that the senate decreed that the practised fraudster should be
escorted in chains to Hannibal.

But the really significant part of the story is this.* Hannibal held   114
8,000 prisoners whom he had not seized in the battle-line, nor had
they fled from it in fear of death. They had been left in the camp by
the consuls Paulus and Varro. The senate decreed that they should
not be ransomed, even though a small payment could have sufficed
for the purpose, the intention being to instil into our troops the message that they must conquer or die. The same Polybius writes that
when Hannibal heard of this, his morale was shattered, because the
Roman senate and people had reacted to their desperate situation in
such a lofty spirit. Thus apparently useful policies are outweighed
when set in the balance against the honourable.

115   However, Gaius Acilius,* who wrote his history in Greek, states
that several soldiers returned to the camp with the same deceitful
ploy of freeing themselves from their oath, and that the censors subjected them to every possible mark of shame.

This topic must now be concluded, for it is perfectly clear that
behaviour motivated by a cowardly, submissive, abject, broken
spirit—such as Regulus would have exemplified if his proposal
about the prisoners had met his own apparent need rather than that
of the state, or if he had sought to remain at home—is not beneficial,
because it is disgraceful, foul, and shameful.

116   We are left with the fourth subdivision, which comprises propriety, restraint, moderation, self-control, and temperance. Can anything, I ask, be useful if it is opposed to this chorus of virtues? Some
philosophers—the Cyrenaics who derived their name from Aristippus of Cyrene, and the Annicerii so-called—* have argued that all
good lies in pleasure, and have maintained that virtue is praiseworthy merely because it is productive of pleasure. These schools are
now defunct, but Epicurus is fashionable, and he is the supporter
and sponsor of virtually the same doctrine.* If we intend to defend
and preserve the honourable, these are the foes with whom we are to
117   fight it out, 'on foot and on horseback' as the saying goes. For if not
merely the useful, but also the happy life in its entirety depends
solely on the vigour of our bodily constitution and the considered
prospect of its remaining so, as Metrodorus has written,* it is
inevitable that this concept of the useful, even considered at its
highest (as these philosophers advocate it) will be at war with the
honourable.

For to begin with,* what role will be afforded to practical wisdom?
Is its function merely to seek out pleasant experiences from every
quarter? How wretched the servility of that virtue would be, playing
handmaid to low pleasure! What duty is assigned to wisdom? To
deploy our understanding to discriminate between pleasures? Even
assuming that no task is more pleasant than this, what more degrading duty can be imagined? Again, if a man argues that pain is the
greatest evil, what role in his thinking is there for courage, which dis-
dains pains and toils? Granted that Epicurus speaks in many places,
as he does, quite bravely on the subject of pain, we must examine not
what he says, but what consistency his words have when he confines
goods to pleasure, and evils to pain. Likewise if I listen to him on

self-control and temperance, he has much to say about them at many points, but his flow falters, as the saying goes; for how can he praise temperance, yet define pleasure as the highest good? Temperance is the foe of lusts, and lusts are enthusiasts for pleasure.

Yet these philosophers equivocate as best they can, and not with- 118 out subtlety, on these three categories of virtue. Prudence they present as the knowledge which affords pleasures and banishes pains. Courage too they promote in some sense, when they propound a rationale for disregarding death and enduring pain. They even usher in temperance, which is by no means easy for them, but they deal with it as best they can; for they state that what sets bounds to the summit of pleasure is the absence of pain. But for them justice wobbles or rather falls flat, together with all the virtues visible in social life and in the fellowship of the human race; for goodness or generosity or courtesy cannot be in evidence any more than friendship, if these virtues are not sought for their own sake, but are directed towards pleasure or advantage.

So let us draw these considerations together briefly. I have 119 demonstrated that the useful is never found in opposition to the honourable, and I likewise maintain that all low pleasure is opposed to the honourable. This leads me to the conclusion that Callipho and Dinomachus* are all the more to be condemned for believing that they would settle the dispute if they joined the pleasurable with the honourable, which is like mating an animal with a human. The honourable does not accept this alliance; indeed, it spurns and despises it. The greatest of goods and the greatest of evils must in fact be uncompounded; they cannot be a mixture and combination of totally different things. But I have discussed this large-scale topic at greater length elsewhere;* let us turn to the issue before us.

We have earlier discussed at sufficient length how a judgement is 120 to be made between the apparently useful and the honourable, on the occasions when they conflict with each other. But if pleasure as well is to have the appearance of the useful, it cannot be reconciled with the honourable. To make some concession to pleasure, it will perhaps add some spice to life, but will certainly offer nothing beneficial.

So here, Marcus my son, is a present from your father—an import- 121 ant one as I see it, though its value will depend on how you receive it. You must, however, take in these three books as guests, so to say, among the lecture-notes of Cratippus.* If I had visited Athens (as indeed I would have done if my country had not so loudly called me back when I was on my way),* you would eventually have heard me discoursing as well; so now in these volumes my words have embarked on their journey to you, and accordingly you must devote as much time to them as you can; 'as you can' here will mean 'as you wish'. Once I am aware that you take delight in this branch of knowledge, I shall both discuss it with you soon in person, I hope, and as long as you are away, from a distance.

So farewell, my dear Cicero. Reassure yourself that you are most dear to me, but you will be much dearer if you are pleased to receive such advice and instruction as this.

Explanatory Notes

BOOK ONE

§§ 1–10: Introduction to the subject

1 *a whole year . . . a pupil of Cratippus*: Cicero's son Marcus had left for
Athens in early April 45 BC (*Att.* 15. 15. 4); Books 1–2 of this treatise
were finished by early November 44 (*Att.* 16. 11. 4), and this Preface
was composed perhaps a month or two earlier. Cratippus, whom
Cicero had met at Ephesus when en route to his province in 51, later
became President of the Lyceum at Athens. Here and elsewhere
(*Div.* 1. 5) he is praised as the outstanding Peripatetic of the day.

her examples: At *Fin.* 5. 2 (part of a conversation set in the gardens of
the Academy), the Peripatetic Pupius Piso instances Plato, Speu-
sippus, Xenocrates, and Polemo as such inspirational figures. Cicero
himself cites the Academic Carneades, and his nephew Lucius recalls
visiting the haunts of Demosthenes and Pericles (*Fin.* 5. 3, 5. 5).

in both learning and discernment: 'learning' renders the reading *discen-
dum*, which is supported by a similar comment at *N.D.* 1. 8. The variant *dicendum*, which would imply that Cicero's acquaintances were in
the habit of declaiming in Greek, would be more appropriate to his
own activities (cf. *Att.* 9. 4, Plutarch, *Cic.* 4. 4–5) than to theirs. 'Discernment' probably refers to insight into philosophical problems.

2 *satisfied with your progress*: here and at greater length at 3. 6, Cicero is
clearly exercised by the possibility that his son is wasting his time (and
his father's money) at Athens. Marcus in fact abandoned his studies
later to enrol in the forces of Brutus, who in April 43 showers praise on
him in a letter to his proud father (*Ad Brut.* 3. 6).

followers of Socrates and Plato: as an adherent of the Academics, Cicero
claimed spiritual descent from them. Though he shared the scepticism of Carneades in the fields of epistemology and physics, his friendship with the reforming Academic Antiochus reinforced his Roman
traditionalism to draw closer to the Stoic–Peripatetic position,
especially in ethics. See the Introd., p. xxxii f.

3 *my dear Cicero*: though at the commencement of each book in this treatise Cicero uses the more affectionate address 'Marcus my son', here and elsewhere he frequently uses his *cognomen*. By becoming a senior magistrate and a senatorial, 'he had ennobled his son, and he was zealous to employ . . . the *cognomen* which that ennoblement entitled the boy to expect' (J. N. Adams, *CQ* 72 (1978), 158–9).

almost as many: that is, by computing the individual books of the philosophical and rhetorical works combined; they number 56 against the 70 speeches published by this date.

Demetrius of Phalerum: this Athenian statesman and philosopher (b. *c*.350) had been appointed governor of Athens (313–307) by the Macedonian Cassander. As a disciple of Theophrastus, when he was exiled from Athens he wrote philosophy as librarian at Alexandria. His mastery of the Middle Style (intermediate between the Plain Style which instructs, and the Grand Style which persuades by carrying an audience with it, wins further applause from Cicero at *Brutus* 285, *Orator* 92 ('he excelled the rest'), etc.

Theophrastus: as successor of Aristotle to the headship of the Lyceum, he in Cicero's words 'handled topics previously treated by Aristotle' (*Fin.* 1. 6). Cicero was greatly impressed by his mellifluous style, which he terms 'sweet' (*Brutus* 121) and 'divine' (*Orator* 62).

4 *Plato . . . Demosthenes . . . Aristotle . . . Isocrates*: Cicero correctly observes that Plato and Aristotle did not practise in the courts, though Aristotle in his *Rhetoric* was closely engaged with the theory of oratory, and Demosthenes and Isocrates did not write philosophy. Elsewhere Cicero praises Plato's style as dignified and mellifluous (*Orator* 62), but adds that it lacked sting and sinew as court-oratory demanded. The tradition that Demosthenes studied under Plato but subsequently abandoned philosophy for oratory was widespread in later days (see Cicero, *De oratore* 1. 89; *Brutus* 121; *Orator* 15; Plutarch, *Dem.* 5). The tradition of rivalry between Aristotle and Isocrates is often mentioned by Cicero (*De oratore* 3. 141; *Orator* 62; *Tusc.* 1. 7). For the contrast between the styles appropriate to oratory and philosophy, see *Brutus* 120f.

Honourable behaviour . . . neglecting them: the Latin words *honestas* and *turpitudo* (rendering the Greek *kalon* and *aischron*) are to be interpreted predominantly in the social rather than the personal context.

5 *several schools . . . supreme evil*: at *Fin.* 2. 39ff., Cicero condemns not only the Epicureans but also the Cyrenaics, who argued that physical

gratification was the primary goal in life, and the eclectic school under Hieronymus of Cardia, who reckoned that freedom from pain was the chief good. He adds a word of criticism of Carneades, founder of the Third Academy, whose theories of epistemology and physics he accepts, but not his ethics.

5 *pain . . . self-controlled*: the Epicureans are primarily in Cicero's mind, but for a more nuanced analysis of their doctrine, see Rist, *Epicurus*, ch. 8. Courage and temperance ('cannot be brave . . . cannot be self-controlled') are two of the four cardinal virtues which Cicero assumes that all accept as fundamental norms of human conduct.

6 *elsewhere*: the *De finibus*, in which Cicero discusses the various Hellenistic theories of the highest good, discusses virtue at 2. 35 ff.

right behaviour alone . . . discredited: in *Fin.* 5, Pupius Piso the Peripatetic spokesman praises Antiochus, the first-century Academic, for reverting to the view of the Old Academy that virtue is the chief good, and that externals such as health, wealth, beauty are subsidiary goods; hence the Academy of Cicero's day could contribute positively to the present discussion. On the other hand, Aristo, Erillus (both heterodox Stoics) and Pyrrho (founder of the Sceptics) condemned the Stoic doctrine of 'things preferred' (health, wealth, noble birth, etc.) and 'things not preferred' (sickness, poverty, low origins, and the like), claiming that all such intermediate things were indifferent, and thus restricting moral choices. Further, Erillus pronounced knowledge, not virtue, to be the sole good (*Fin.* 2. 43).

in whatever way, my judgement and inclination dictate: this statement is important as qualifying the modest claim made for Cicero's philosophical writings at *Att.* 12. 52. 3: 'These writings are mere copies, produced with no heavy labour; I supply only the words, of which I have a rich store.' This comment may in fact refer only to the more technical writing (the *Academica*) on which he was then engaged. He makes further claims of originality at *Att.* 13. 13. 14.

7 *Panaetius*: for his importance as a major source of Books 1–2, see the Introd., p. xxvii ff.

ought to begin with a definition: Cicero as punctilious Academic frequently insists on this necessary preliminary to logical argument (see *Rep.* 1. 38; *De oratore* 1. 209 ff., 2. 108).

8 *katorthoma . . . meson*: on these terms, see Rist, *Stoic Philosophy*, 97 ff. *meson* is Winterbottom's conjectural supplement to the text, which I accept.

10 *in such classification of a topic*: the threefold division by Panaetius outlined in the previous paragraph dictates the structure of the treatise; Book 1 discusses the honourable, Book 2 the useful, and Book 3 the relationship between the two.

§§ 11–17: Human reason and the virtues associated with it

11 *Our starting-point*: Cicero here as in *Fin.* 2. 45–7 echoes the Stoic thesis that moral behaviour develops from natural instinct.

man is endowed with reason . . . the causes of things: this Stoic view of the fundamental difference between man and the lesser animals is adapted from Aristotle's *Politics* (1253a) and more extensively from his *De anima*.

13 *the search and scrutiny into truth*: Cicero now outlines the four cardinal virtues from which obligations stem. They first appear in Plato (*Rep.* 427d ff.) as wisdom, justice, courage, and temperance; Aristotle extends the discussion of them in his *Nic. Eth.* and *Politics* (see D. Ross, Aristotle⁵ (London 1949), 202 ff.). In Cicero's analysis, a distinction is later made between wisdom and prudence as the first of the four (see 1. 153), justice is expanded into social virtue and combined with liberality, courage is more widely defined as greatness of soul, and the fourth virtue becomes the concept of the fitting, in which moderation and self-restraint play a leading part. At this stage of the presentation, the important point is that men aspire to these virtues by their possession of reason.

15 *in Plato's words*: the citation is from *Phaedrus* 250d, a description of *phronesis* or wisdom.

§§ 18–19: Wisdom

18–19 *two faults . . . also unnecessary*: the first fault, overdogmatism in metaphysical questions, is in Cicero's view especially associated with Epicurean theology and physics; see *N.D.* 1. 18, where the Epicurean Velleius dogmatizes 'with the breezy confidence customary with Epicureans, fearing nothing so much as to give the impression of doubt about anything'. The second fault echoes the Stoic view that learning should be sought merely to attain virtue, and that the disinterested spirit of curiosity recommended by Aristotle should not be pursued for its own sake. I outline this controversy between Peripatetics and Stoics in *GR* 35 (1988), 78 ff. At *Fin.* 4. 13, 5. 48, Cicero shows himself more sympathetic to the Peripatetic position than appears here.

19 *Gaius Sulpicius . . . Sextus Pompeius*: C. Sulpicius Galus (cos. 166 BC), the outstanding student of Greek culture of his day, was renowned for his astronomical lore (Cicero, *Rep.* 21–2; *Sen.* 49), and he allegedly prophesied a lunar eclipse before the battle of Pydna (Livy 44. 36. 5 ff.). This Sextus Pompeius was the uncle of Pompey the Great; according to Cicero, *Brutus* 175, he was well versed in civil law and Stoic philosophy as well.

denial of one's duty: this Stoic observation on the greater importance of public service was congenial to Cicero's order of priorities; he reverts to the topic at 1. 153 ff. Others like Sallust regarded such written research as an alternative form of public service (cf. *Jug.* 4. 5 ff.). This is a reflection of the older Stoic view (see *SVF* 3. 172) that both the active and the contemplative lives were things preferred.

§§ 20–41: Justice, its impediments and obligations

20 *the title of* boni: the word has not only moral overtones (cf. 2. 38) and a status in Roman law (cf. 3. 70 and 77) but also a political nuance. The *boni* are 'the politically sound elements in the state' (so *OCD* 6), and in the context of later 44 BC, when Cicero delivered the first four Philippics against Mark Antony and hoped to revitalize the senate, they represent those who defend the republic against tyranny.

beneficence . . . generosity: the Stoics here subsume under the second cardinal virtue the Aristotelian doctrine of magnificence (*Nic. Eth.* 1122a ff.) in its emphasis on enlightened giving.

21 *Arpinum . . . the Tusculans*: the examples combine Cicero's native town in Volscian territory with the site of his favourite villa near Frascati where the *Tusculans* and other philosophical dialogues were composed.

22 *as Plato . . . put it*: the reference is to Plato's *Ep.* 9 (358a) addressed to Archytas. In that passage Plato additionally cites parents between country and friends. Since Cicero emphasizes our obligations to parents at 1. 58 and 1. 160, it is curious that he omits them from the quotation here.

as the Stoics have it: see *N. D.* 2. 154 ff., where the Stoic Balbus details this teaching of his school.

23 *fides . . . fiat*: the Stoic zest for etymologies as rationalizing explanations of fables and cults was taken to extreme lengths. The fanciful
derivations of the Stoic Balbus at *N. D.* 2. 66ff. are taken to task by the
Academic Cotta later in that treatise (3. 62): 'Your strained interpretations are quite pathetic.' There is no etymological connection
between *fides* and *fiat*; though Cicero here waxes sceptical about it, he
cites it with approval elsewhere (*Rep.* 4. 7; *Fam.* 16. 10. 2).

25 *Marcus Crassus observed*: the citation is not found elsewhere. For
Crassus' career and his vision of 'the key to success in wealth', see
OCD, Crassus (4). The anecdote at 3. 73–5 may be part of the same lost
citation.

26 *those words of Ennius*: the quotation is from an unknown play, perhaps
Thyestes.

The shameless conduct of Gaius Caesar: this treatise, composed only a few
months after the assassination of the dictator, repeatedly castigates
the dead man's career; see the Introd, p. x, and 2. 27ff., 3. 36, 3. 82–3.

most outstanding talent: though Cicero condemned Caesar's political
ambition which precipitated the end of the Republic, he admired his
abilities and much preferred him as a person to Pompey.

28 *Plato's remark*: see *Theaetetus* 173d–e.

30 *in Terence*: the citation is from *The Self-Tormentor*, 77.

31 *to restore a deposit*: in the text following this phrase the words *etiamne
furioso?* ('even to a madman?') appear, but modern editors delete them.
The corruption must have entered early, because Ambrose, whose
De officiis is modelled on Cicero's treatise, writes at 1. 254: 'If you do
not refuse to a madman the sword deposited with you.' An attempt has
been made to make sense of the insertion with the additional gloss of
gladium (the sword).

32 *the third of his three wishes*: the story goes back to Greek tragedy. In
Euripides, *Hippolytus* 887ff., however, this was the first of Theseus'
three wishes. As W. S. Barrett explains in his edition of *Hippolytus*
(Oxford 1966, *ad loc.*), an alternative, possibly earlier, version of the
story existed, reflected in Seneca, *Phaedra* 949 as well as here.

33 *Give the law its head, and injustice rules instead*: so Terence, *The Self-
tormentor*, 796.

A notorious case: Plutarch, *Moralia* 223A, ascribes this trickery to
Cleomenes I of Sparta (*c.*519–488 BC); Herodotus 6. 78–9 describes

the ruse differently. Cicero may have omitted the name of the king as being of little interest to his readers, or more probably he could not recall with certainty who he was.

33 *Quintus Fabius Labeo*: this anecdote is recounted in similar terms by Valerius Maximus 7. 3. 4. Labeo was consul in 183; the story finds no mention in Livy, but it could none the less be historical, either omitted by the historian for patriotic reasons, or having occurred after 167 where his account is lost.

35 *living peaceably without suffering injustice*: this doctrine of the theory of the just war goes back (presumably through Panaetius) to Plato, *Laws* 628d, and Aristotle, *Nic. Eth.* 1177b.

to confer citizenship . . . Carthage and Numantia . . . Corinth: in his attempt to reconcile Roman imperial policies with the Greek philosophical principles of just war and enlightened treatment of conquered communities, Cicero here idealizes the privileges accorded to Rome's Italian subjects. It is true that Tusculum received the full citizenship, probably as early as 381 BC, and other Latin towns gained it fifty years later; the citizenship awarded to communities among the Aequi, Volsci, Sabines, and Hernici was initially without voting rights, though some later graduated to full citizenship. But Rome's jealous refusal to award full citizenship to all her Italian allies, while demanding from them contingents for her military campaigns, led to the Social War of 91 BC (on which, see 2. 75 and n.). Cicero's defence of the destruction of Carthage in 146 BC, and of Numantia in Spain in 133 BC, on the grounds of 'cruel monstrosities' is specious; both incidents reflect the increasing ruthlessness of Roman foreign policy which brooked no opposition. His qualified apologia for the treatment of Corinth, destroyed by Mummius in 146 BC as an object lesson to the defiance of the Achaean Confederacy, is equally feeble; the Corinthians had not waged war cruelly, which on Cicero's own admission would have been the only justification for the destruction of the city. Note the later condemnation of the sack of the city at 3. 46.

one far from ideal . . . now we have none: Cicero on the eve of the Great Civil War of 49 BC remained true to his philosophical principles and supported the senatorial party, but made strenuous efforts to mediate with Caesar, preferring 'even the most unjust peace to the justest of wars' (*Fam.* 6. 6. 5). The 'seeds of future treachery' referred to here was   Caesar's cloaked ambition for tyrannical power. Cicero believed that peace might have been established with Caesar in such a way as to preserve the republic, however weakened (cf. *Fam.* 6. 1. 6).

35 *even if a battering ram has shattered their city wall*: there seems to be a conscious criticism of Caesar's response to the Aduatuci (*Bell. Gall.* 2. 32. 1): 'He said that in accordance with his custom rather than their merit, he would preserve their city if they surrendered before the ram was applied to the wall . . . '. The Roman tradition of sparing those who surrendered (epitomized in Virgil's 'parcere subiectis et debellare superbos' (*Aen.* 6. 853), is repeatedly emphasized in Livy; see e. g. 30. 42. 17, 37. 45. 8f.

became their patrons in accordance with ancestral custom: see the examples in *OCD, s. v.* Patronus.

36 *the fetial code of the Roman people*: there was a college at Rome of twenty 'fetial' priests, allegedly dating from the Regal period, who advised on issues of war and peace. If a declaration of war was imminent, its representatives visited the offending state to demand solemn satisfaction; if this was not forthcoming within 33 days, a formal denunciation followed. The fetials then returned home, war was declared, and a fetial signalled the existence of hostilities by dispatching a spear into enemy territory. See Livy 1. 32. 5 with the note and bibliography in R. M. Ogilvie, *Commentary on Livy I–V* (Oxford 1965), 127 ff.

[*The commander Popilius . . . in initiating warfare*]: this anecdote is rightly excised by modern editors. First, it conflicts with the version immediately following. Secondly, there are linguistic peculiarities (the mood of *patitur*, the tense of *obliget*, the phrase *militiae sacramentum* not otherwise found before the third century AD). M. Popilius Laenas as consul in 173 BC fought against the Ligurians. His barbaric treatment of the captured enemy was condemned in the Roman senate (Livy 42. 8–9, 21–2). This condemnation could have afforded Cicero an apposite example of Roman concern for justice in war. The final sentence ('Such was the degree . . . ') is retained by some scholars, but it does not follow on logically from the first two sentences of § 36.

37 *a letter of Marcus Cato the elder to his son Marcus*: for young Marcus' service in Macedonia, see Valerius Maximus 3. 2. 16, Iustinus 33. 2. 1. The consul mentioned here as commanding the Roman forces in the Third Macedonian War against Perseus in 168 BC was L. Aemilius Paulus (Livy 44. 19 ff.).

Phrases in the Twelve Tables: originally drawn up by a special commission in 451/50, the tablets on which they were written were destroyed in the Gallic invasion of 387/6; the later reconstruction of them contained archaisms such as those cited here. Cicero's contemporary Varro, in his *De lingua Latina* 5. 3, makes the same point as is made here about the earlier meaning of *hostis*; Cicero may have derived his information from that book, for it was issued about the same time as the *De officiis*, and was addressed to Cicero.

38 *fought for dominion . . . glory sought is for empire*: Cicero makes a distinction between the long and bloody engagements against the Celtiberi in Spain (195–133 BC) and against the German Cimbri on Italy's northern border (113–101 BC), in which the conditions for just warfare outlined at 1. 35 were to be maintained, and the 'glory sought for empire' in the extension of Roman rule in Italy (against Latins and Sabines in the sixth to the fourth centuries, against the Samnites (343–290 BC), and against Pyrrhus of Epirus (280–275 BC) and subsequently against Carthage (264–241, 218–202, 149–46 BC)).

that celebrated speech of Pyrrhus: the poet Ennius devoted Book 6 of his epic poem *Annales* to the war with Pyrrhus. In this fragment (*Annales* 186–93 Warmington) he records how after his victory over the Romans at Heraclea in 280, the king responded to the request of the Roman leader C. Fabricius (consul 282) to ransom Roman prisoners. In the Roman tradition of that war, Fabricius is the figure more frequently depicted as a model of incorruptibility; see 3. 86 below, and the brief mention of the same story at 1. 40.

the race of the Aeacidae: the alleged descendants of Aeacus, king of Aegina and later one of the three judges in the underworld.

39 *Regulus*: M. Atilius Regulus (consul 267, 256) was captured during the First Punic War in 255 by Xanthippus, the Spartan mercenary commander of the Carthaginians. The Roman tradition that when sent on parole to Rome to arrange exchange of prisoners, he urged the senate not to comply, and chose to return to Carthage to be tortured and executed, is of doubtful historicity. Cicero discusses the episode further at 3. 99–100; Horace, *Odes* 3. 5, is a memorable poetic evocation of the legend.

40 [*In the Second Punic War . . . an unprovoked aggressor.*]: The whole of this section has dubious manuscript authority. A further reason to doubt its authenticity is that the story of the ten captives and the crafty individual who discharged himself from his oath (cf. Polybius 6. 58; Livy 22. 58. 6–61. 10) is recounted in greater detail at 3. 113–14; the celebrated anecdote concerning Pyrrhus and Fabricius is also found at 3. 86. See the notes on these passages.

41 *Slaves . . . give them their due*: the abrupt sequence of thought from justice in warfare to justice to slaves mirrors Cicero's earlier discussion

at *Rep.* 35 ff. Behind the advice offered here to treat slaves as hired hands is the Stoic doctrine that no man is a slave by nature; the Stoic Chrysippus is quoted as saying that a slave is 'a hired hand for ever' (Seneca, *De beneficiis* 3. 22. 1). Stoicism refined the traditionally brutal attitude to slaves; see e.g. Petronius, *Satyricon* 71 ('slaves too are men') which probably parodies Seneca *Ep.* 47. 11.

§§ 42–60: Beneficence and liberality as adjuncts to justice

This topic is given prominence by Aristotle (*Nic. Eth.* 1120a ff.); its development in Stoic thought is expounded at length by Seneca, *De beneficiis*, which draws on the *Peri kathekontos* of Hecato, pupil of Cicero's source Panaetius.

42 *his worth*: I take this as the sense of *dignitas* here rather than 'social standing', in view of the discussion which follows at 1. 45.

43 *When Lucius Sulla and Gaius Caesar . . . gave it to outsiders*: as regularly in this treatise, Cicero glosses Panaetius' principles with *exempla* from his own experience. Sulla's notorious proscriptions, condemned also at 2. 27, were familiar to him when he delivered his speech *Pro Roscio Amerino* in 80 BC. Though Sulla himself is not attacked in the speech, his freedman Chrysogonus was. Julius Caesar's sale of property owned by casualties of The Great Civil War (cf. 2. 83) is condemned by Cicero in his *Philippics* (2. 108; 5. 17).

44 *that our benevolence does not go beyond our means*: this principle is derived from Aristotle, *Nic. Eth.* 1120b, and echoed by Seneca, *De beneficiis* 2. 15. 1.

48 *as Hesiod bids us*: See *Works and Days* 349–50, a favourite quotation of Cicero's; see *Brutus* 15; *Att.* 13. 12. 3.

49 *by affection for the world at large*: the transmitted text, *uel morbo in omnes*, is corrupt; I speculatively read and translate *uel amore in omnes*.

50 *they lack reason and speech*: this doctrine of the nature of the superiority of man over the lower animals, taken over from Aristotle by the Stoics, is emphasized by Balbus in *N.D.* 2. 147 ff., and echoed by Seneca, *Ep.* 76. 9.

51 *'all things shared by friends'*: the proverbial phrase is found repeatedly in Plato (*Phaedrus* 279c; *Rep.* 424a; *Laws* 739c) and Aristotle (*Nic. Eth.* 1159b; *Politics* 1263a).

51 *Which Ennius applies*: the citation is from an unknown tragedy.

52 *'his own lamp still shines'*: that is, a person should not deprive himself of all his possessions by giving to others. Contrast Christ's recommendation at Matt. 19: 21.

53 *the same city-state*: for this account of the characteristics of the *ciuitas*, cf. Cicero's *Rep.* 41.

54 *From such procreation . . . states have their beginnings*: this account of the evolution of human societies from the primary unit of the family goes back to Aristotle, *Politics* 1252a–b.

55 *None . . . more pre-eminent . . . than the friendship between good men of like character*: Aristotle devotes two books (*Nic. Eth.* 8–9) to the subject of friendship, discussing in turn that based on utility, on pleasure, and (at the highest level) on goodness. Cicero has earlier discussed friendship at length in his *De amicitia*; in that dialogue Laelius argues that true friendship can exist only between good men (§ 18).

56 *Pythagoras' requirement for friendship is met*: it was natural that the notion of unity out of plurality should be ascribed to the quasi-religious community of Pythagoras at Croton, on which see W. K. C. Guthrie, *A History of Greek Philosophy*, i (Cambridge 1962), 181 ff.

57 *the barbaric conduct of these contemporaries of ours*: these bitter comments are aimed at Julius Caesar and more particularly at Mark Antony and his associates, who after the assassination of Caesar had continued to implement his plans. The first four of the fourteen *Philippics*, which date to September–December 44 when this treatise was composed, repeatedly echo this condemnation. 1, delivered on Sept. 2, is 'a comprehensive attack on Antony's political record in recent months'; 2, 'a pamphlet in political form' dating to November 44, 'is *par excellence* a political and personal attack on Antony'. 3–4, both delivered on Dec. 20, attack Antony and his brother Lucius, and claim that Mark Antony is now *de facto* a public enemy. The above citations are from D. R. Shackleton Bailey, *Cicero, Philippics* (Chapel Hill, NC 1986).

58 *our country and our parents must take first place*: Cicero here echoes the Roman tradition that our primary allegiance is to our country; the satirist Lucilius (fr. 1207 f. Warmington) similarly ranks country, parents and family in that order as proper recipients of obligations. The reasons for putting country first are outlined at 1. 53.

    flourish best in friendships: Aristotle expresses similar sentiments at *Nic. Eth.* 1172a.

59 *when he gathers in his harvest*: Cato, *De agricultura* 4, advises close relations with neighbours so that they will be helpful in such circumstances; cf. Hesiod, *Works and Days* 343 ff.

a relative or friend . . . rather than a neighbour: it is surprising that in this
context of obligations to particular groups and individuals, no mention is made of the patron–client relationship—perhaps an indication
that Cicero is following his Greek source at this point.

§§ 61–92: Greatness of soul and the obligations which stem from it

Following Panaetius, Cicero replaces the third traditional cardinal virtue,
courage, with the broader concept of *megalopsuchia* or *magnitudo animi*.

61 *You young men . . . that maid a man's*: the source is unknown. One speculative suggestion is that it comes from the *Meleager* of Accius, in
which case the maid would be Atalanta; others would ascribe the line
to a *fabula togata* which celebrates the heroine Cloelia (on whom,
cf. Livy 2. 13. 6 ff.).

O son of Salmacis . . . sweat or blood: this is a citation from the lost play
Aiax of Ennius. With Testard, I take Salmacida as vocative rather than
as an adjective with *spolia*, but both are possible.

the battles at Marathon, Salamis, Plataea, Thermopylae, and Leuctra:
the engagements of the Greeks against the Persians at Marathon
(490 BC), Salamis (the sea-battle of 480 BC), Plataea (479 BC), and
Thermopylae (480 BC), were frequently cited by orators and by
students in the schools of rhetoric as examples of victories for Greek
liberty against the might of Persia. The battle of Leuctra (371 BC), in
which Thebes prevailed over Sparta, provided testimony of the
decline of the greatest military power in Greece.

Horatius Cocles, the Decii, Gnaeus and Publius Scipio, Marcus Marcellus:
the epic legend of Horatius Cocles' defence of the wooden bridge to
save Rome, and his subsequent swim across the Tiber when the
bridge was cut down (508 BC) is described sceptically by Livy 2. 10
(cf. Polybius 6. 55. 1 ff.). The Decii, father (340 BC), son (295 BC), and
grandson (279 BC), are all said to have devoted their lives to gain the
gods' favour and victory in war (Livy 8. 9. 6, 10. 28. 12; Cicero,
Tusc. 1. 89); the claims of the grandson are dubious. The two Scipios,
father and uncle of the great Africanus, were killed in Spain in 211 BC
(Livy 25. 32 ff.). Claudius Marcellus, the hard man of the Second Punic

War, was celebrated as the avenger of Cannae by worsting Hannibal in the open field, and by his capture of Syracuse (Livy 23. 16. 16, 25. 23 ff.).

62 *'the virtue which champions the right'*: this definition attributed to the Stoics is not attested elsewhere. Cicero clearly has in mind the example of Julius Caesar when he qualifies the force of this virtue by insisting that it be consonant with justice, which means with the rights of the community.

63 *Plato puts it very well*: the quotation is a combination of passages from *Menexenus* 246c and *Laches* 197b.

64 *We read in Plato*: see *Laches* 182e. This treatise of Plato is devoted to consideration of the virtue of courage. Socrates rejects the purely military concept of refusal to run away from battle in favour of 'wise endurance of the soul' based on knowledge of good and evil.

   to wield sole power: though Julius Caesar is the obvious target here, the additional comments which follow bring to mind other first-century personalities, including Catiline and Pompey, who according to Caesar (*Bell. Civ.* 1. 4. 4) could not bear an equal.

65 *fame as reward for what he has achieved*: earlier in 44 BC Cicero had composed a treatise on fame (*De gloria*) which is unfortunately lost. But the gist of the content can be gathered from the discussion in this treatise at 2. 31 ff.

66 *disregard for external circumstances . . . should not lie down before . . . emotional disturbance or twist of fortune*: Cicero summarizes the fundamental tenets of Stoic ethics. Virtue is the only good (in Stoic thought, the possession of any virtue means possession of all). Though Stoics make a distinction among externals between 'things preferred' and 'things not preferred', all are indifferent. The emotions are to be excised, and reason is to be our sole guide in the attainment of virtue. The caprices of Fortune are to be despised. For the texts, see Long–Sedley, i. 354 ff., 377 ff., 410 ff.

68 *by greed, by base pleasure . . . greed for glory*: these exemplify the emotional disturbance condemned in the two previous sections.

69 *desire and fear, anguish and excessive pleasure and anger*: the four chief emotions condemned by older Stoicism are supplemented here by *iracundia*, proneness to anger, earlier regarded as a subdivision of desire. Later Stoicism as represented by Posidonius and Panaetius advance it to the status of a fifth vicious emotion, and Seneca devotes a treatise (*De ira*) to it.

69 *renounced affairs of state . . . had recourse to a life of leisure*: in earlier
    Stoic thought, kings, men active in the state, and those who devote
    themselves to knowledge all live lives that are 'preferred' (see 1. 19n.).
    Apart from the casual reference to kings in the next section, Cicero
    concentrates on the other two. Though here and later he is respectful
    to the contemplative life, he makes it clear especially at 1. 153ff. that
    the active life of politics is more important in his eyes.

    philosophers of the greatest fame . . . austere and serious men: many Greek
    philosophers from Plato and Aristotle onwards took no part in public
    life; Seneca, *De tranquillitate animi* 1. 10, lists the Stoics Zeno, Clean-
    thes, and Chrysippus among them. Among Cicero's contemporaries
    Lucilius Balbus, the Stoic spokesman in *The Nature of the Gods*, and
    Atticus, Cicero's friend and confidant (see Nepos, *Atticus* 6. 1–2) simi-
    larly avoided public life. Atticus was an adherent of the Epicurean
    school, which advocated a life of retirement which offered freedom
    from anxiety; see Lucretius 2. 1ff.

71 *men hindered by ill-health*: so Publius, son of the great Scipio Africanus
    and the adoptive father of Scipio Aemilianus, was a sickly scholar and
    could not try to emulate his father. Cicero may also have had his father
    in mind; at *Leg.* 3 he remarks that his father 'was in poor health', and
    so 'spent most of his time . . . among his books'.

74 *a belief which must be toned down*: the Greek examples that follow make
    it likely that Panaetius had played down the superiority of military
    achievement. But clearly Cicero found this standpoint congenial in
    view of his own career.

75 *Themistocles . . . Solon*: to regard the Athenian Themistocles merely as
    the victor at Salamis (480 BC) is to undercut his achievement. He trans-
    formed Athens into the strongest naval power in Greece from the time
    he became archon in 493/2. Admittedly Salamis was his greatest
    moment, but his later fortification of Athens and the Piraeus, and his
    defiance of the hegemony of Sparta, were equally significant. Solon
    was chief archon in 594/3 BC; his social and constitutional reforms are
    to be dated somewhat later. It would be more precise to say that he
    broadened rather than founded the Council of the Areopagus by
    including all ex-archons, thereby making the body more democratic.
    He set down its powers in writing.

76 *Pausanias and Lysander . . . Lycurgus' laws and system of training*: the
    Spartan Pausanias is cited here primarily as victor over the Persians at
    Plataea in 479 BC, a victory which gained Sparta still higher prestige
    among the Greeks. Lysander's fame arises from his naval victories

over Athens in the Peloponnesian War, especially at Aegospotami
(405 BC), and from the geographical expansion of Spartan influence
that followed. Some authors date the laws of Lycurgus to the ninth or
eighth century BC (so Herodotus 1. 65. 4; Thucydides 1. 18. 1;
Plutarch, *Lycurgus* 1), others from the late sixth century. See D. M.
MacDowell, *Spartan Law* (Edinburgh 1986), ch. 1.

76 *Scaurus . . . Marius . . . Catulus . . . Pompeius*: Scaurus, a senior consular
(consul 115 BC) became *princeps senatus* and later (109 BC) censor; he
was 'the last great *princeps senatus*, exercising that power through
factio and *auctoritas*' (so E. Badian in *OCD*). Gaius Marius by the 90s
(the period of Cicero's boyhood) had made his name as a soldier in
Spain, against Jugurtha in Africa, and above all on the Italian northern
frontier against the Teutones and Cimbri in 102–1; later, in 90, he
commanded on the northern front in the Social War. Quintus
Lutatius Catulus, consul in 78, was a leading senatorial in the 70s and
60s, becoming censor in 65; Pompey in the meantime had gained
military eminence against Sertorius in Spain (76–3), against the
pirates (67), and against Mithridates in 66.

Africanus . . . Publius Nasica . . . assassinated Tiberius Gracchus:
the Africanus mentioned here is Scipio Aemilianus, additionally
called Africanus because he had been adopted into the family of the
great Africanus' son. After fighting with distinction in the Third
Punic War, he captured and destroyed Numantia in Spain in 133. In
that same year Cornelius Scipio Nasica Serapio (consul 138) opposed
the re-election as tribune of the reformer Tiberius Gracchus; when
the consul Scaevola failed to disqualify Tiberius, Nasica led an attack
on the tribune and killed him.

77 *Let arms . . . to men's praise*: this is a line from Cicero's autobiograph-
ical poem *De consulatu*, composed in 60 BC. It became an object of derision to Calpurnius Piso (consul 67) and Mark Antony among others;
see Cicero, *In Pisonem* 74; *Philippic* 2. 20. 1; G. B. Townend, 'The
Poems' in *Cicero* (ed. T. A. Dorey, London 1964), ch. 5. As the
following sentences indicate, Cicero's suppression of the Catilinarian
conspiracy was the major theme of the poem.

78 *Gnaeus Pompeius . . . paid me this tribute*: Cicero was so gratified by this
testimonial from Pompey that he reported it not only privately to
Atticus (*Att.* 2. 1. 6) but also publicly in his *Second Philippic* (2. 12).
A comment in an earlier speech (*Cat.* 4. 21) is on the same lines.

his third triumph: Pompey had actually celebrated three triumphs earlier—in 81 (for operations in Sicily), in 79 (recovery of Africa to the

Sullan cause), and in 71 (defeat of Sertorius in Spain). Thus his triumph over the pirates and Mithridates in 61 was his fourth, but perhaps the first two were regarded by Cicero or by Pompey himself as virtually one.

79 *the Third Punic War, begun at the behest of Marcus Cato*: in 150 the Carthaginians finally lost patience with the depredations of Masinissa, and by counter-attacking afforded the hawks at Rome, led by Cato, the excuse to demand a declaration of war in 149. Cato died in that year, but his ruthless policy was continued after his death when Scipio Aemilianus destroyed the city of Carthage in 146.

80 *with the intention of establishing peace*: see 1. 35.

82 [*So far as the destruction . . . cruel behaviour.*] This sentence is deleted from the text by Winterbottom and others since it intrudes upon the more general level of philosophic discussion before and after it. Perhaps the gloss was prompted by the phrase 'to punish the guilty, to spare the great majority' which follows.

84 *Callicratidas*: this Spartan admiral defeated the Athenian fleet under Conon at Mytilene in 406, but in a further engagement off the Arginusae Islands in the same year, his force was defeated and he himself fell overboard and was drowned.

a modest reverse: Sparta subsequently restored its lost fleet, and Lysander's subsequent victory at Aegospotami in 405 was followed by Athens' capitulation to Sparta in 404.

Cleombrotus . . . Epaminondas: the reference is to the battle of Leuctra (1. 61 n.), in which Cleombrotus of Sparta was worsted by the great Theban leader Epaminondas.

Quintus Maximus, of whom Ennius writes: Quintus Fabius Maximus Verrucosus, elected dictator for the second time after the disaster at Lake Trasimene (217), pursued a policy of dogging Hannibal's footsteps to deny him supplies whilst refusing to engage in open battle. The title Cunctator ('Delayer'), initially abusive (hence the 'common talk' in the second line of the citation), became a badge of honour. The poet Ennius (239–169), whose poem the *Annales* described the history of Rome from the fall of Troy to his own day, celebrates the manner of his achievement in the extract (frr. 360–2 Warmington).

85 *the two precepts which Plato lays down*: in moving on the discussion from obligations in warfare to those in civil government, Cicero (doubtless following Panaetius) aptly supports the arguments with

citations from Plato's discussions of the ideal state (*Rep.* 342e) and ideal laws (*Leg.* 715b).

85 *'men of the people'* . . . *'the best citizens'*: these terms, *populares* and *studiosi optimi cuiusque* (= *optimates*) do not describe political parties in the modern sense. The *optimates* were men who defended the authority of the senate, jealously preserving its political control and the economic interests of its members. The term *populares* was applied to those individuals who claimed to stand for the sovereignty and interests of the people, and who strove to overturn the dominance of the closed circle in the senate. The Great Civil War of 49 BC found Pompey, as leader of the *optimates*, confronting Julius Caesar, the latest in the series of *populares* who sought to overthrow the entrenched senatorials.

86 *The Athenians experienced great dissensions . . . baneful civil wars*: following the Athenian capitulation to Sparta in April 404, the oligarchs at Athens invited the Spartan Lysander to intervene in their interests. As a result, the Thirty Tyrants seized control and initiated a reign of terror, with executions and confiscations rampant. Democracy was restored in later 403. At Rome, there had been intermittent disorders throughout Cicero's life; he thinks especially of the struggle between Sulla and Marius in the 80s, and of the Great Civil War of 49–45 from which Caesar emerged as master of the Roman world.

87 *Plato . . . provides a splendid commentary . . . He further recommends*: at *Rep.* 488a–b, Plato presents the analogy of sailors without experience vying with each other to seize the helm. There is no close parallel to what 'he further recommends' in the extant dialogues, but compare his *Leg.* 856b.

    the disagreement between Publius Africanus and Quintus Metellus: the Africanus mentioned here is Scipio Aemilianus (1. 76 n.); Quintus Metellus was a senior consular (consul 143, censor 131). When in 133 Tiberius Gracchus as tribune put through a bill distributing public land among the poorer citizens, and a commission proceeded to carry it out, Aemilianus opposed the measure, while Metellus supported it. Cicero reports the disagreement as conducted on amicable terms at *De amicitia* 77; at *Rep.* 1. 31, however, it is described as a bitter feud. See Powell's n. in the Oxford World's Classics edn. of *The Republic, The Laws* (Oxford 1998), 180 f.; A. Lintott in *CAH* 9^2 (Cambridge 1994), 74.

88 *what some call 'a high level of tolerance'*: the Latin *altitudo animi*

translates Aristotle's *megalopsuchia*; for the sense of political moderation, cf. Livy 4. 6. 12.

88 *all punishment*: I translate the alternative reading *punit* rather than *punitur* (in Winterbottom), which I cannot understand.

89 *which the Peripatetics uphold*: Aristotle's celebrated account of the moral virtues as the mean between opposing vices (for example, the virtue of courage between the vices of cowardice and rashness) is at *Nic. Eth.* 1107a–1108b, 1115b–1128b; see Ross, *Aristotle*, 202 ff. The criticism of the Peripatetic view that follows underlines the Stoic belief that anger is a vicious emotion, whereas the Peripatetics argue that it is nature's useful gift; see Cicero, *Tusc.* 4. 43.

90 *Socrates and Gaius Laelius did this*: Socrates' imperturbability was the focus of anecdotes, e. g., the alleged comment of his wife Xanthippe recorded at Cicero, *Tusc.* 3. 31, and Seneca's account (*Ep.* 104. 28) of how he bore his condemnation and death ('they did not change even the expression on his face'). Laelius' reputation as the Stoic sage who bore reverses impassively is underlined by the account of his attitude to his friend Scipio Aemilianus' death recorded by Cicero, *De amicitia* 7 ff.

Philip . . . the more affable and considerate of the two: this contrast in temperaments between Philip II (king of Macedon 359–336 BC), whose affability is attested by Aeschines and Demosthenes amongst others, and his hot-tempered son Alexander the Great was emphasized by Pompeius Trogus in his *Historiae Philippicae*, as Justin's *Epitome* 9. 8 reveals.

Africanus . . . fond of making this comparison: for Panaetius' friendship with Scipio Aemilianus, see Introd., p. xxviii. Though the comparison with the frisky horse is well-worn (cf. Livy 39. 25. 13, with reference to Philip V of Macedon), Aemilianus ingeniously extends it.

92 *On the earlier question*: I follow Miller in his Loeb edition in translating *illud* in this way. In concluding this section on Greatness of Soul (§§ 61–92) Cicero reverts to the topic raised in §§ 70–2, the relative merits of the active and contemplative life, from which he diverged to discuss first military achievement and then civic activity.

The man who observes these injunctions: perhaps a flattering reference to Cicero's friend Atticus (cf. 1. 69 n.).

§§ 93–151: The concept of the fitting, and the virtues associated with it

The fourth of the traditional cardinal virtues, temperance, is subsumed into the broader notion of the fitting in this discussion, the framework of which is laid down by Panaetius. It may be objected that 'the fitting' sits oddly in the catalogue of virtues, being an aesthetic rather than a moral concept, but it is an appropriate criterion of correct behaviour.

94 *inseparable from the honourable*: Cicero is aware of the anomaly which has arisen from Panaetius' presentation of the fitting (*prepon*) as the fourth virtue following knowledge/prudence, justice, magnanimity/ courage, and in what follows he assigns to it a more general status associated with all the cardinal virtues, which in Stoic thought merge into the concept of the honourable.

96 *as present in the honourable as a whole*: 'the fitting' is the manifestation of the honourable in action. In the definition of this first sense of the concept, man's 'excellence' refers to his possession of reason which the lower animals do not have; this faculty allows men to discern what is seemly in every circumstance.

relevant to each subdivision of the honourable: though Cicero proceeds to discuss its relevance only to the fourth subdivision, there is no need to emend the text. 'The deportment of a free spirit' covers the rest.

97 *which the poets pursue . . . in a context different from this*: Horace, at *Ars Poetica* 92, echoing traditional Greek theory, offers 'a universal declaration' of the fitting in tragedy and comedy (so Rudd in his edition of Horace, *Epistles II and Ars Poetica* (Cambridge 1989), 65). See also Cicero, *Orator* 70 ff.

if Aeacus or Minos were to say . . . But when Atreus utters the lines: Aeacus, renowned for his piety, and king Minos of Crete both became judges in Hades after death, symbolizing their concern for justice. Atreus, 'that notorious figure who prepared a feast of death for his brother' (Cicero, *N.D.* 3. 68) by serving up to Thyestes his children in a dish, was the central character of the tragedy *Atreus* by Accius. The first citation here, 'oderint dum metuant', was said to be a favourite saying of the emperor Caligula (Suetonius, *Cal.* 30. 1). In the second quotation, 'the father' is Thyestes, who unwittingly buried his children in his stomach. The texts are at frr, 168, 190 Warmington.

101 *the reason commands, and the appetite obeys*: in the Stoic psychology as delineated by Chrysippus and by Cicero's source Panaetius, the soul's

authoritative part (*to hegemonikon*) embodies the powers of reason and appetite. Panaetius diverges from earlier Stoicism in regarding the appetite as an irrational element, perhaps being influenced by Plato's myth in the *Phaedrus* (246b) in which the soul is envisaged as a charioteer endeavouring to control two horses, one good and one wayward.

102 *anger, ... lust or fear ... excessive pleasure*: Panaetius/Cicero here visualizes appetite, when it defects from the control of reason, as lapsing into the irrational emotions which the Stoics condemn (see 1. 69 n.).

103 *Nature has not fashioned us ... for fun and games*: this curious sequence of thought from the bipartite nature of the soul into 'fun and games' goes back through Panaetius to Aristotle's *Politics* (1333a): 'The soul of man is divided into two parts, one of which has reason itself, and the other ... able to obey reason ... The whole of life is further divided into two parts, business and leisure' (tr. Jowett). Cicero's fondness for urbane humour leads him to discuss witticisms rather than leisure in general until the close of § 104.

104 *The first is ill-bred ... the second is refined*: one is initially taken aback to find Plautus as well as Aristophanes placed in the second category, but Cicero is doubtless contrasting them with the crudities of Fescennine performances and mimic shows. On 'the books of Socratic philosophy', see *Brutus* 292, where Atticus says: 'I regard as witty and elegant the irony ascribed to Socrates which he employs in the books of Plato, Xenophon, and Aeschines.'

by old Cato ... under the title of Apophthegms: at *De oratore* 2. 271 ff., Cicero states that old Cato (234–149 BC) recorded many *bons mots*, and cites some examples of them.

Activities ... of sportive recreation: after diverging to discuss witticisms, Cicero returns to the theme of leisure activities in general. The campus Martius to the north-east of the city was the regular exercise-ground where ball-games, wrestling, riding were often followed by a dip in the Tiber. See J. P. V. D. Balsdon, *Life and Leisure in Ancient Rome* (London 1969), 160.

108 *Lucius Crassus ... Lucius Philippus ... Gaius Caesar, Lucius' son*: Lucius Licinius Crassus (140–91 BC), a leading statesman in Cicero's boyhood (consul 95, censor 92), became Cicero's model as an orator; he is the chief spokesman in the *De oratore*, and his combination of high seriousness and urbane wit is praised in the *Brutus* (143). Lucius Marcius Philippus (consul 91 BC) is likewise praised in the *Brutus* (173) for his sharp wit, examples of which appear at *De oratore* 2. 245, 249. Gaius

Iulius Caesar Strabo Vopiscus (curule aedile 90 BC) is praised for his urbane wit at *Brutus* 177, and is the spokesman on humour at *De ora-tore* 2. 217–89.

108 *Marcus Scaurus and the young Marcus Drusus*: Cicero characterizes Marcus Aemilius Scaurus (consul 115 BC) as a wise and highly serious man (*Brutus* 111; cf. *Pro Fonteio* 24), but Sallust takes a more cynical view (*Jug.* 15), doubtless reflecting his different political perspective. Marcus Livius Drusus (consul 112 BC and father of the tribune of 91 BC) shared the censorship with Scaurus in 109. His serious demeanour as an orator is noted in the *Brutus* 109.

Gaius Laelius . . . Scipio . . . more austere: Gaius Laelius (consul 140 BC and intimate friend of Scipio Aemilianus) enjoyed a high reputation as a virtuous sage; as spokesman in the *De amicitia* and *De republica* he emerges as a man of genial temper. His friend Scipio Aemilianus is here described as having had a *uita tristior*. If *tristior* is taken as mean-ing 'more melancholy', the phrase conflicts with the description of his 'most affable ways' at *De amicitia* 11. Some scholars interpret the phrase *uita tristior* as a reference to his early and mysterious death in 129 BC, but the Latin can scarcely bear that sense; moreover, a contrast is being apparently made with Laelius' genial bearing. It seems best to take *tristior* as 'more solemn', 'more austere' (so *OLD, tristis* 4).

Socrates . . . Pythagoras and Pericles . . . without recourse to gaiety: for Socrates, see 1. 104n. Such anecdotal comment about Pythagoras, deriving from his role as founder of a quasi-religious community, and attributable to late source-material, is apocryphal. For Pericles' high seriousness in oratory and bearing, see Plutarch, *Pericles* 5.

Hannibal . . . Quintus Maximus: such characteristics of Hannibal are admiringly detailed by Cornelius Nepos, *Hannibal* 5. 2 ff; compare Livy's famous sketch at 21. 4. 3ff. Quintus Fabius Maximus gained his reputation for craftiness by dogging Hannibal's footsteps (see 1. 84n.) and notably by his stratagem in recapturing Tarentum, as a result of which Hannibal is said to have exclaimed: 'The Romans too have their Hannibal!' (Livy 27. 16. 10).

Themistocles and Jason of Pherae . . . that trick of Solon: on Themisto-cles, see 1. 75n. He was famous for the ruses by which he lured Xerxes into the sea-battle at Salamis (Herodotus 8. 75; Plutarch, *Them.* 12), and protracted negotiations with Sparta until the protective walls of Athens were built (Thucydides 1. 90; Plutarch, *Them.* 19). Jason, tyrant of Pherae (*c.*385–70 BC), used guile to win over Pharsalus and thus to become the chief magistrate of Thessaly. After Leuctra (1. 61n.), he persuaded the Thebans to make peace with Sparta, and thus furthered his own ambitions in the ensuing balance of power, but was assassinated in the following year (Xenophon, *Hellenica* 6. 1ff.). On the ruse of Solon (on whom, 1. 75n.), see Plutarch, *Solon* 1. 8: when Salamis was ceded to Megara, and a law was passed at Athens forbidding any claim to the island, Solon feigned madness, declaimed his poem *Salamis* in the agora, and proceeded to capture the island.

109 *as we saw with Sulla and Marcus Crassus*: for Sulla's career, see *OCD*. According to Plutarch's biography, the future dictator gained the praetorship by a combination of solicitation and bribery (ch. 5). 'He courted those whose help he wanted . . . one could not tell whether he was by nature more haughty or more subservient' (ch. 6). He offered extravagant gifts to his own troops in order to win over those of rival commanders (ch. 12). For Crassus, see 1. 25n.

Lysander . . . Callicratidas: on Lysander, see 1. 76n. For his complaisant ways, see Plutarch, *Lysander* 2, where it is claimed that he 'paid court to the great, and readily endured the insolence of the powerful'. For Callicratidas' *amour propre* and independence, see 1. 84.

the Catuli . . . Quintus Mucius [Mancia]: the elder Quintus Lutatius Catulus (consul 102) and his son (consul 78) are both praised for their elegant Latin, though not regarded as outstanding orators, at *Brutus* 132–3. The Quintus Mucius mentioned here is probably Quintus Mucius Scaevola (consul 117 BC), for he is described as an 'old jester' at *Att.* 4. 16. 3. Mancia is to be excluded from the text as a gloss, perhaps inserted by a scribe who had read mention of him as a wit at *De oratore* 2. 274.

Publius Scipio Nasica, whereas his father . . . was never genial in conversation: On the father's murder of Tiberius Gracchus, see 1. 76n.; for his imperious and sharp manner of address, *Brutus* 107. For the son (consul 111 BC), see *Brutus* 128: 'He was equal to each and all in Latin speaking, and superior to all in spice and wit.'

110 *in the face of Minerva*: Minerva as the goddess of learning and intelligence is invoked in the phrase *inuita Minerua* to express the notion of 'against one's natural intelligence'.

111 *inserting Greek words, as some do*: Cicero at *Fin.* 1. 8ff., in claiming that Latin has a richer vocabulary than Greek, cites satirical lines by Lucilius condemning T. Albucius for his fondness for using Greek.

112 *Marcus Cato's situation*: Marcus Cato Vticensis (95–46 BC) supported Pompey in the Great Civil War; after Pompey's defeat at Pharsalus in

48, he joined the Pompeians in Africa, where after the defeat at Thapsus in 46 he committed suicide rather than accept pardon from the victorious Caesar. As a committed Stoic, he regarded suicide as a duty in such special circumstances; see M. Griffin in *GR* 33 (1986), 72ff., 194ff.

113 *the many hardships which Ulysses endured*: for the courtesies shown to Circe and Calypso (Cicero politely refrains from calling them witches), see Homer, *Odyssey* 10. 480ff., 5. 203ff.; for his patience with underlings on his return to Ithaca in the face of insults, 18. 10ff., 327ff.; 19. 66ff.

Ajax with that fabled temper of his: the contrast between the demeanour of Ulysses and Ajax, stemming from their claims to the arms of Achilles, was already a commonplace in Roman drama by Cicero's time. The *Ajax* of Sophocles, on which Roman tragedies were based, depicts the hero as insane with rage and disappointment, until he kills himself.

114 Epigoni *and* Medus . . . Melanippa *and* Clytaemestra; *Rupilius . . . in* Antiope . . . *Aesopus not often in* Ajax: of the two actors mentioned here, Rupilius is not elsewhere attested; Cicero waxes sarcastic about a stage-appearance of Aesopus which he witnessed in September 55 (*Fam.* 7. 1. 2). The plays cited are all Roman tragedies now lost; the *Epigoni* by Accius, *Medus* by Pacuvius, *Melanippa* by Ennius, *Clytae-mestra* by Accius, *Antiope* by Pacuvius, and *Ajax* by Ennius. For the plots and extant fragments of these plays, see Warmington, *Remains of Old Latin*, i–ii, 2nd edn. (London 1956).

115 *the twin roles which I mentioned earlier*: see 1. 107 for our roles as rational men, and secondly as individuals of the human species.

116 *Quintus Mucius, son of Publius, in civil law, and Africanus, son of Aemil-ius Paulus, in soldiering*: Publius Mucius Scaevola (consul 133 BC), a senior supporter of Tiberius Gracchus, was the preeminent jurist of his day, but his son Quintus (consul 95) outshone his father, publish-ing the first systematic treatise on civil law. Lucius Aemilius Paulus Macedonicus (consul 182, 168) gained his early military experience in Spain and Liguria, and achieved his greatest fame by his victory over Perseus at Pydna in the Third Macedonian War. For the military achievements of his second son Scipio Aemilianus, adopted by Publius Scipio son of the great Africanus (hence his title Africanus fre-quently in this treatise), see 1. 76n.; for his eloquence, see Cicero, *Brutus* 77, 82. For his career in general, see A. E. Astin, *Scipio Aemil-ianus* (Oxford 1967).

116 *Timotheus, the son of Conon*: Conon (*c*.444–392 BC) achieved eminence as Athenian admiral in the Peloponnesian War, and subsequently enlisted support from Persia to achieve further success against Sparta at Cnidos (394 BC). His son Timotheus emulated his father's distinction in naval operations against Sparta in 376/5, and in extending the second Athenian empire in the Chalcidice in 364–362. A pupil and later a friend of Isocrates, he is saluted as a man of great learning by Cicero at *De oratore* 3. 139.

118 *According to Xenophon*: Prodicus, to whom this celebrated myth of the choice of Hercules is attributed, was a sophist contemporary with Socrates. Cicero has recorded the story in terms virtually identical with those of Xenophon, *Memorabilia* 2. 1. 21. The description of Hercules as 'sprung from the seed of Jupiter' suggests by its poetic language that it is a citation from a lost tragedy (so Winterbottom).

120 *nature plays the greatest part, closely followed by fortune*: this section, on the roles played by nature and by fortune in shaping our manner of life, is strongly influenced by the atomist philosopher Democritus (see the texts in Dyck); he argues that nature is the firmer, and fortune less reliable. In one fragment which we possess, fortune grapples not with nature, as here, but with wisdom.

121 *the elder Africanus' son . . . in the way that his father could do*: on the sickly Publius Scipio, see 1. 71n. Scipio Africanus Major, the hero of the Second Punic War, was the son of Publius Cornelius Scipio (consul 218), who fought against Hannibal in northern Italy at Ticinus and the Trebia (218), and against the Carthaginians in Spain in 217–211.

123 *men in old age . . . surrendering to tiredness and idleness*: the first part of this paragraph is a distillation of one of the four themes of Cicero's *De senectute*, that old age offers abundant scope for intellectual activity. The spokeman in the dialogue, old Cato, represents Cicero's ideal in this respect, and he parades the names of other aged Greeks and Romans to convince his addressee Atticus and himself that old age can be a fruitful period of life.

124 *the obligations of magistrates*: it appears from Cicero's reference to Panaetius at *Leg.* 14 that the Greek discussed this question in considerable detail.

'*a good citizen*': See 1. 20n.

125 *Foreigners and resident aliens*: Plato in *The Laws* has an extended discussion (952d ff.) on the reception of foreign visitors. Cicero has

presumably abbreviated Panaetius' account drawing on Plato, to exclude issues irrelevant to Roman practice.

126 *Nature at the outset*: this section on 'the fitting' as it concerns the human body is a riposte to the doctrine of the Cynics, as the reference to them at § 128 suggests. Diogenes (*c.*400–*c.*325 BC), founder of the Cynic school, argued that we should satisfy our basic needs in a 'natural' and shameless way; the school derived its name of Cynics ('dog-like') from this attitude. Panaetius/Cicero presents arguments against such liberated behaviour claiming to be natural.

127 *keep out of sight the parts which nature has hidden*: at *N.D.* 2. 141, the Stoic Balbus argues that just as architects keep the drains of a house away from our eyes and ears, so nature keeps the equivalent features in our bodies away from the organs of sense (somewhat similarly, Xenophon *Memorabilia* 1. 4. 6 earlier).

128 *such Stoics as were virtually Cynics*: early Stoicism, and notably its founder Zeno, adopted with much else the frankness of the Cynics in speaking of sexual and other social matters; see Diogenes Laertes 7. 4, and Cicero, *Fam.* 9. 22. 5, citing Zeno: 'The wise man will call a spade a spade.' Cicero himself rejects this attitude in this letter and at *De oratore* 2. 242.

the effort of begetting children is honourable, but a filthy expression: Cicero avoids the verb *futuo* for sexual intercourse with a woman; such explicit expressions are found mainly in epigrams and graffiti; see J. N. Adams, *The Latin Sexual Vocabulary* (London 1982), 118 ff.

129 *unmanly conduct on the one hand, and boorish and uncouth behaviour on the other*: Cicero argues for the Aristotelian mean between extremes.

sons . . . do not bathe with their fathers, nor sons-in-law with their fathers-in-law: the first part of this observation is echoed at *De oratore* 2. 224. Plutarch, *Cato Maior* 20. 8, also mentions this Roman fastidiousness, adding (rather inconsequentially) that Romans later learned from Greeks to bathe naked, and taught the Greeks to do so even before women.

130 *any adornment unworthy of a man*: compare Ovid, *Heroides* 4. 75–6: 'Young men decked out like ladies, come not near;/A manly form prefers but modest care.' See also *Ars amatoria* 1. 505 ff.

131 *not to saunter along too mincingly . . . nor again to hurry along at break-neck speed*: the Romans were obsessive about such effeminate walking habits: see Cicero, *Fin.* 5. 35; Sallust, *Catiline* 15. 5. Horace, *Satires* 1. 3. 9 ff., urging us to be indulgent to others' faults, instances the man

'running as if fleeing from the foe, often moving like one bearing Juno's sacred offerings'. The reference to 'tray-bearers' can hardly mean the *canephoroi* bearing baskets on their heads, for they were women. In such processions as described by Apuleius, *Metamorphoses* 11. 8ff., the priests carried utensils and other sacred objects.

132 *thought and impulse . . . subject our impulses to reason*: Cicero has already made this point at 1. 101.

   argumentation and in conversation: it seems probable that Cicero has here expanded a line of thought in Panaetius which contrasted the attention paid by rhetoricians to the rules for public discourse (as in Aristotle's *Rhetoric*) with the absence of such stylistic guidelines for philosophical dialogue (note the references to 'philosophical discussions' at § 132, and to 'Socratic dialogues' at § 134). For Cicero, conversation in the wider sense was a vital component of life in community; see his comments at *Fam.* 9. 24. 3. But rules for such informal converse are hardly feasible.

   students crowding round the rhetoricians: the censors for the year 92 BC issued an edict stating their disapproval of 'a new kind of teaching' by 'Latin rhetoricians', 'counter to the customs and traditions of our forebears' (Suetonius, *On Rhetoricians* 1). One of the censors was the Crassus who is the leading spokesman in the *De oratore*. He defends the edict there by claiming that these Latin rhetoricians, unlike the Greek, were incompetent. But the attempted suppression had little effect; see M. L. Clarke, *Rhetoric at Rome* (London 1953), ch. 2.

133 *the Catuli*: see 1. 109 and n.

   Lucius Crassus: see 1. 108 and n.

   Caesar, brother of the elder Catulus: see 1. 108 and n. He was the younger half-brother of Q. Lutatius Catulus. Their mother Popilia had married first the elder Quintus Lutatius Catulus, and subsequently Lucius Iulius Caesar.

134 *the disciples of Socrates are the supreme masters*: see 1. 104 and n.

135 *as long as those present consent to this*: I speculatively propose and translate *si adnuunt qui aderunt* for the corrupt *sed utcumque aderunt* which is obelized by Winterbottom.

136 *as physicians turn to cautery and the knife*: compare 1. 83, where Cicero similarly exploits the image of the physician's extreme measures, but in the different context of dangers to be faced.

136 *anger should be kept at bay*: see 1. 88 f., where the Stoic condemnation of anger is invoked under the different heading of greatness of soul.

137 *imitating 'the braggart soldier'*: Cicero clearly alludes to Pyrgopolyn-ices, the boastful soldier of Plautus' *Miles Gloriosus*.

138 *Gnaeus Octavius . . . Scaurus*: Octavius (consul 165 BC) achieved celebrity when as praetor of the Aegean fleet he received the surrender of Perseus of Macedon at Samothrace in 168 BC. After celebrating a triumph in the following year, he built the Porticus Octavia at Rome. As a member of the commission sent to destroy the Seleucid fleet and to hamstring the elephants, he incurred odium and was assassinated in a Syrian uprising in 162(?). Marcus Aemilius Scaurus, son of the con-sul of 115 who was eminent as *princeps senatus*, later became stepson of Sulla. He reached the praetorship in 56 BC and governed Sardinia in 55. Complaints of extortion were laid against him in 54, and Cicero (amongst others) defended him in the *Pro Scauro*, achieving his acquittal. But on standing for the consulship of 53, he was accused of bribery, convicted, and forced into exile.

139 *'A fine old house! How different is your owner!'*: the quotation from a lost tragedy has not been traced. Cicero cites it in part again at *Phil.* 2. 104 in condemning Mark Antony for occupying the house of Marcus Varro at Casilinum. The speech provides further evidences of appro-priations, including the house of Pompey (2. 64 ff.).

140 *the case of Lucius Lucullus*: Lucius Licinius Lucullus (consul 74) enjoyed a distinguished military career, first as Sulla's lieutenant in the Social and Civil Wars, and later as commander in the Third Mithridatic War (74–66), though these campaigns in the east ended ultimately in failure. He retired from active politics in 59 BC to live an Epicurean life in his splendid villas, which were a byword for luxury (Cicero, *Leg.* 3. 30; Plutarch, *Lucullus* 39, etc.).

142 *by which is understood maintenance of due order*: according to *LSJ*, *eutaxia* means (1) good arrangement (2) disciplined behaviour. Cicero translates with the word *modestia*, but warns us that this Latin word is not being used in the second sense of *eutaxia*, but in the first.

143 *The same definition . . . at the outset of the treatise*: Cicero's treatment of *prudentia* is not wholly clear or consistent. At 1. 15 he labels the first of the four virtues 'wisdom and prudence', without making a distinction between the two. At 1. 18 that first virtue is now called *ueri cognitio*, knowledge of the truth, which can embrace both wisdom and pru-dence. In the passage here, *prudentia* is equated with knowledge of the

opportunity for action. Only at 1. 153 is the useful distinction made
between wisdom (*sophia*) and prudence (*phronesis*), the latter being
practical awareness of what to seek and what to avoid.

144 *the response of Pericles*: this anecdote, also recorded by Valerius Maximus under 'Restraint and Self-control' (4. 3. Ext. 1) in all likelihood
goes back to the *Epidemiai* ('Visitations') of Ion of Chios, the tragic
poet. Ion entertained Sophocles (see Athenaeus 13. 603E) in 441–440
BC, at a time when Pericles was putting down the revolt of Samos. The
anecdote is to be ascribed to this period.

145 *singing in the forum*: at 3. 75, 3. 93 dancing in the forum is similarly
regarded as unseemly.

146 *when masters mimic them*: one wonders whether Cicero recalls his own experience when under instruction from Molon at Rhodes. See *Brutus* 316.

147 *not only what each of them says, but also their feelings*: when Cicero
makes this distinction between words and feelings elsewhere (1. 40
and 124), he is referring to our own responses where a difference may
be perceptible. Here, however, one wonders how other people indicate their feelings if not by what they say.

148 *Socrates and Aristippus . . . against the established custom of the city*: the
Aristippus indicated here must be the older of the two, since his grandson as a Cyrenaic will not have recommended himself to Cicero. The
grandfather, a rhetorician and close associate of Socrates, must have
been seen as sharing in Socrates' condemnation of Greek theology
deriving from Homer and Hesiod (Plato, *Rep.* 377d ff.). For the repercussions of this criticism and of Socrates' moral enquiries in general,
see W. K. C. Guthrie, *The Greeks and their Gods* (London 1950), ch. 12.

As for the Cynics: see 1. 126, 128, and nn.

150 *professions and gainful occupations*: there is dispute among scholars
whether this and the next paragraph reflect predominantly Greek attitudes (as transmitted from Panaetius) or Roman thinking. M. I. Fin-
ley, *The Ancient Economy* (London 1973), 50 ff. sees mainly Roman
ideas here but with the incorporation of some Greek influence; P. A.
Brunt, *PCPS* NS 19 (1973), 26 ff., inclines to the view that Panaetius'
depiction of Greek standards is strongly present here.

customs officials and money lenders: collection of customs-duties (*porto-
ria*) was leased to the *publicani* at Rome; their officials were unpopular if
they did their job conscientiously. See Plautus, *Menaechmi* 114 ff.,
where Menaechmus complains that he might as well have married a cus-

toms officer because his wife asks him to declare all his activities. Though moneylenders traditionally had a bad image (see the remark of old Cato at 2. 89 below, and again his comment at *De agricultura* 1, where he rates the moneylender as lower than the thief), respectable contemporaries of Cicero like Brutus, Atticus, Pompey, and Caesar lent money at interest. It was the low-class operator like Milo in Apuleius, *Metamorphoses* 1. 21, who was despised.

in Terence's words: see *Eunuch* 257.

151 *for those of the appropriate social class*: the reservation is significant. These occupations were not regarded as appropriate for sons of senators like Marcus.

winning possible praise: Cicero takes it for granted that his readers know that he is again referring to an occupation appropriate for equestrians rather than senatorials.

in my Cato Maior: in this work (known more familiarly as *De senectute*), old Cato speaks lyrically of the pleasures of agriculture in old age (51 ff.). Such joys in a slave-society are those of knowledgeable ownership and aesthetics rather than direct acquaintance with the spade and hoe.

152–160: Comparison of the virtues, and priority of obligations

152 *which Panaetius has omitted*: Cicero has already drawn attention to this lapse at 1. 10; he repeats the criticism at 1. 161.

153 *than do those which stem from knowledge*: Cicero here implicitly opposes the view of Aristotle, who at *Nic. Eth.* 1176a ff. argues that intellectual virtue and the life of contemplation rank before the moral virtues and the obligations that stem from them. Cicero lays greater stress on the importance of community, and the fact that man is 'by nature a creature of the city'. That is of course Aristotle's definition (*Politics* 1253a), and Cicero's implication that the life of contemplation isolates the thinker from the life of the community not only misrepresents Aristotle, but is qualified by Cicero himself in 1. 155–6.

he would die: since Cicero has granted the solitary philosopher 'abundant provision of everything', it is hard to see the justification of this statement. If on the other hand he were dependent on others for life's necessities, the statement would be justified.

Now chief of all the virtues . . . ranked higher than that from knowledge: some scholars (e.g. Griffin's note ad loc.) suggest that there is textual corruption, or alternatively a lack of logic, in this section. But Cicero is arguing that *sapientia* (wisdom) is not merely the first of the virtues in order of presentation; it actually embraces sense of community, the second virtue, whereas mere *cognitio* (knowledge) does not. Obligations deriving from the sense of community (in other words, justice) can therefore be regarded as deriving in the wider sense from *sapientia*.

155 *Lysis who taught Epaminondas . . . Plato who taught Dion of Syracuse*: Lysis of Tarentum was the elderly tutor of the youthful Theban, 'who was so devoted to him that he counted the gloomy and austere old man as preferable in friendship to all his contemporaries' (Cornelius Nepos, *Epaminondas* 2. 2; cf. Plutarch, *De genio Socratis* 579 C, 583 C). For Plato's influence over Dion, brother-in-law of Dionysius I of Syracuse, in the 380s, and his return to Syracuse after the death of the tyrant in 367 with the vain aspiration of making a philosopher-king out of Dionysius II, see *OCD*, svv. Dion, Plato.

my teachers and their learning: Cicero's interest in philosophy was fostered in his teens by acquaintance with the Epicurean Phaedrus, who thereafter became a close friend. He attended the lectures of the Stoic Diodotus, who became a resident in his house. Philo, the celebrated Academic who came as a refugee to Rome about 87 BC, was a conspicuous influence. In his two years abroad in 79–77 BC, Cicero struck up a close friendship with the Academic Antiochus in Athens, and forged close connections with the Stoic Posidonius in Rhodes.

157 *It is the same with humans*: in this long-standing argument whether men are gregarious by nature, or whether they form societies to satisfy human needs, Cicero here and again at *Rep.* 1. 39 ('not so much weakness as an innate desire . . . to form communities') upholds the position of the later Stoics. The most explicit statement of the opposite theory, that they united initially through human weakness, and that only subsequently the fondness for community developed, is at Polybius 6. 5. 4ff. This was one of the political issues which divided later Stoics and Epicureans; as Lucretius makes clear (5. 1011ff.), the Epicureans argued that communities are formed for mutual protection.

158 *the magician's wand, as the saying goes*: Cicero presumably thinks of such Greek examples as Circe's wand (Homer, *Odyssey* 10. 238, 319 etc.), for the phrase *uirgula diuina* is not found earlier, and Virgil's golden bough has no predecessor in extant Latin literature.

159 *Posidonius has listed many of these*: for Posidonius, and Cicero's marginal use of him as source especially in Book 3, see the Introd., p. xxix. He is cited again at 3. 8 and 10.

160 *The first duty is owed to the immortal gods . . . on a descending scale*: at
1. 58 above the order of priorities in obligations is to (1) our country
and parents, (2) our children and household, (3) congenial relatives.
The gods are excluded there because Cicero is concluding his discussion of levels of human fellowship, and the obligations thereby
entailed; here he widens his perspective. It is not wholly clear at 1. 58
whether obligations to parents are considered as great as those to one's
country, but in any case the intervening discussion on the importance
of obligations to the community at 1. 154, 157–8 may have led him to
distinguish between them, and to put country first.

161 *passed over by Panaetius*: see 1. 152n.

BOOK TWO

1–8; Introduction: The theme of the book (§ 1), followed by Cicero's defence of philosophical study (§§ 2–6) and of the Academics' approach to philosophy (§§ 7–8)

1 *As I have mentioned*: see 1. 10.

2 *mention of philosophy is abhorrent to some men of integrity*: Cicero's
apologia for philosophical study is directed at the 'good men' who
devote themselves to politics rather than to studies which they believe
undermine the state. He explains to them that service to the state has
always been his primary concern, but that the present political climate
makes it impossible for him to make a positive contribution. Though
philosophy is for him a *pis aller*, it is the best of choices if politics is
ruled out (§§ 1–6). He then responds to learned critics with knowledge
of the philosophical schools who are critical of his Academic viewpoint
(§§ 7–8). The arguments he presents have earlier been rehearsed in the
Academica, *De finibus*, and *De natura deorum*.

the dominion of a single man: for Cicero's retirement from politics
following the Roman revolution inaugurated by Julius Caesar, see
Introd., p. ix f.

the men of the highest calibre: Cicero refers especially to Pompey and the
Younger Cato, and to lesser figures like Marcellus (whom he defended
in the *Pro Marcello*, and who was murdered in May 45), and Publius
Servilius Vatia, censor in 55, who had recently died at an advanced age
(*Phil.* 2. 12).

2 *feelings of anguish*: these were prompted not only by political humiliation, but also by domestic crises, especially the death of his daughter
Tullia in childbirth in February 45.

3 *as I often did*: for the 70 speeches published by this date, see 1. 3n.

4 *a great deal of time in educating myself . . . time was spent entirely in
reading*: Cicero's youthful encounters with eminent Greek philosophers (the Epicurean Phaedrus, the Stoic Diodotus, the Academic
Philo), and his later friendships with the Stoics Antiochus and
Posidonius at Athens and Rhodes, led him to continue his philosophical studies throughout a busy political and forensic career; see
my Introduction to *The Nature of the Gods* (Oxford World's Classics,
Oxford 1998), pp. xii ff.

5 *As philosophers of old defined it*: Cicero summarizes the views of
Socrates, Plato and Aristotle; see, e.g., Xenophon, *Memorabilia* 4. 6. 7;
Diogenes Laertius 3. 6. 3; Aristotle, *Nic. Eth.* 1141a–b.

6 *this is the discipline*: it is notable that Cicero's apologia for philosophy
centres here on ethics, the dominant concern of Hellenistic and
Roman philosophers, and the central issue of this treatise.

in another book: this is the *Hortensius*, an exhortation to philosophy
now lost which Cicero wrote as introduction to the series of philosophical works composed in 46–44 BC. It has achieved immortality as
the book which implanted in Augustine a longing for 'the immortality
of wisdom', setting him on the path to Christian conversion
(*Confessions* 3. 7).

7 *objections are raised against me*: in the *Academica* (2. 7 ff., 2. 103 ff.) the
criticisms of the Academic school mounted by Lucullus and Antiochus are rebutted at length. A brief justification of Cicero's philosophical outlook appears at *N.D.* 1. 12.

minds adrift . . . never have a guiding star to follow: the criticism is
directed at the followers of Pyrrho of Elis, the founder of Greek scepticism (*c*. 365–*c*. 275 BC). Their doctrine that no positive knowledge was
possible was taken up by the Academics of the third and second centuries BC, but not to the point at which non-reliance on the evidence
of the senses paralysed any capacity for action. Cicero adopts the
stance of Carneades, whose doctrine of probability is expounded at
Acad. 2. 99, see Introd., xxxii.

The other schools say that some things are certain and others uncertain:
Cicero refers here primarily to the Peripatetics and Stoics, who argue

that all knowledge comes through the senses; these perceptions provide certainty in some things, but in others our sense-impressions are mistaken, so that we must suspend judgement in those cases. The Epicurean standpoint is rather different: for them sense-impressions are infallible, but faulty mental judgement may misinterpret them.

8 *in my book, the* Academica: Cicero followed publication of the *Hortensius*, which recommended philosophy as preeminently a subject for study, with this treatise devoted to epistemology. The first version (completed in April–May 45 and known as *Academica Priora*) was written in two books; the second (published in June 45 and called *Academica Posteriora*) was expanded into four. A single book from each has survived; in the modern text of two books, Book 1 is the first book of the *Posteriora*, and Book 2 is the second book of the *Priora*.

Cratippus as your spokesman: see 1. 1 n. Young Marcus had attached himself to the Peripatetic school at Athens.

akin to yours: such a claim is relevant only to the field of ethics, in which the reforming Academic Antiochus had drawn closer to the position of Peripatetics and Stoics; see the Introd., p. xxxii f.

§§ 9–10: The useful is inseparable from the honourable

9 *five approaches*: see 1. 9–10, where Cicero augments Panaetius' three topics (the honourable, the useful, and the potential conflict between them) with the further considerations of choice between differing honourable courses, and choice between differing useful ones.

10 *these three intermingled concepts*: Winterbottom obelizes *tria genera* in recognition of a long-standing dispute detailed in Dyck's commentary, the problem being that the previous discussion centres on only two concepts, the honourable and the useful. It is possible to argue, however, that the phrase *tria genera* points forward to the three concepts in the syllogism that follows—the just, the honourable, and the useful; Cicero is claiming that while philosophers assert the distinction between the three, they acknowledge their interrelationship. I therefore translate the MSS reading, rather than accept the emendation from *tria* to *duo*, with Dyck and other modern editors.

whatever is honourable is also useful: the syllogism, the tool of logic which the Stoics inherited and developed from the Peripatetics, suggests that Cicero draws on Panaetius here.

§§ 11–20: Elements useful or deleterious to human life

11 *the things which make for the maintenance of human life*: Cicero here
mounts the rungs of 'the ladder of nature', which Aristotle in the
De anima had tabulated in distinguishing differing levels of life and of
the soul, and which becomes a commonplace in Stoic thought.

and bees: there is a good case for excising (with some modern editors)
apes from the text here, not only because they intrude upon the four-
footed animals which precede (and incidentally ruin the tricolon), but
also because bees were widely thought to have 'divine intelligence' (so
Virgil, *Georgics* 4. 220; cf. Aristotle, *Generation of Animals* 3. 10). They
may have been inserted by a scribe because of what follows ('their
labour makes a contribution . . .').

mostly produced by men's labours: in what follows, Cicero reduplicates
many of the arguments of the Stoic Balbus at *N.D.* 2. 150 ff., where
such human skills, reflecting reason in man, are adduced as proof of
the providential ordering of the world.

13 '*iron, copper, gold and silver, hidden deep within*': the citation is from a
lost tragedy, perhaps the *Prometheus* of Accius, who may have incorporated echoes of Aeschylus, *Prometheus Vinctus* 500 ff.

how could they have been repaired . . . ?: reading *subueniri* (sc. *iis potuisset*)
for *subuenire* in Winterbottom.

men sharing life in community: at 1. 158, Cicero argues that human societies develop from a natural desire to congregate, rather than from the
need of men to seek each other's help; see 1. 157 n. The passage here
does not necessarily contradict that view, but emphasizes the benefits
that accrue from such life in community.

16 *Panaetius' verbose observations*: for Cicero's adaptation of Panaetius'
treatise, here by condensation, see Introd. p. xxvii f.

Themistocles . . . Alexander: see the entries in the Glossary. The choice
of these leaders suggests that Panaetius remarked on the influence
of teachers and philosophers on great men; e.g., the influence of
Mnesiphalus on Themistocles (Plutarch, *Them.* 2), of Anaxagoras on
Pericles (Plutarch, *Per.* 4 ff.), of Xenophon on Agesilaus (Xenophon,
Agesilaus), of Aristotle on Alexander (Plutarch, *Alex.* 7). It is not clear
whether the Cyrus cited here is the founder of the Achaemenid empire
(559–529), whose education was romanticized in Xenophon's
Cyropaedia, or the younger Cyrus, whom Xenophon accompanied on

the expedition against Artaxerxes II. The chronological order of the *exempla* favours the second.

Dicaearchus, that great and prolific Peripatetic: Cicero was a great admirer of this pupil of Aristotle ('Dicaearchus, my favourite', *Tusc.* 1. 77). He wrote extensively on philosophy (as here), history, geography, and literary matters; see the entry in *OCD*. The observation here about the greater ravages to human life caused by men echoes Aristotle, *Pol.* 1253a; cf. Seneca, *Ep.* 103. 1.

18 *centres . . . on three things*: at 1. 18ff., Cicero divided the honourable (which is identifiable with virtue) into the four subdivisions of wisdom, justice, greatness of soul, and 'the fitting'; here the analysis is different. The first of the three things corresponds with wisdom, the first of the four in the earlier analysis. The second, restraint of the emotions and subjection of the impulses to reason, appears earlier under the discussion of the fitting which is relevant to all the subdivisions of the *honestum* (see 1. 94). The third thing here, the social virtue of treating others with consideration, falls partly under justice, the second of the virtues in Book I, but is also associated with temperance, a concomitant virtue of the fitting.

19 *Fortune plays a major role*: Cicero briefly discussed the impact of Fortune at 1. 120.

20 *three most recently*: these are the three defeats sustained at Pharsalus in Thessaly in 48 BC, at Thapsus in Africa in 46, and at Munda in Spain in 45.

an eminent and exceptional man: this is Pompey, defeated at Pharsalus and subsequently assassinated on landing in Egypt.

the exile . . . of citizens who are often well-deserving: Cicero refers to his own bitter experience when exiled for 20 months in 58–57 BC, and also to such worthy figures as the Stoic Rutilius Rufus, exiled for extortion by an equestrian jury after incurring the hostility of the equestrian tax-collectors in Africa (see *N.D.* 3. 80).

§§ 21–22: Motives which induce men to lend support to leaders

21 *kings or 'people-pleasers'*: Cicero adduces both Greek examples (see the comments on the later Spartan kings at 2. 80; Nabis in particular sought popular support by exiling his bourgeois opponents and confiscating their property) and his Roman bugbears the *populares*, from

the Gracchi (see 2. 43, 2. 78 ff.) to Julius Caesar, who is excoriated at 2. 84.

22 [*Further . . . may be bribed.*]: There is little doubt that this paragraph is to be deleted from the text (so Winterbottom and other editors) since it merely restates in more pedestrian fashion the content of the previous paragraph.

§§ 23–29: Affection is more effective than fear in gaining support

23 *Ennius*: the citation may be from the *Thyestes*, for Accius later echoes the phrase in his tragedy *Atreus* (see 1. 97 n.), which handles the same theme.

The death of this tyrant . . . more especially now that he is dead: this illustration from the death of Julius Caesar of the thesis that love wins support rather than fear is an echo of Cicero's speech at *Phil*. 1. 35: 'If the end met by Gaius Caesar cannot convince you that it is better to be loved than feared . . .'. The speech, delivered on 2 Sept. 44 BC, at a time when this treatise was being composed, details Mark Antony's continuation of Caesar's policies.

24 *in verdicts passed silently in court or in secret ballots for magistracies*: in view of the pessimism expressed at 2. 29 ('the republic we have lost utterly'), it is surprising that Cicero puts faith in the survival of republican institutions. I take *iudiciis tacitis* to refer to verdicts in the criminal courts rather than to vaguer judgements in general; juries restricted to senators and equestrians by Caesar's reforms would not expose themselves to danger by their secret verdicts. Likewise the elections in the popular assembly could ensure the advancement of honourable candidates without fear of reprisals.

25 *the elder Dionysius*: Dionysius I of Syracuse (432–367 BC) was a powerful tyrant who successfully resisted Carthaginian pressures, extended his influence into Magna Graecia, and enjoyed close relations with Sparta. Cicero has recorded this anecdote of the fearful monarch with greater detail earlier in *Tusc*. 5. 57 ff.

Alexander of Pherae: this tyrant, who ruled the Thessalian city between 369 and 358 BC, had good grounds for apprehension of danger since he was constantly opposed by neighbouring states of Thessaly, especially Larissa, and also by Thebes, whose leader Pelopidas intrigued with Alexander's wife Thebe to oust the tyrant. There are slightly verying accounts of the manner of the assassination, and the reason for it, in other sources (Xenophon, *Hell.* 6. 4. 35 ff., Diodorus 16. 14, Plutarch, *Pelopidas* 35).

26 *Phalaris*: this tyrant of Akragas (= Agrigentum) in Sicily, who ruled *c.*570–554 BC, was notorious for his cruelty, especially for the brazen bull in which he roasted opponents alive. This tradition is as old as Pindar (*Pyth.* 1. 185 ff.), and Diodorus (13. 90. 4–5) claims that the bull was still in Agrigentum in his day. For an anecdotal account of the circumstances of his death, see Diodorus 9. 30.

this tyrant of ours: Cicero repeatedly refers to Julius Caesar in these disparaging terms.

Demetrius . . . Pyrrhus: in 287 BC, in the warfare between the forces of Pyrrhus of Epirus and the Macedonians under their king Demetrius Poliorcetes, Pyrrhus seized the Macedonian town of Beroea, and thereafter the Macedonians seceded from the king, who subsequently lost his throne. See N. G. L. Hammond and F. W. Walbank, *A History of Macedonia, iii* (Oxford 1988), 224 ff.

their debacle at Leuctra: 1. 61 n. The Spartan defeat in July 371 BC was attributable in part to the superior generalship of Epaminondas, but partly to the reluctance of Sparta's allies to fight wholeheartedly under her oppressive leadership.

The senate was a haven . . . for kings, tribes, and nations: this idealized account of Roman arms abroad in the period of the middle republic is echoed in the pages of Livy's history. For the enlightened treatment of kings and nations after defeat, see, for example, Livy's version of a letter sent by Scipio Africanus the Elder to Prusias of Bithynia at 37. 25. 8 ff.

27 *Even before Sulla won his victory*: ancient historians held varied theories about the commencement of Roman moral decline, to which they attributed the collapse of political order in the first century BC. The view that the rot was setting in as early as 187 BC with the return of Manlius Volso's troops from Asia was propounded by the annalist of the second century BC, Calpurnius Piso, and this was echoed by Livy, though he adds that 'these were barely the seeds of the luxury to follow' (39. 6. 7). Polybius (6. 57. 3, 31. 25. 3) made the destruction of the kingdom of Macedon in 167 BC the starting-point. Sallust marks the fall of Carthage as the beginning of decline, but claims that Sulla's return from Asia in 83 BC was the occasion of major infection (*Cat.* 11. 4 ff., *Jug.* 41–2), the view which Cicero takes here. Elsewhere (*Rep.* 3. 41) Cicero blames his *bête noire* Tiberius Gracchus for

initiating the ill-treatment of Roman allies with which Cicero is particularly concerned here.

27 *he erected the auction-spear in the forum*: after his victorious return to Rome in 83 BC, Sulla was elected dictator. He restored senatorial government ('an honourable cause'), but then published lists of proscribed citizens. The property of those listed was sold in public auction; the Roman procedure to signal such a sale was to erect a spear and to conduct the auction beneath it. The citation of Sulla's bogus claim that he was 'selling booty he had won' echoes the remark of *In Verrem* 2. 3. 81.

laid hands on whole provinces and districts: this phrase describes Caesar's systematic conquest of senatorial forces and their allies as they gathered in provinces overseas.

28 *the city of Massilia borne in triumph*: after marching on Rome and thus initiating the Great Civil War in 49 BC, Caesar first laid siege to Massilia, whose leaders had been persuaded to block his army's advance into Spain (see Caesar, *Bell. Civ.* 1. 34 ff.). This city (modern Marseilles), founded from Phocaea *c.*600 BC, was a venerable Roman ally; the Romans believed that the alliance went back to the Regal period. Hence Cicero's indignation that Caesar incorporated the capture of the town in his triumph over Gaul, one of four triumphs which he celebrated in September 46. Representations of captured cities were a regular feature of triumphal processions at Rome.

His estate has been inherited by the few: Caesar's last will is documented by Suetonius, *Iul.* 83. 2. Three of his sisters' grandsons were the main beneficiaries.

29 *Publius Sulla . . . still more crime-laden*: the Publius Sulla cited here was the nephew of the dictator. Elected as consul for 65, he was disqualified for bribery. In 62 he was defended by Cicero when charged with involvement in the Catilinarian conspiracy, and acquitted. In the Great Civil War he supported Caesar, and was a subordinate commander at the battle of Pharsalus. Subsequently he profited from the proscriptions, as this passage indicates.

Yet another Publius Sulla: he is otherwise little known. His rise from humble scribe under Sulla to city quaestor under Caesar signals for Cicero evidence of corrupt government. Caesar doubled the number of quaestors to forty; as the lowest of the regular magistrates, they mostly served in the provinces and in Italian cities as financial agents. Tenure of the office in the capital was a more august position.

§§ 30–51: The importance of glory, and how to attain it

30 *the faithful intimacy of friends*: though Cicero adverts initially to friendships as a means of gaining glory, he is distracted from his main theme
through emphasizing the value of friendship in its own right.

31 Laelius... *two books of mine on the subject as well*: Cicero wrote *Laelius*
(more popularly known as *De amicitia*) in the summer of 44 BC, shortly
before embarking on this treatise. Laelius is chosen as title and as
interlocutor because of his proverbial friendship with Scipio Aemilianus, and also because of his reputation as an incorruptible Stoic.
Laelius has survived, but the two books of *De gloria* are lost; the long
section here (§§ 31–51) is doubtless a resumé of that earlier work.

another approach: this is detailed in §§ 44–51 (so Griffin) rather than in
§§ 54–64 (as Dyck), because there is more emphasis in the first on the
effects on the community as a whole, and in the second Cicero condemns rather than commends such large-scale allocations of money.

33 *can anticipate future events*: the literal meaning of *prudentia* (prudence)
is 'foresight'.

'good men': 1. 20n.

35 *the man who possesses one virtue possesses them all*: Chrysippus, the most
influential of the early Stoics, argued that although virtues are different from each other, they cannot exist in isolation; 'all depended on the
knowledge of what was good and bad, and a man who had that knowledge must possess all the virtues' (F. H. Sandbach, *The Stoics* (London 1975), 43). To claim, as Cicero does, that 'all philosophers' agree
to this thesis, is an exaggeration, though the Stoics develop it from the
teachings of Plato and Aristotle. Cicero himself argues the case at
length at *Tusc.* 3. 14 ff.

Panaetius adopted the same practice: the standpoint that the virtues are
to be distinguished from each other was adopted by Panaetius from
Chrysippus (see the previous note). It is the proposition that a man can
possess one virtue and not another which Cicero advances as a concession to popular belief; Panaetius is depicted as arguing for this practice
in a different context at *Fin.* 4. 78 f.

36 *'who profit neither themselves nor their neighbour'*: similar to the expression 'good for neither man nor beast'.

37 *when the flaming brands of physical pain are applied to them*: by this strik-
ing metaphor Cicero recalls his account (*Tusc.* 2. 61) of Pompey's visit

to the Stoic philosopher Posidonius, who was crippled with arthritis. When Posidonius felt such 'burning brands of pain', he would repeat: 'You are wasting your time, pain; you are troublesome, but I shall never confess that you are an evil.'

38 *justice . . . the single virtue which bestows the accolade 'good' on men*: see 1. 20.

tried by fire: at *Tusc.* 4. 26, Cicero defines avarice as 'the strong belief that money is eminently desirable', in a catalogue of mental diseases which stems ultimately from the account of the Stoic Chrysippus. The metaphor 'tried by fire' to define those not susceptible to the disease is an apt one, for it refers to the way in which gold is tested for its purity; similarly, the incorruptible man is the genuine currency in the state.

40 *without some small element of justice*: the 'honour among thieves' motif may stem via Panaetius from Plato, who at *Rep.* 351c employs it in his discussion of the nature of justice with the sophist Thrasymachus. But pirates were a hazard familiar in the lifetime of Cicero, as was demonstrated when Pompey was given unprecedented powers in 67 BC to clear the eastern Mediterranean of them.

Bardylis the Illyrian brigand . . . Viriathus the Lusitanian: Bardylis I (*c*.448–358 BC), king of the Illyrian Dardani, made his presence felt not only on the high seas but also in attacks on the Molossians in Epirus and against the Macedonians, until he was defeated by Philip II in 358. Viriathus was a Lusitanian shepherd who rose to become commander-in-chief in 147 BC. He defeated one Roman commander after another until he was treacherously assassinated by fellow-countrymen in 139 BC. The role of Laelius as praetor in 145 BC (cf. *Brutus* 1. 84) is exaggerated here; so far from becoming an easy target for subsequent Roman commanders, Viriathus forced the Roman general of 140 BC, Fabius Maximus Servilianus, to conclude a humiliating peace, and to declare Viriathus a friend of the Roman people. Viriathus remains a national hero in Portugal to this day.

the sobriquet 'The Wise': cf. 1. 90 n., 3. 16.

41 *as noted by Herodotus*: at 1. 96 ff. Herodotus claims that Deioces as judge won such a reputation for justice that he was elevated to king and thus became the founder of the royal line, ruling for 53 years (700–647 BC). The name is certainly historical, but little else; cf. W. W. How and J. Wells, *A Commentary on Herodotus I* (Oxford 1912), App. III. 3.

42 *When this failed to obtain, laws were devised*: this interpretation of early Roman history, that a legal framework was established only after

Roman kings failed to ensure justice for all, is derived from Posidonius, who is cited by Seneca (*Ep.* 90. 5–6): 'But when vices crept in,
and kingships turned into tyranny, there began to be a need for
laws . . .'. Cicero had earlier argued (*Rep.* 2. 25, 31, 33, 38, etc.) that
laws already existed under the kings, but here he is claiming, as Livy
does in an impressive passage in 2. 1, that with freedom the rule of law
now becomes the basis for a just society.

43 *Socrates nobly declared*: cf. Xenophon, *Mem.* 2. 6. 39: 'The shortest,
safest, and finest way, Critobulus, is to strive to become the good man
which you would like to appear to be.'

Tiberius Gracchus . . . his sons . . . deserved to be slain: Tiberius Sempronius Gracchus (consul 177, censor 169) came to prominence in 190 BC,
when he negotiated the safe passage of the Roman army under the
Scipios through Macedonia and Thrace with Philip V. In 'the trials of
the Scipios' (187–4) he was the leading spokesman on their behalf. He
had outstanding success as commander in Spain in 180–79, both in
warfare and in diplomacy. Thereafter he was the leading senatorial
figure up to his death in 154, renowned for his austerity and his incorruptibility. His sons Tiberius and Gaius, tribunes in 133 and 123–2
respectively, proposed agrarian legislation highly unpopular with the
dominant conservatism of the senate. Tiberius sought to relieve urban
poverty by his proposals, which he put directly to the people to cir-
cumvent senatorial opposition; when his fellow-tribune Octavius
vetoed the bill, Tiberius successfully proposed his removal from
office. Such untraditional behaviour incensed his opponents, so that
when he sought re-election as tribune, he was assassinated (1. 76n.).
His younger brother Gaius in his two-year tenure of the tribunate continued and extended his brother's policies. He legislated for a corn-
dole (2. 72), further land distribution, and foundation of colonies; he
unsuccessfully proposed to bestow citizenship on the Latins, and
Latin rights on other Italians. When he failed to secure re-election for
a third year, he resorted to violence, and was killed in a riot. In Cicero's
claim that 'in life' the Gracchi gained no support from 'good men', the
term *boni* relates to the senatorials who were defending simultaneously
ancestral tradition and economic and political self-interest; his condemnation of them 'in death' is coloured by his later experiences with
more corrupt *populares*, including Catiline and Caesar.

described in the previous book: 1. 3n.

45 *to command a cavalry squadron*: this is the sole evidence which we possess for the service of young Marcus as a cavalry-officer at Pharsalus in

48 BC at the age of 17. Subsequently his ambition for military glory overrode his political allegiance; he had to be dissuaded from joining the Caesarean forces in Spain in 45 BC (*Att.* 12. 7. 1). By April 43 BC he had joined the army of Brutus and was winning plaudits for his soldiering; see 1. 2 n.

47 *Publius Rutilius in the house of Publius Mucius*: for Mucius Scaevola (consul 133 BC), the leading jurist of his day, see 1. 116 and n. For Rutilius Rufus, consul in 105 and a committed Stoic unjustly exiled, see 2. 20 n., 3. 10.

Lucius Crassus . . . that celebrated and famous speech: this speech, which Lucius Crassus (on whom, see 1. 108 n.) made in 119 BC at the age of 21, was the prosecution of Gaius Papirius Carbo (consul 120 BC), who in the outcome committed suicide. See A. E. Douglas' edition of Cicero's *Brutus* (Oxford 1966), § 103. 17.

as we are told Demosthenes did: there is ambiguity of meaning here. Does the phrase, as the order of the Latin suggests, point backward (so Dyck), or forward (so Atkins)? Demosthenes was certainly involved in civil litigation to recover his property at an early age (perhaps 18), but his first entry into a public trial (*Against Androtion*) was at the age of 29. A further complication is the tradition that he was a student of rhetoric under Isaeus whilst claiming his property. My translation supports the interpretation that Demosthenes was still practising in the schools at the age when Crassus was shining in the courts.

48 *two forms of discourse . . . conversation and . . . argumentation*: see 1. 132 and n.

Letters . . . sent by Philip to Alexander . . . by Antipater to Cassander . . . by Antigonus to his son Philip: these letters need not have been genuine; such compositions were a favourite exercise in schools of rhetoric. Philip II ruled Macedon 359–336 BC, and his son Alexander the Great, 336–323 BC. Antipater (397–319 BC) was Philip II's trusted lieutenant in diplomacy and war; after Alexander's death, he governed Macedon and Greece (and was responsible for Demosthenes' suicide). His son Cassander (*c.*358–297 BC), who accompanied Alexander on his epic expedition, succeeded after his father's death in consolidating his leadership in Macedon. Antigonus (*c.*382–301 BC), friend and fellow-general of Antipater, became commander of the Macedonians in Asia after Alexander's death, and assumed the title of king in 306, but was killed at the battle of Ipsus in Phrygia by an alliance between Cassander, Ptolemy, and Seleucus. His son Philip, overshadowed by his brother Demetrius I Poliorcetes, was famous only for youthful indiscretions (Plutarch, *Demetrius* 23).

49 *Marcus Antonius . . . Publius Sulpicius . . . indicted . . . Gaius Norbanus*: Antonius was regarded as the other outstanding orator of his day besides Crassus, and the two are the leading spokesmen in Cicero's *De oratore*. The earliest attested speech of Antonius was his prosecution of Gnaeus Papirius Carbo, brother of the Carbo indicted by Crassus, in 112 BC; as Antonius was three years older than Crassus, he was 31 at that time. Publius Sulpicius Rufus, a youthful follower of Crassus, indicted Gaius Norbanus in 95 BC on a charge of treason; for the details, see A. Lintott, *CAH* 9² 102. Cicero is scathing about Norbanus because he was a *popularis* who had successfully prosecuted one of the old guard of the senate, Servilius Caepio, for his negligence in sustaining a notorious defeat at Arausio in 105 BC at the hands of the Cimbri; Norbanus achieved this success after violently removing tribunes who sought to veto the indictment.

50 *the two Luculli . . . my action on behalf of the Sicilians . . . Julius on behalf of the Sardinians*: the two Luculli (consuls in 74 and 73 respectively) successfully prosecuted the augur C. Servilius for negligence after Servilius had indicted their father for peculation while governor of Sicily (hence Cicero's phrase 'as an act of revenge'). Cicero indicted Verres, proconsul of Sicily 74–71 BC; he had become the patron of the Sicilians following his quaestorship in western Sicily in 75 BC. Gaius Iulius Caesar in 103 BC indicted Titus Albucius, ex-governor of Sardinia, for extortion in that province; for Caesar's reputation as a witty performer in the courts, see 1. 108 and n.

Lucius Fufius in indicting Manius Aquilius: as governor of Sicily in 100 BC, Aquilius quelled a slave insurrection there; on returning to Rome he was prosecuted for extortion by Fufius. His careful indictment failed because Aquilius' counsel, Marcus Antonius, tore open his client's shirt to reveal the wounds sustained in single combat with the leader of the insurrection. Cicero does not rate Fufius highly as an orator; see *Brutus* 222.

This is what happened to Marcus Brutus: the elder Brutus was a distinguished jurist who had published three books on civil law; see *De oratore* 2. 224; *Pro Cluentio* 141. The son, however, incurred general notoriety through his enthusiasm for the role of prosecutor ('accusator vehemens et molestus', *Brutus* 130).

51 *if Panaetius . . . did not approve the practice*: Cicero is pleased to find philosophical justification for his own practice; for example, under

pressure from the triumvirs he defended Vatinius in 54 BC, though he had prosecuted him two years earlier, and Gabinius, clearly guilty of extortion, in the same year.

51 *that speech . . . still survives*: in the year 80 BC Cicero at the age of 26 successfully defended Sextus Roscius from a charge of parricide when two of Roscius' relatives, backed by Sulla's henchman Chrysogonus, sought to have him proscribed and his property confiscated. The speech *Pro Sexto Roscio Amerino*, Cicero's second major foray in the courts, is extant today.

§§ 52–64: Two means of imparting benefits: (1) gifts of money

52 *beneficence and generosity*: Cicero has already discussed these in 1. 42–60 from the aspect of the honourable; here he is concerned with their utility. Such giving had been treated by Aristotle at *Nic. Eth.* 1119b, and there are two citations here from another Peripatetic, Theophrastus, at § 56 and § 64. The Peripatetic doctrine is presumably mediated through Panaetius.

you exhaust the very source of your generosity: there are good grounds for arguing that personal service ranks higher than financial help, but this is not one of them; Cicero does not credit the donor with the intelligence to be generous within his means, the very advice which he gives in § 54.

53 *a noteworthy rebuke of Philip's*: for the letter, see 2. 48 and n.

54 *profligate giving is followed by seizure from others*: Cicero's thoughts revert to the public confiscations ordered by Sulla and Caesar, and to attempts made to recoup from provincials the outlays on public shows (see 2. 57 n. on Scaurus); they have little relevance to private benefactions.

55 *'The pot of giving has no bottom'*: though Cicero states that this is a Roman saying, the Latin phrase is not otherwise attested. But there is a Greek equivalent, 'Like water poured into a leaking cask' (Aristotle, *Pol.* 1320a, with reference to the demands of the poor becoming greater and greater).

civic feasts, distributions of meat: perhaps an implicit criticism of Caesar's lavish giving. See Suetonius, *Iul.* 38. 2, where Cicero's phrase *epulum ac viscerationem* is echoed. Such distributions of meat followed solemn sacrifices.

gladiatorial shows . . . public games . . . wild-beast chases: Cicero, like Seneca and the Younger Pliny after him, was contemptuous of these popular entertainments; cf. *Pro Archia* 13; Seneca, *Ep.* 7. 4; Pliny, *Ep.* 9. 6. 'Wild-beast chases' refers to spectacles in the arena; Cicero is especially critical of them (*Fam.* 7. 1. 3).

redeeming captives from pirates: for the hazards of first-century sea-travel, see 2. 39 and n., 3. 107.

56 *Theophrastus . . . his book* On Riches: on Theophrastus, 1. 3n. He was a prolific writer, but most of his works including this one have not survived.

Aristotle's rebuke . . . He adds: this treatise of Aristotle has not survived. I propose and translate *adicit* for the corrupt *at ii* of the manuscripts.

a mina for a pint of water: a *mina* is worth 100 drachmas; during the Peloponnesian war Athenian sailors were paid half a drachma a day (Thucydides 8. 45. 1; Xenophon, *Hell.* 1. 5. 4ff.), the same rate as Athenian jurors. Thus the hypothetical cost of a pint of water would be the equivalent of 200 days' pay.

57 *Publius Crassus . . . Lucius Crassus . . . adorned the office*: amongst their other city duties, aediles mounted the public entertainments. Ambitious individuals exploited this duty to win popularity in the furtherance of their careers, often augmenting the state allowance with money from their own pockets. The Publius Licinius Crassus cited here is probably the consul of 97 BC, whose aedileship will have been held about 102 BC (it is doubtful if he had the *cognomen* Dives). Lucius Licinius Crassus was aedile about five years later.

Gaius Claudius . . . and many others . . . did likewise: Gaius Claudius Pulcher's aedileship (99 BC) was memorable for the introduction of elephants to the arena. The brothers Luculli (2. 50n.) held the aedileship jointly in 79 BC; they introduced a revolving stage for dramatic performances, and pitted bulls against elephants in the arena. Q. Hortensius Hortalus (consul 69, and the most celebrated orator at Rome till Cicero outshone him) put on notable games in 75 BC; Decimus Iunius Silanus was aedile *c.*70 BC (*MRR* 2. 127).

Publius Lentulus . . . Scaurus . . . my friend Pompeius: Lentulus Spinther, consul 57 and earlier aedile in 63, was one of Cicero's devoted supporters; he took custody of one of the Catilinarian conspirators in 63, and supported the demand for Cicero's recall from exile in 57. Scaurus, having bankrupted himself on public shows as aedile in 58, sought to recoup his losses as propraetor in Sardinia in 54; hence the indictment noted at 1. 138n. Pompey, invariably (3. 82 excepted) mentioned in complimentary terms in this treatise, by contrast with Cicero's acerbic judgements during the Great Civil War, was consul for the second time in 55 BC, the year in which he dedicated his famous theatre (2. 60n.) with games marked by a glut of wild beasts.

58 *Mamercus ... sidestepped the aedileship*: the aedileship was not a compulsory rung on the ladder of offices, but those who skirted it to avoid the expense often suffered reverses in their later careers. Mamercus (Oscan form of Marcus) Aemilius Lepidus finally attained the consulship in 77 BC, having been rejected for it at an earlier date.

This is what I myself did: the implication of Cicero's remarks is that if sound men cannot attain higher offices without tenure of the aedileship, they should suppress their reservations for the greater good of Rome. For the games which he mounted in 69 BC as aedile, see *In Verrem* 2. 5. 36.

Orestes ... Marcus Seius ... Milo: Cn. Aufidius Orestes was consul in 71; the date of his aedileship is uncertain. Sulla and Crassus exemplify such provision of religious tithe-offerings. In the public feasting which followed Sulla's offering to Hercules 'a great quantity of food was thrown into the Tiber every day; wine forty years old or even older was drunk'. When Crassus similarly honoured Hercules, 'he fed the people at ten thousand tables, and distributed three months' ration of corn' (Plutarch, *Sulla* 35; *Crassus* 12). Seius' distribution of corn was when he was aedile in 74 BC, at a time when piracy was causing severe shortages; the price of an *as* per peck was less than a sixth of the normal cost. Milo's hiring of gladiators took place when he was tribune in 57 BC; they were employed in counter-violence against the hoodlums of Cicero's enemy Clodius. Cicero identifies the defence of the republic with his own safe return from exile later in that year.

59 *Lucius Philippus ... Cotta and Curio ... I too can make the same boast up to a point*: Lucius Philippus failed in his candidacy for the consulship of 93 BC, but was elected two years later. C. Aurelius Cotta (spokesman for the Academics in Cicero's *The Nature of the Gods*) reached the consulship in 75 BC, and C. Scribonius Curio a year earlier. For the shows mounted by Cicero, see § 58n. above. He topped the poll for the aedileship of 69 and the praetorship for 66 BC; he was praetor at 40 and consul at 43, the minimum ages laid down by the legislation of Sulla.

60 *Out of respect for Pompeius*: for Cicero's deferential attitude towards the dead Pompey, see 2. 57 n. Pompey's stone theatre, the first

permanent theatre at Rome, was dedicated following his triumph in 55 BC. The complex of buildings embodied colonnades and a shrine to Venus Victrix; Cicero's condemnation of new temples indicates his preference for restoration of the old.

though not word for word: a specific indication of the nature of Cicero's debt to his main source; see Introd., p. xxviii.

Demetrius of Phalerum . . . the famous Propylaea: on Demetrius, see 1. 3 and n. The Propylaea is the roofed gateway on the west side of the Athenian Acropolis; designed by Mnesicles *c.*435 BC, it took five years to complete, and is still largely intact. It was financed, together with the other new buildings on the Acropolis, from the tribute paid by members of the Delian Confederacy, and was criticized at Athens on that account (Plutarch, *Pericles* 12). Presumably Demetrius criticized excessive outlay on what was a mere adjunct to the Parthenon itself.

in the books which I have written: this section of *The Republic* has not survived.

61 *that motivated by generosity*: Cicero is still discussing financial outlays, but here distinguishes private generosity (§§ 61–4) from public extravagance (§§ 51–60).

62 *As Ennius well says*: the tragedy from which this trochaic septenarius has been taken has not been identified.

63 *a published speech of Crassus*: Cicero almost certainly refers to the speech which L. Licinius Crassus delivered in 106 BC in support of the Servilian bill to divide jurors equally between senators and equestrians (the equestrian monopoly of juries had earlier led to the conviction of several senators). In Crassus' speech as reported by Cicero (*Pro Cluentio* 140), Crassus 'adorned the senate with the highest praises'; these will have included reference to the ransoming of captives by members of the senate.

64 *praised by Theophrastus*: on Theophrastus, see 1. 3 n. The passage describing Cimon's hospitality (see the n. below) will have come from the lost *On Riches* (see 2. 56).

distinction on our state: this perhaps refers to the furnished quarters and hospitality extended to visiting ambassadors in the *villa publica* on the Campus Martius; see Livy 33. 24. 5.

Cimon . . . offered hospitality even to the Laciads: Cimon (*c.* 510–450 BC), the celebrated general and statesman of Athens, served with distinction in the military operations of the Delian Confederacy (476–63 BC) and thereafter became influential as leader of the aristocratic party, a thorn in the flesh of Themistocles and later of Pericles. The tradition that he was a genial and hospitable host to people of his deme (the ten Athenian tribes were divided into some 150 demes or local communities) goes back to Aristotle, *Ath. Pol.* 27. 3, and is repeated in Plutarch, *Cimon* 10, who reports an alternative version that his table was available to 'any poor Athenian'.

§§ 65–85: Benefits (2) by personal service

65 *Safeguarding the interests of individuals at law*: this is the primary way in which Cicero interprets the notion of personal service to others.

the man who has easily surpassed his predecessors in knowledge of the law: this is Servius Sulpicius Rufus (consul 51 BC), friend of Cicero to whom he wrote the celebrated consolation on the death of his daughter Tullia (*Fam.* 4. 5). The ninth Philippic, delivered in February 43 shortly after Sulpicius' death, praises his political career and his distinction as jurist: 'If all from every age who had knowledge of law in this city were assembled in one place, they would not be on a par with Servius Sulpicius' (*Phil.* 9. 10).

66 *without payment*: according to Tacitus, *Annals* 11. 5 (cf. also 13. 42, 15. 20) the *lex Cincia* of 204 BC forbade anyone to receive money or a gift for pleading in court. But there were other inducements: 'Cicero was once left a library in a will and was given a large loan in order to buy a house' (Griffin, ad loc.). For the loan of two million sesterces by P. Sulla, defended by Cicero in 62 BC, see Aulus Gellius 12. 12. 2.

67 *the cessation . . . of eloquence*: Tacitus was later to echo this lament, and to connect it, as Cicero implicitly does, with the loss of political freedom, in his *Dialogus de oratoribus*. In Cicero's case the political situation was interlinked with stylistic controversy; a new generation of orators centring on C. Licinius Calvus proclaimed allegiance to the spare 'Attic' style of Lysias, and condemned the 'Asianism' or highflown style of Ciceronian oratory. See A. E. Douglas' edition of *Brutus*, XII ff.

69 *It is an honourable claim to make*: in fact in discussing the honourable at 1. 45–6, Cicero argues that we should look to character when dispensing benevolence. Here, in the context of the useful, he concedes that a person's wealth and standing can affect our attitudes, before urging us to assist the needy man if he is virtuous, and to realise that a well-endowed recipient is not always grateful.

Someone put it well: Cicero had earlier exploited the epigram, the provenance of which is unknown, in 54 BC in the *Pro Plancio* 68, when defending the man who as quaestor in Macedonia had comforted Cicero during his exile there.

being greeted as 'clients': 'clients' is used here in the Roman sense of social dependants; Cicero's claim that wealthier people strongly objected to having this label pinned on them is echoed by Seneca at *De beneficiis* 2. 23. 3.

71 *Themistocles as our authority*: for Themistocles, see 1. 75 and n. The anecdote recorded here became a great favourite with moralizing historians. See Plutarch, *Them.* 10. 3, who makes Themistocles the father of the bride; Diodorus 10. 12; Valerius Maximus 7. 2 ext. 9.

72 *Gaius Gracchus . . . Marcus Octavius was modest*: for Gaius Gracchus, see 2. 43 n. His corn law ordained that the state was to sell a monthly ration to any citizen who applied for it at 6⅓ asses a peck; Cicero repeatedly condemns the measure. The date of the legislation of M. Octavius, who repealed the law of Gaius Gracchus and either raised the price or restricted the recipients, is uncertain. P. A. Brunt, *Italian Manpower* (Oxford 1971), 377, argues for *c.* 120 BC; Douglas, *Brutus*, 163, and G. Rickman, *The Corn Supply of Ancient Rome* (Oxford 1980), 161–2, for about forty years later.

73 *an agrarian law by Philippus*: L. Marcius Philippus (see 1. 108, 2. 59 nn.) was tribune probably in 104 BC; though he courted popular favour at that time with his bill, he later showed his true colours as 'a pillar of the Sullan establishment' (E. Badian, *OCD*). His suggestion in this 'pernicious speech' that of the half-million inhabitants of Rome (see N. Purcell, *CAH* 9², 648) less than 2,000 owned property is criticized but not challenged by Cicero.

in the hope of guarding their possessions: see 2. 13 n. (*men sharing life in community*).

74 *to avoid the imposition of a property tax*: this tax had been abolished in 167 BC following the Third Macedonian War, when the proceeds from overseas provinces made such a tax superfluous (see 2. 76). The philosophical basis on which Cicero's views rest is that the levying of taxes by the state is as unjust as the assault on an individual's private property by a neighbour.

which our ancestors often imposed: Cicero doubtless thinks of the elder Cato's budgetary measures in his censorship of 184 BC, which were 'harsh and oppressive to all ranks' (Livy 39. 44. 1, who furnishes the details).

74 *the solution is obvious*: Cicero accepts that some provision of welfare is necessary, but on the modest scale laid down by M. Octavius (2. 72), the cost of which could be met by revenue from overseas.

75 *Gaius Pontius the Samnite*: the reference is probably to the Samnite general who trapped the Roman army at the Caudine Forks in 321 BC in the Second Samnite War, rather than to his father of the same name, who is mentioned in *De senectute* 41. The remark attributed to him here is presumably the invention of a Roman annalist who makes him idealize the incorruptibility of Roman leaders like L. Papirius Cursor or M'. Curius Dentatus; it is anachronistic because Pontius could not have foreseen such a decline in Roman morals.

He would surely have had to wait for many generations: for varying Roman theories of the commencement of moral decline, see 2. 27 n. When Cicero speaks of 'recently', he may have Sulla's return to Rome in mind.

since Lucius Piso pioneered a law on extortion: L. Calpurnius Piso (consul 133 BC and censor 120 BC, and a distinguished Roman annalist) put through the first law against extortion, which was aimed at unscrupulous officials in the provinces who were squeezing money from their hapless subjects. Once the special court (*quaestio*) for this offence had been set up, and the *lex Acilia* of 122 BC had transferred the panel of jurors to the equestrians, a stream of indictments against senatorial officials ensued. In spite of the spate of subsequent legislation (*lex Servilia* 111 BC, *lex Cornelia* 81 BC, *lex Iulia* 59 BC) exploitation of provincials remained rife.

so fierce a war: this was the Social War of 91 BC, which Cicero appears to believe was caused by the removal of *equites* from the panel of jurors. But this was a relatively minor issue in the context of the Italians' frustration at being denied citizen-rights. For the issue of debarment of equites, see E. Gabba, *CAH* 9^2, 111 ff.

76 *Panaetius praises Africanus for his incorruptibility*: as at 1. 90, the Africanus discussed here is Scipio Aemilianus, with whom Panaetius was on friendly terms; see 1. 116 n., and Introd. p. xxviii.

Paulus acquired all the massive treasures of the Macedonians: for the career of L. Aemilius Paulus, see 1. 116 n. After his victor over Perseus at Pydna in 167 BC, a massive amount of booty was transported to

Rome (Livy 45. 33. 5ff.) Paulus then devastated Epirus, looting all gold and silver from the cities, and selling 150,000 into slavery. Polybius (18. 35. 4–5) states that he lodged more than 6,000 talents of gold and silver in the treasury; Roman writers offer varying figures, Livy 120 million sesterces (45 40. 1), Velleius 210 million (1. 9. 6), Pliny 300 million (*NH* 33. 56).

Africanus followed the example of his father: Scipio Aemilianus, son of Aemilius Paulus (1. 116n.) was the Roman commander in the Third Punic War, which culminated in the destruction of Carthage in 146 BC. According to Polybius (18. 35. 9), 'On becoming master of Carthage, reputedly the wealthiest city in the world, he took literally nothing from it for his own use.'

his fellow-censor Mummius was not a penny richer: Lucius Mummius Achaicus (consul 146 BC and fellow-censor with Scipio Aemilianus in 142) sacked the city of Corinth in 146, and disbanded the Achaean Confederacy. He is credited with the embellishment of Rome and other Italian cities, while leaving himself too poor to give his daughter a dowry (Pliny, *NH* 34. 36).

77 *the oracular utterance of Pythian Apollo*: this warning from the oracle at Delphi (Apollo is 'Pythian' because he slew the python, the guardian dragon there) was allegedly addressed to the eighth-century kings of Sparta, Alcamenes and Theopompus (Plutarch, *Moralia* 239F).

78 *'people-pleasers'*: for Cicero's abhorrence of the *populares*, see 2. 21n.

   as I remarked earlier: see 2. 73.

80 *the expulsion of the ephor Lysander . . . the Spartans . . . put king Agis to death*: the ephors, five in number and elected annually, had both executive and judicial powers, and exercised a degree of control over the two kings. Lysander, as ephor in 243 BC, supported king Agis IV's attempt to introduce agrarian reforms; the other king, Leonidas II, led conservative opposition to the measure. After Lysander quitted office (rather than was expelled), Leonidas and the conservative faction engineered Agis' execution. See Plutarch, *Agis* 6ff.

   From that time onward: the conflict between the two factions in the state continued after the death of Agis in 241 BC. Cleomenes III was more successful with plans for social revolution, including cancellation of debts, allotments of land, and increase of the citizen-body. But his policy of military expansion in the Peloponnese ultimately led to defeat and suicide, and to a succession of tyrants at Sparta,

conspicuously Nabis, who was defeated by the Romans in 195 BC, and
later assassinated.

80 *the Gracchi here at home*: for the earlier explicit contrast between
Tiberius and Gaius on the one hand, and their father on the other, see
2. 43 and n. The father had earlier married the daughter of Scipio
Africanus, hero of the Second Punic War (Livy 38. 57. 2); hence
'grandsons' here.

81 *Aratus of Sicyon*: Sicyon, which lies to the west of Corinth, had been
founded from Argos. Aratus (271–213 BC) was educated at Argos,
from where at the age of 20 he delivered his native city from the tyrant
Nicocles. For detail of his capture of the city, see Plutarch, *Aratus* 6 ff.

82 *a huge subvention . . . from the wealthy king*: the king was Ptolemy II
Philadelphus. Plutarch states that Aratus had sent him paintings by
the eminent artists of the day, and having thus gained his favour, he
received 150 talents in instalments from the king (*Aratus* 12–13).
Plutarch also records Aratus' consultation of fifteen leading citizens,
'to decide upon the claims of the exiled families for their inheritances'.

83 *on two occasions*: that is, in the confiscations by Sulla and Julius Caesar.

'Let them dwell in the property of another without payment': Cicero
quotes selectively from the measures backed by Caesar in 48 BC, which
were much more moderate and desirable than Cicero suggests. See
Caesar, *Bell. Civ.* 3. 20–1; Dio 42. 22. 3: E. Rawson, *CAH* 9^2, 431–2,
457–8.

84 *stronger than in my consulship*: in 63 BC Catiline, frustrated by Cicero in
his ambition for the consulship, took up the causes of debt and land.
For Cicero's opposition to the measures for debt relief, see T.P. Wiseman, *CAH* 9^2, 351 ff.

though our present-day victor was defeated then: it is highly improbable
that Caesar was implicated in the Catilinarian conspiracy; see
Wiseman (§ 84), 351 ff.

§§ 86–7: The usefulness of good health and money

86 *Antipater of Tyre*: though he was the author of several works (listed in
OCD, 'Antipater (4)', including *On the Fitting*, which Cicero has con-
sulted here), Antipater's main claim to fame was as Stoic mentor to
Cato the Younger (Plutarch, *Cato Minor* 4).

87 *Xenophon . . . in his book* Oeconomicus: this book by the disciple of Socrates takes the form of two dialogues on the management of country estates, in which Socrates stresses the importance of moral behaviour in country life. Cicero's translation, made *c.*85 BC at the age of 21, has not survived.

at the central gate of Janus: Roman bankers carried on their business of moneylending at this central archway, which lay to the east of the Roman forum. See Horace, *Sat.* 2. 3. 18–19, *Ep.* 1. 1. 54; Cicero, *Phil.* 6. 5. 15.

§§ 88–9: Comparison between useful things

88 *which Panaetius left out*: Cicero has already noted this omission at 1. 10, and repeats it here to publicize his own original contribution to the discussion.

89 *The celebrated mot of old Cato*: on Cato the Censor and his reputation for witticisms, see 1. 104 and n. His work *De agricultura*, composed *c.*160 BC and still surviving, deals with grazing for profit in Latium and Campania, as well as with cultivation of vines, olives, and fruit-trees.

How about money-lending?: for traditional Roman attitudes to usury, see 1. 150n.

BOOK THREE

§§ 1–6: Introduction. Contrasting uses of leisure

1 *Publius Scipio . . . as his contemporary Cato noted*: Cicero repeats from *Rep.* 1. 27 the epigram of Africanus, probably garnered from Cato's *Apophthegmata* (1. 104n.) rather than from the preface to the *Origines* as Leo suggested. Scipio gained the title Africanus for his exploits in the Hannibalic War; appointed to the Spanish command at 24, he drove the Carthaginians out of Spain, and in 204 invaded Africa, bringing the war to a close at Zama in 202. His profitable use of leisure must date to the subsequent years. Though his domestic career prospered (censor 199; princeps senatus 199–184; second consulship 194), he was never entrusted with another military command overseas. He served as legate to his brother Lucius in the war against Antiochus (191–189); it was as a result of this campaign that he was accused of peculation, and died under a shadow in self-imposed banishment at Liternum in 184 BC.

1 *I pursue a life of leisure . . . I roam the countryside*: in the face of intimidation from Mark Antony (hence 'the force of sacrilegious arms'
here), detailed in Cicero's *Second Philippic* (never delivered, but sent
to Atticus on 25 October 44 (*Att.* 15. 13. 1)), Cicero left Rome in the
second week of October to reside in his Campanian villas, and to continue his writing there.

2 *the senate has been snuffed out and lawsuits have been abolished*: though
there is an element of exaggeration in the language here, Antony was
dominating the senate with a show of military force (see *CAH* 9², 478),
and the work of the courts was paralysed by the absence of the praetors
Brutus and Cassius; see Introd., p. x.

3 *to choose the least of evils*: for the phrase, see Aristotle, *Nic. Eth.* 1109a;
Cicero resurrects it in discussion of Regulus' alleged return to
Carthage at 3. 102 below.

4 *Africanus has merited the greater praise . . . fruit of his solitude*: the
element of 'mock diffidence' (Griffin's phrase *ad loc.*) is underlined by
the strongly contrasting statements at 1. 156 and *Pro Archia* 12 on the
importance of communicating one's learning to others.

  I have written more: referring not to his total literary output
(see 1. 3 n.), but to his works on philosophy and rhetoric.

5 *my friend Cratippus*: see 1. 1 n.

6 *If you are to emulate my capacity for work*: like many an over-ambitious
father, Cicero foolishly parades his own achievements to persuade his
son to apply himself more enthusiastically to his studies. He had asked
his friend Atticus to keep a friendly eye on the boy, and Atticus must
have sent back a worrying report. Marcus' tutor in rhetoric, a certain
Gorgias, was dismissed for encouraging him in dissolute ways
(Plutarch, *Cic.* 24. 8; *Fam.* 16. 21. 6). Hence the comments earlier at
1. 2, and Cicero's earlier intention to visit Athens to encourage his son
face to face (see 3. 121 below). For a full account of the father-son relations at this time, see Dyck, 10 ff.

§§ 7–13: The conflict between the honourable and the apparently useful, a topic raised but never treated by Panaetius

7 *I have followed him very closely*: see Introd., p. xxviii.

  He suggested three headings: see 1. 9 above.

8 *Panaetius lived for thirty years longer*: on Panaetius, see Introd., p. xxviii ff. His death is speculatively assigned to 110–109, which would date his treatise to 140–139, but both dates could be a decade or more early; for the subjective evidence, see Dyck, 21 ff.

Posidonius . . . touched so briefly on this subject: on Posidonius, see 1. 159n. Two letters addressed to Atticus on 5 and 12 November 44 help to elucidate this statement. *Att.* 16. 11. 4 reports that Cicero has written to a certain Athenodorus Calvus asking him to send a list of contents of Posidonius' book (presumably *On the Fitting*). *Att.* 16. 14. 4 states that he has received in reply a commentary (doubtless a more detailed account of the contents of the book). Since Cicero was moving between his Campanian villas, he probably did not have available Posidonius' text, and he bases his statement that Posidonius has not discussed the third topic at length on the summary which he received.

9 *that he deliberately left it out*: the identity of these commentators is unknown, but they are presumably Stoic spokesmen for whom the issue is a non-question.

10 *Publius Rutilius Rufus, a former pupil of Panaetius*: a committed Stoic, after service as military tribune at Numantia and in the Jugurthan war, he reached the consulship in 105 BC. His unjust condemnation for extortion in Asia (2. 20n.) led him to exile and the life of a man of letters first at Mytilene and then at Smyrna.

the painting . . . which Apelles had left unfinished: the fourth-century painter from Colophon was in the process of painting a second portrait of Venus rising from the foam at Cos when he died (Pliny, *NH* 35. 92); he had completed the head and the upper part of the body (Cicero, *Fam.* 1. 9. 15).

11 *Socrates, so we are told*: the sentence that follows suggests that Cicero derived the ascription to Socrates from a Stoic source. He had already cited it earlier at *Laws* 1. 33, and Clement of Alexandria, *Stromateis* 2. 131, also records it.

12 *those who assess the honourable by the criterion of pleasure or absence of pain*: the Epicureans are the target here.

neither improved by the addition, nor worsened by the subtraction, of things which are apparently useful: Cicero attributes to Panaetius the traditional Stoic view that virtue alone is the highest good to be sought to achieve happiness. By contrast Diogenes Laertius (7. 128) ascribes to him the belief that health, financial expenditure, and strength were also necessary. Panaetius perhaps regarded these, which for Stoics would fall into the category of 'things preferred' among those morally indifferent, as preconditions for some kinds of virtuous action (so F. H. Sandbach, *The Stoics* (London 1975), 127–8). It seems improbable that Panaetius diverged from the central view of Stoic ethics that virtue is the only good.

13 *some people think it was wrong to enter the comparison*: the comparison, that is, between the honourable and the apparently useful. 'Some people' can scarcely refer to Panaetius, since he expressed his intention to discuss it; Cicero is generalizing about the reaction of traditional Stoics.

sages: the Stoic sage or wise man, exemplified by Hercules and Socrates, 'is not found in everyday life. He is a perfect man, whose character mirrors the perfection of nature' (A. A. Long, *Hellenistic Philosophy* (London 1974), 204).

§§ 14–18: The distinction between 'perfect' and 'intermediate' obligations

14 *described by Stoics as 'intermediate'*: the Greek word *meson* which Cicero translates here must mean intermediate between good and evil, but here and elsewhere Cicero uses *medium officium* as the equivalent of *commune officium*, the obligation which ordinary mortals share. It is contrasted with 'perfect' or 'right' obligation, which, as Cicero explains in the following sentence, only sages can fulfil.

'it fulfils all the numbers': this Stoic phrase descriptive of the virtuous action of the sage (*katorthoma*) may derive ultimately from the Pythagorean theory of numbers, in which even abstractions like truth and justice are equated with individual numbers. For the wide currency of the phrase, see Cicero, *Fin.* 3. 24; Seneca, *Ep.* 95. 5.

16 *the two Decii or the two Scipios . . . men of courage, . . . Fabricius or Aristides is named 'The Just'*: on the two Decii, father and son, and the two Scipios as exemplars of Roman courage, see 1. 61n. On Fabricius' incorruptibility, see 3. 86n. below, where he is acclaimed as the Roman Aristides. For Aristides as 'The Just', see Plutarch, *Aristides* 6f., a section which includes the anecdote about his being ostracized for being known as 'The Just'; see also 3. 49 below.

Marcus Cato and Gaius Laelius . . . the famous Seven: Cicero earlier designates Cato the Censor as wise at *De senectute* 4, and Laelius likewise in *De amicitia* (see 1. 90 n.). The Seven Sages (Greeks of practical wisdom living in the seventh and sixth centuries BC) are usually listed as Cleobulus of Lindos, Periander of Corinth, Pittacus of Mytilene, Bias of Priene in Caria, Thales of Miletus, Chilon of Sparta, and Solon of Athens.

17 *financial profit*: the topic is introduced by Cicero here as the obvious example of the apparently useful.

18 *not that 'they should be'*: Cicero resumes the assertion made earlier that Panaetius intended to raise the comparison between the apparently useful and the honourable; not however to attempt to reconcile the two, but to note that some men are exercised by the dilemma in which they are placed.

§§ 19–39: Establishing a formula or criterion for behaviour, when the apparently useful conflicts with the honourable

19 *if a man murders a tyrant . . . the most noble of illustrious deeds*: Cicero repeatedly describes the assassination of Julius Caesar as the just murder of a vile tyrant, both in the *Second Philippic* (85 ff., 110, 116) and in his correspondence (*Att.* 14. 6. 2, 9. 2, 13. 2, etc.). At 3. 32 below he offers the philosophical basis for the view: it is the amputation of a diseased limb from the body-politic. The same argument lies behind the justification for the murder of the Gracchi at 2. 43. Cicero in the *Second Philippic*, and in his correspondence, repeatedly claims that the assassination of Caesar had the support of public opinion, but the events following the murder scarcely bear this out; see T. N. Mitchell, *Cicero, the Senior Statesman* (New Haven and London 1991), 289 ff.

20 *whatever position seems most probable*: Cicero continues to maintain his allegiance to the Academics (Introd., p. xxxii), and justifies his espousal of Stoic ethical tenets by appealing to the doctrine of probability. But there is little doubt that he is increasingly drawn to Stoicism in his final years; see the closing sentences of *The Nature of the Gods*.

21 *If a person . . . furthers his own advantage by another's loss . . . it undermines the fellowship between members of the human race*: this is the foundation, so to say, for the mode of behaviour which those who contemplate action apparently useful must observe.

22 *Take this parallel*: Livy (2. 32. 8 ff.) ascribes a similar version of the fable to the plebeian Menenius Agrippa in the early days of the

struggle of the orders (494 BC). There is general agreement that the fable derives from Greek philosophical sources (cf. Xenophon, *Memorabilia* 2. 3. 18). It later becomes a commonplace, pressed into service by St Paul, 1 Cor. 12: 12 ff., and Seneca, *De ira* 2. 31. 7.

23 *the law laid down by gods and men*: Cicero recapitulates here the doctrine of natural law which he had expounded at length in the first book of *Laws*. As the Introduction to the Oxford World's Classics edition of *The Republic, The Laws*, pp. xxvii ff., explains, this thesis rests on the suppositions (1) that the universe is maintained by a rational Providence (2) that man lies below God but above all other creatures as a distinct species (3) that the human laws which man promulgates should harmonise with that natural law. This third principle may not always obtain (see 3. 69 f.), but it would in an ideal world.

24 *mere living*: translating *vita*. It seems curious to argue that life itself is less 'natural' than the social virtues, but the suggestion is that mere existence is shared with the brute beasts, whereas man's nature rises higher.

25 *the fabled Hercules . . . exalted to the council of the gods*: Hercules by reason of his labours on behalf of suffering communities throughout the known world became the ideal Stoic sage. At 1. 118 above, the story of his choice of the path of virtue in preference to the path of pleasure establishes him as a Stoic as against an Epicurean. His cult at Rome was probably the earliest importation of foreign worship; see Livy 1. 7. 3 ff. with Ogilvie's n.

27 *Since the premise is true, so likewise is the conclusion*: Cicero presents the argument in the form of the extended syllogism beloved of the Stoics:

1. If we safeguard the individual's interests because of his membership of the human race,

2. and if all men are constrained by the one law of nature,

3. then we are forbidden to do harm to each other.

28 *does not involve injustice*: I read and translate here *quae <non> vacent iustitia*. Winterbottom and other editors retain *quae vacent iustitia* and argue that several words have fallen out immediately before the phrase.

29 [*Certainly not . . . my own profit.*]: Editors exclude this sentence from the text because the objection raised is answered at length in § 30; this is an intrusive gloss.

that cruel and monstrous tyrant Phalaris: see 3. 26 n.

30 *your deed is not blameworthy*: this dubious argument, open to abuse through self-interest as Cicero himself acknowledges in § 31, is implicitly contradicted at 3. 89 below.

32 *once the savagery and brutality of the beast takes human shape*: a similar metaphor is used at *Rep.* 2. 48 in condemnation of the tyrant.

33 *Panaetius would have taken up these topics*: this comment should be read in association with 3. 7 ff. above; Cicero reiterates the point to remind the reader that the previous observations are his own contribution, not copied from the Greek source.

   If Cratippus does not permit you to accept this: young Marcus' teacher as a Peripatetic would argue that the honourable (= virtue) is preeminently to be sought, but that there are other goods such as health, wealth, noble birth which the Stoics categorize as 'things indifferent'.

   sometimes the one, and sometimes the other appears more probable: Cicero maintains his standpoint as an Academic; see Introd., p. xxxii, and 3. 20 n.

34 *the belief of those who have prised the two apart*: the criticism is earlier (see 3. 11 and n.) ascribed to Socrates; presumably Panaetius has quoted Socrates' alleged words with approval.

   battling it out by myself, as the saying goes: this statement is immediately followed by Cicero's own qualification. He has clearly consulted other works, including the writings of Hecato (see 3. 89 ff.; criticized at 3. 63), and the summary of Posidonius' work (3. 8 n.).

35 *(as Zeno thought) . . . (as Aristotle argues)*: curiously, this is the first mention of Zeno of Citium in Cyprus (*c.*335–263 BC), founder of the Stoic school; the view ascribed to him is so generally representative of Stoic thought that it does not appear in *SVF*. Similarly Aristotle is cited for the view central to Peripatetic ethics, deriving from *Nic. Eth.* 2–6.

36 *finally regal status*: Cicero is reflecting bitterly on Julius Caesar and his successor Mark Antony.

   that imposed by their own base conduct: the argument that men's base conduct is its own punishment is a leading theme in Plato's *Gorgias*, and is prominent in Boethius' *Consolation of Philosophy* (4. 4).

38 *the celebrated figure of Gyges*: the story of Gyges is found in different versions in Plato, *Rep.* 359c ff. and Herodotus 1. 7 ff. Plato (whose version Cicero acknowledges and follows here) recounts the original folk-tale. In Herodotus' rationalizing version, Gyges was a member of

his predecessor Candaules' bodyguard; Candaules was so proud of his wife's exceptional beauty that he invited Gyges to spy on her naked form; she detected him, and the outcome was that she enticed him to kill Candaules and to supplant him on the throne.

38 *as the king of Lydia*: Gyges is an historical figure, king of Lydia *c.*685–657 BC; see *OCD*.

39 *True, it could never happen*: I read and translate *nequaquam* (Manitius) for *quamquam* which Winterbottom retains. Though men could remain ignorant of such behaviour, Roman traditional theology could hardly envisage the gods failing to observe and to visit such immoral behaviour.

§§ 40–9: The apparently useful and the demands of justice

40 *When Brutus deposed ... Collatinus from the consular power*: according to the tradition as represented by Livy 2. 2. 2–11, Iunius Brutus and Tarquinius Collatinus were elected as the first consuls in 509 after the last king Tarquinius Superbus was deposed, but popular prejudice against the Tarquins forced Collatinus to resign from the office. The tradition is fictitious, since Collatinus could not have been Brutus' colleague in the consulship; on the historical problems, see Ogilvie's *Commentary*.

41 *he slew his brother*: Livy (1. 7. 1 ff.) records differing traditions of the murder of Remus by Romulus. In the first, rivalry for the throne (as here in Cicero) is the motive; in the other, Remus is slain for impiously jumping over the rising walls of the new city. The two stories represent Romulus variously as villain and Roman hero, an ambivalence which persists throughout Roman literature.

Quirinus, or if you prefer, Romulus: at *Rep.* 2. 20, Cicero describes how the peasant Proculus Iulius claimed to have seen a vision of the dead Romulus on the Quirinal, and to have received the message that Romulus was now a god bearing the name Quirinus. Thus Cicero jocularly refers to him in his two roles as god and man.

42 *Chrysippus as usual put it neatly*: Chrysippus (*c.*280–207 BC) was the third and most illustrious president of the Stoic school; his writings became the canon of Stoic orthodox beliefs. Cicero's approval of his remark here has been criticized as inconsistent with his rejection of Hecato's similar comment at 3. 63, but there is greater emphasis here on the importance of not wronging another.

43 *must never take precedence over friendships*: Cicero recalls (or records from an intermediate source) Aristotle's similar emphasis on the priority of friendship at *Nic. Eth.* 1169a.

to the detriment of the state . . . his oath or pledged word: The same trio of exceptions to the prior claims of friendship were earlier listed by Cicero in *De amicitia* 19.

to arrange a date for pleading the case: Cicero has in mind his own behaviour as praetor in 66 BC, when his friend the tribune Manilius was indicted on laying down his office. Cicero arranged the date of the trial for December 29, when he would be the presiding judge before demitting the praetorship; see T. P. Wiseman, *CAH* 9², 942.

44 *to do all he can with integrity of faith*: in civil cases the competing parties cited this formula in binding the presiding praetor to adjudicate honestly.

conspiracies rather than friendships: Cicero here recapitulates the observations which he places in the mouth of Laelius at *De amicitia* 38ff., where the same contrast between sages and ordinary mortals is made.

45 *Damon and Phintias*: this anecdote recording the exemplary friendship was earlier recounted by Cicero in *Tusc.* 5. 63, where the affectionate pair are stated to be Pythagoreans. A variant of the story is recounted by Iamblichus, *Life of Pythagoras* 33, according to which Dionysius II was testing the Pythagoreans' capacity for friendship. The story is probably apocryphal.

46 *when we perpetrated the destruction of Corinth*: see 1. 35 and n., where Cicero offers a qualified apologia for the destruction of the city by L. Mummius in 146 BC.

Even harsher was the decree of the Athenians: (this is the obvious sense of the Latin, as against Dyck's 'The Athenians also acted too harshly'; it is true that if Cicero had cited the slaughter of the male population and the enslavement of women and children, the comparison would be ludicrous, but he refers here only to the destruction of the city). For the decree, see Aelian, *Varia Historia* 2. 9, specifying the severing of the right thumbs of the Aeginetans 'to prevent their ability to wield a spear while still being able to row'. Plutarch, *Lysander* 9. 7, restricts the application of the decree to prisoners-of-war; it is uncertain if the decree was ever carried out.

47 *Pennus . . . and Papius*: M. Iunius Pennus as plebeian tribune in 126 BC passed his measure either to discourage public disorder at elections or

more generally to restrict the ever increasing flow of aliens into Rome. In 65 BC the plebeian tribune C. Papius put through a bill expelling from Rome non-citizens who claimed to have the franchise. The measure was probably directed at the Transpadanes, whose aspiration to the citizenship was being supported by Crassus and Caesar.

47 *the law of Crassus and Scaevola*: for L. Licinius Crassus, see 1. 108 n.; for Q. Mucius Scaevola, 1. 116 n. They were colleagues as aediles, praetors, and finally consuls in 95 BC. Their *lex Licinia Mucia*, passed in that year, debarring aliens from claiming the rights of citizens, was a contributory cause of the Social War of 91 BC, when the Italians resorted to armed rebellion to obtain access to citizen privileges.

   the disaster at Cannae: this was the scene of the greatest military humiliation in Rome's history, when in 216 BC Hannibal crushed the Roman forces in Apulia. For the idealized Roman reaction to the defeat, see 3. 114.

48 *Cyrsilus urged them . . . to admit Xerxes*: in 480 BC Themistocles persuaded the Athenians to evacuate the city in the face of the Persian invasion led by Xerxes. Demosthenes, *De corona* 204, records that the citizens stoned to death not only Cyrsilus but also his wife. In the outcome, the Persian naval forces were defeated at Salamis (1. 75, 1. 108 nn.)

49 *a plan for the safety of the state*: the anecdote that follows characterizes Themistocles as a devious trickster (cf. 1. 108 n.) in contrast to Aristides, who is idealized as a man of honour (cf. 3. 16, 87). According to Plutarch, *Them.* 20. 1–2, Themistocles' plan was to burn the entire Greek fleet, not the Spartan ships alone, and the fleet was drawn up at Pagasae, not in the Spartan port of Gytheum.

   while allowing the pirates to pay nothing: when Pompey settled more than 20,000 pirates in Cilicia after he cleared the Mediterranean of them in 67 BC, taxes were not levied from them, whereas the provinces after the final defeat of Macedon were obliged to make contributions.

§§ 50–7: Can reticence in applying the principle of Caveat emptor be reconciled with the honourable?

50 *As an example*: Cicero will probably have drawn this example from Hecato, together with similar cases listed at 3. 89. Hecato may well

have presented the case as a dialogue between two Stoic spokesmen (on whom, see the next note) offering differing interpretations.

51 *Diogenes of Babylon ... his pupil Antipater*: Diogenes (*c.*240–152 BC) was a pupil of Chrysippus (3. 42 n.); he himself later became the head of the Stoic school. He visited Rome with the Academic Carneades and the Peripatetic Critolaus in 156/5 BC, and stimulated interest in the Stoic philosophy there. Antipater of Tarsus succeeded him as head of the Porch. Both Diogenes and Antipater were teachers of Panaetius.

52 *the nature of the gods or the highest good*: Cicero selects two centrally important topics in Stoic philosophy which he had previously treated in separate dialogues, *De natura deorum* and *De finibus*.

53 *that forbids a man to possess anything of his own*: this statement attributed to Diogenes is irrelevant to the argument. Antipater is not claiming that all property is owned in common, but that in commercial transactions both buyer and seller should observe equity.

54 *a lapse which at Athens incurs a public curse*: such a discourtesy was associated with refusal to offer water or fire (see 1. 52), in that all three attracted a public curse.

55 *When a buyer is free to exercise his judgement*: the relevant provision in Roman law (*Digest* 18. 1. 43) stipulated that a vendor was not bound by the claims made in advertising the sale so long as the buyer was able to judge the situation for himself. See 3. 68–9 below.

57 *The answer, then, seems to be*: Cicero's 'rule' is echoed by Aquinas at *ST* 2a2ae 77. 3, where Diogenes' rhetorical question at the end of § 55 (what is so lunatic ... ?) is cited and answered as follows: 'A man is not bound to announce through the auctioneer any fault in what he is to sell, for if he did so, buyers would be put off ... But he must inform a potential buyer individually, who can then weigh all the features, good and bad, with each other.'

§§ 58–64: Dishonesty and scrupulousness in business-transactions

58 *Gaius Canius, a Roman knight not devoid of native wit*: Cicero may have heard the anecdote which follows when he was quaestor in Sicily in 75 BC. Since Canius appeared in court on behalf of P. Rutilius in the trial of 116 BC, the incident may date to the final years of the second century. Cicero recounts an example of Canius' wit at *De oratore* 2. 280.

59 *completed the transaction*: this was done either by formal contract drawn up by the banker (so Alan Watson, *The Law of Obligations in the Later Roman Republic*, Oxford 1965, 30 ff.), or, if Pythius was a Greek not holding Roman citizenship, by *stipulatio* (by which the vendor elicited a formal guarantee from the purchaser).

60 *Gaius Aquilius*: the celebrated jurist, praetor with Cicero in 66 BC, put through his bill condemning fraud either during his praetorship or more probably in the years following. At *N.D.* 3. 74 Cicero says that he 'swept every kind of deception into that net of his. Aquilius indeed believes that malicious fraud has been netted when there has been a pretence of doing one thing and actual performance of another'.

61 *the Twelve Tables . . . the Laetorian law . . . as good faith demands*: the Twelve Tables, the earliest code of laws at Rome drawn up almost certainly in 451–450 BC, included provision for the proper disposition of wills. Nothing is known of the Laetorius (his name itself is disputed; here and at *N.D.* 3. 74 some editors read Plaetorius) who passed a bill to protect minors. The reference in Plautus, *Pseudolus* 303 (staged in 191 BC) suggests that the bill was passed in the years immediately before that date. For the types of case in which the formula AS GOOD FAITH DEMANDS was invoked, see 3. 70 below.

fairer and better . . . honest negotiation as between honest parties: the first of these formulas was invoked when after a divorce, a claim was advanced for the return of a dowry, and the second when property was assigned to another on the understanding that it would later be restored.

62 *Quintus Scaevola*: see 1. 116n., 3. 47.

led Ennius to say: the citation, which Cicero again quotes in a letter to Trebonius (*Fam.* 7. 6. 2), is from the *Medea* (fr. 271 Warmington). A similar sentiment from *Medea* of Euripides is quoted by Cicero in Greek in a letter to Julius Caesar (*Fam.* 13. 15. 2).

63 *Hecato of Rhodes*: this Stoic philosopher, pupil of Panaetius and fellow-student of Posidonius, flourished about 100 BC. The work which Cicero calls here and at 3. 89 below *On Obligation(s)* was actually entitled *On the Fitting*. The Quintus Aelius Tubero to whom it was addressed was a friend of Panaetius, who dedicated his work *On Enduring Pain* to him (so Cicero, *Fin.* 4. 23). Cicero respected him more as a philosopher than a literary stylist (*De oratore* 3. 87; *Brutus* 117–18).

64 *We do not readily encounter an honest man who fills the bill*: Cicero

candidly admits that his recommendations for behaviour are far removed from the everyday practices of first-century Rome.

§§ 65–72: Sharp practice in commercial transactions, and the civil law

65 *defects specified by word of mouth*: that is, specified by the buyer.

the penalty incurred should be doubled: see Watson (3. 59 n.), 81 ff.

any defect . . . must be made good: this certainly became statutory later, but in Cicero's day may have rested on the judge's interpretation of 'good faith' (see 3. 70).

66 *An example*: Cicero may have been made aware of this case after being elected to the college of augurs in 53 BC. It had been contested some 40 years earlier. 'The citadel' refers to the observation-post on the Capitol, from where the augurs watched the flight of birds to ensure good augury for the conduct of public business. The house on the Caelian hill to the east apparently impeded the view. Centumalus is not otherwise known; Lanarius played a minor military role in the suppression of the rising of Sertorius, when in 81 BC he routed and killed Sertorius' lieutenant Julius Salinator, who was controlling the passage through the Pyrenees (Plutarch, *Sertorius* 7. 3).

Marcus Cato, father of our contemporary Cato: for Cato Vticensis ('our contemporary'), see 1. 112 n. His father, Marcus Porcius Cato, was a plebeian tribune in 99 BC but died whilst contesting the praetorship (Gellius 13. 20. 4).

67 *Marcus Marius Gratidianus . . . Gaius Sergius Orata*: the family connection of Gratidianus with Cicero was remote: Gratidianus' father was the brother-in-law of Cicero's grandfather. Gratidianus was a *popularis* in politics, supporting Marius against Sulla; he was plebeian tribune in 87 and praetor twice, probably in the successive years 85 and 84 BC. After Sulla's march on Rome he was manhandled and killed, and his head was carried through the streets by no other than Catiline (see B. Marshall, *CQ* 35 (1985), 124 ff.). This lawsuit revolved round the fact that Sergius Orata had bought a property on the Lucrine Lake, and before selling it to Gratidianus had allocated the fishing rights to others. Orata then bought back the property to develop oyster-ponds there, but when the fishermen objected he sought to rescind the sale.

67 *Crassus acted for Orata, and Antonius defended Gratidianus*: these two
were the leading advocates during Cicero's boyhood; for Crassus, see
1. 108n., and for Antonius, 2. 47n. At *De oratore* 1. 178, Cicero represents Crassus claiming, in reference to this case, 'our entire defence
was surely concerned solely with the law'. The final comment in this
section ('To make it clear to you that our forbears disapproved of tricksters') strongly suggests that Antonius won the case.

68 *as a sort of snare*: I omit the words that follow in the MSS, *domum
propter uitia uendas* ('sell a house because of its faults'), since editors
bracket them as a gloss.

69 *I have often made the point earlier*: see 1. 50–8, especially 53 and 57,
where especial emphasis is laid on the link between citizens of the same
state.

international law and civil law: at *Laws* 2. 10–11, Cicero expatiates at
greater length on the distinction between divine law, which is the
source of international law, and the civil law which 'meets the tempor-
ary needs of communities'.

a ... model of true law ... its outline and hazy appearances: Cicero makes
oblique reference to Plato's Theory of Forms, as outlined in the
Phaedo (which he had earlier translated) and the *Republic* (476a), to
indicate that absolute law and justice exist only in the realm of the
Forms, of which in this world we have only a hazy representation; perhaps Plato's celebrated myth of the cave is in his mind (*Rep.* 514aff.).

70 *Quintus Scaevola the chief priest*: for Scaevola, see 1. 116, 3. 47nn. He
became chief priest in 89 BC; Cicero gives him the designation here
to distinguish him from the Quintus Mucius Scaevola mentioned
at 1. 109.

71 *By edict of the aediles*: the aediles were charged with the maintenance
and supervision of public buildings, including regulation of the slave-
market. This edict is cited by Gellius 4. 2. 1 and by the *Digest* 21. 1. 1. 1.
The phrase 'who should have had knowledge' suggests that in Cicero's
day the vendor could plead ignorance as excuse for a defective sale,
whereas later (*Digest* 21. 1. 1. 2) it was not accepted as an excuse.
If conscious suppression of such defects was proved, the sale was
rescinded.

in a different category: it was assumed that those who had recently
inherited a slave could not be expected to know his earlier history.

72 *ill-will posing as rational thought*: ill-will (*malitia*) is defined by Cicero

at *N.D.* 3. 75 as 'the crafty and deceitful intention of doing harm'. The comment here should be read as postscript to 3. 62, where Ennius claims that the wise man (i.e., 'using rational thought') will look to his own self-interest (the implication being that he will do someone else down).

§§ 73–8: So-called 'good men' who pursue the apparently useful

73 *Marcus Crassus and Quintus Hortensius, the most influential men of the day*: M. Licinius Crassus (1. 25 n.) and Q. Hortensius Hortalus (2. 57 n.) were consuls in 70 and 69 BC respectively; this discreditable incident is to be dated shortly before that time.

great affection for one . . . no repugnance for the other: earlier in his career, Cicero had attracted Hortensius' resentment when he outshone him in the courts, and there was coolness between them when Cicero was exiled, but subsequently relations between them were cordial. Cicero praises Hortensius' oratory warmly in the *De oratore* (3. 228 ff.), and their common intellectual interests were signalled when Cicero entitled his protreptic to philosophy *Hortensius*. Crassus on the other hand was Cicero's *bête noire*; in addition to the criticism of him here in § 75, the sardonic comments on the rich man at *Paradoxa* 45–6 are clearly directed against him. Crassus died at Carrhae in operations against Parthia in 53 BC.

74 *Marcus Satrius*: having taken his uncle's name, he became L. Minucius Basilus. A Caesarian supporter, he obtained the praetorship in 45 BC, and in the summer of 44 was appointed patron of Picenum and the Sabines. Cicero waxes indignant here about this ('what a shameful stain on our times!'), because Basilus was a henchman of Mark Antony and had allegedly gained this preferment by force of arms (so Cicero's *Second Philippic* 107). He is to be distinguished from the Minucius Basilus who was a conspirator in the assassination of Caesar.

as I argued in the first book: see 1. 23, 28–9.

even legitimate legacies . . . with evil intent: legacy-hunters (*captatores*) were a notorious blot on Roman society, and the satirists targeted them for abuse; see Horace, *Satires* 2. 5; Juvenal 5. 98, 12. 93 ff.; Petronius 141.

75 *he would have danced a jig in the forum*: that is, he would stoop to activities which no Roman with a sense of decorum would contemplate; see 3. 93 below.

76 *the notion of the good man which lies enveloped in his mind*: 'notion' (*notio*)
is here used technically in the Stoic–Academic sense of 'a concept
implanted and already formed in the mind, requiring elucidation' (so
Cicero, *Topica* 31).

unless he has been the victim of injustice: see 1. 20 above. As Ambrose,
De officiis 1. 131 points out, Christian ideals of behaviour here part
company with those of the Stoics (but not with those of Socrates, who
rebuts Polemarchus' definition of justice ('doing good to friends and
harming enemies') at *Rep.* 335aff.)

77 *my father's story of the former consul Gaius Fimbria*: Gaius Flavius Fimbria was a 'new man' who became consul in 104 BC with Marius. Cicero
expresses admiration for his worthy character also at *Brutus* 129 and
Pro Plancio 12. In this type of case, both sides in the suit deposited
money which was forfeited by the losing party. Fimbria's conception
of 'the good man' usefully epitomizes the Roman ideal of a man of
integrity active in the service of the state (see 1. 20n.). Pinthia's
absence from the political scene disqualifies him.

not merely by Socrates but also by Fimbria: the conjunction of the two is
surprising at first sight, given the specifically Roman sense lent to 'the
good man'. But Cicero thinks of Socrates' alleged fondness for the
expression *kalos k'agathos* ('gentleman'), which may in fact bear a
political connotation.

'to play "How many fingers have I up?" . . . *in the dark'*: this game of
micare, further attested at Petronius 44. 7 (cf. Cicero, *Fin.* 2. 52), is still
played in rural parts of Italy under the title of *morra*.

78 *to Gyges, nor to that hypothetical person I cited*: see 3. 38 and 75.

§§ 79–88: Corruption in high places in pursuit of the apparently useful

79 *Gaius Marius' hopes of attaining the consulship were remote*: Marius
(1. 76 n.), a 'new man' of equestrian family, reached the praetorship in
115 BC. Further political progress was blocked by senatorial conserva-
tives, but Metellus appointed him his legate in the war against
Jugurtha in 109 BC. But when Marius aspired to the consulship,
Metellus ridiculed the notion; Marius accordingly intrigued against
his superior at Rome, and secured not only the consulship for 107 BC,
but also the command against Jugurtha. Cicero's bias against Marius

is counterbalanced by Sallust's political stance in the *Bellum Iugurthinum*.

80 *my kinsman Gratidianus*: see 3. 67 n. It was probably in his first praetorship of 85 BC that he seized this opportunity of gaining popularity. The edict probably included the testing of coins by expert slaves or freedmen; they were then sealed in bags tagged to guarantee the authenticity of the coins.

81 *his election . . . to the consulship*: he did not in fact enter the office, but met the grisly end described in 3. 67 n.

notion: the Latin is *notio*, again as at 3. 76 used in the technical sense cited in the n. there.

82 [*For what difference . . . of the beast?*]: this sentence is excised as a gloss by editors including Winterbottom, or alternatively transposed to 3. 82 or 3. 32 where the contexts make it more appropriate.

the man who even sought . . . would confer power on himself: the reference is to Pompey the Great, hitherto cited (1. 78, 2. 20, 2. 45) respectfully in this treatise. Cicero had been sharply critical in his correspondence of Pompey's lack of leadership in the Civil War, but his attitude towards him softened following his death and the dictatorship of Caesar. Here, however, he recalls with bitterness the so-called 'First Triumvirate' of Caesar, Pompey, and Crassus which when forged in 60 BC presaged the end of senatorial government. Caesar cemented the alliance by giving his daughter Julia in marriage to Pompey in the following year, but she died in 54 BC.

the Greek lines from The Phoenician Women: the citation is from Euripides, *Phoenissae* 524–5; the Greek supports the punctuation as here. The words are spoken by Eteocles, son of Oedipus; the father, after discovering that he had unwittingly killed his father and married his mother, laid a curse on his sons, the working out of which is the theme of the play.

83 *the man who lusted to become king of the Roman people*: Cicero's catalogue of those guilty of political corruption reaches its climax with this impassioned condemnation of Julius Caesar, 'the king' who has undermined Roman law and Roman freedom. Caesar never accepted the title *rex*, well knowing the abhorrence it roused in republican breasts, but his enemies pointed to the honours showered on him (see Suetonius, *Iulius* 76) to depict him as aspiring to it.

the title of Father: Caesar (like Cicero in 63 BC after the Catilinarian conspiracy) was proclaimed *Pater patriae* following his final victory in the Civil War in 45 BC.

84 *As Accius puts it*: this is a citation from an unknown play; the reference
to Tantalus and Pelops, and the kingdom bequeathed to them, suggests that it may have been the *Atreus* (1. 97n.).

85 *the man who deprives him of it*: the reference is to tyrannicides in general, but Brutus, chief assassin of Caesar, is chiefly in his friend
Cicero's mind.

86 *Gaius Fabricius*: Gaius Fabricius Luscinus, consul in 282 and 278 BC,
was a prominent military leader in Rome's subjugation of southern
Italy and notably in the war conducted there with Pyrrhus of Epirus
(280–275 BC). His later fame rested predominantly on this anecdote of
his incorruptibility, recorded variously in the sources. In Plutarch's
version (*Pyrrhus* 21), which dates the incident before the battle of
Asculum (279 BC), Pyrrhus' physician sends a messenger to the
Roman camp offering to poison the king, and Fabricius writes to
Pyrrhus to warn him. Cicero at *Fin.* 5. 64 gives the credit of warning
the king to both consuls Aemilius Papius and Fabricius. According to
Valerius Antias (*HRR* fr. 21), the would-be assassin was Timochares,
friend of Pyrrhus.

87 *the counterpart in this city of Aristides at Athens*: the comparison
between the two is confined to their justice and incorruptibility; for
Aristides' reputation in this regard, see 3. 16 and 49nn.

the well-known proposal of Lucius Philippus: for L. Marcius Philippus
(consul 91 BC), see 1. 108, 2. 59, 2. 73nn. Sulla at the close of the First
Mithridatic War had granted Asian communities immunity from
taxes in return for their contributions made in his support. The
Roman treasury at this date was dependent on the levies from overseas, since citizens were no longer taxed; additional funds were needed
for prosecuting the war with Sertorius in Spain.

the plighted word of pirates is more trustworthy: see 2. 40 and n.

88 *I often disagreed even with my good friend Cato*: for the Younger Cato,
see 1. 112, 3. 66nn. As quaestor (paymaster) in 64 BC, he insisted on all
debts to the treasury being paid promptly and in full, by both citizens
and allies. In 61 BC a company of equestrian tax-collectors had bid too
high for an Asian tax contract; Cato, a powerful voice in the senate,
blocked renegotiation of it, thereby increasing tension between equestrians and senators. Cicero, working for greater harmony between the
two orders, admired Cato's integrity but criticized his political obdu-
racy (*Att.* 1. 17. 9, 1. 18. 7).

Curio too . . . the cause of the Transpadanes: C. Scribonius Curio

(2. 59 n.) was a powerful figure in the senate, becoming consul in 76 and censor in 61 BC. Following the Social War, Italian communities south of the Po received full citizenship; those north of the river were granted the status of Latin colonies by the *lex Pompeia de Transpadanis* of 89 BC. Their subsequent demand for full citizenship was supported by Caesar and Crassus in the mid-6os, the time when Curio probably opposed it. Caesar granted them full citizenship in 49 BC by the *lex Roscia*.

§§ 89–92: Hypothetical cases raised by the Stoic Hecato

89 *Hecato's work* On Obligations: see 3. 63 and n. Hecato there argues that his sole obligation is not to transgress the laws. Since a Roman master had total discretion over his slaves, Hecato presumably argued that he could starve them when food was dear ('what he regards as the useful'), and that in the second case he could save the horse rather than the slave.

on the grounds that it would be unjust: this hypothetical case had been raised by Cicero earlier at *Rep.* 3. 30, though there the persons involved are a stronger man and a weaker. According to Lactantius (to whom we owe this fragment of *Rep.*) Carneades, most influential of Academics, argued that it would be unjust for the stronger man to dislodge the weaker, but that he would be foolish not to do so. Hecato here posits the problem in Stoic terms, replacing the stronger and the weaker man with a sage and a fool, and offers the Stoic solution which Cicero in *Rep.* does not allow the spokesman Laelius to give. In the second problem of ship's owner versus passenger, he has recourse as at 3. 63 to the letter of the law, arguing not from natural justice but from rights of ownership. Presumably if the occupant of the plank had been a stowaway, Hecato would have argued that the captain would be justified in dislodging him!

90 *or a game of chance*: literally, by the game 'How many fingers . . .?', as at 3. 77.

No, that would be impious: the solution advanced here is apparently at odds with Cicero's own order of priorities at 1. 160. He states there that obligations are owed first to the immortal gods (so the father here, by plundering shrines, is guilty of sacrilege and merits punishment), secondly to one's country, and only thirdly to one's parents. (Cicero is himself inconsistent, in that at 1. 58 he ignores the claims of the gods, and brackets fatherland and parents together as taking precedence over all others.) But Cicero would certainly have agreed with Hecato that if the fatherland was in danger of tyranny or other betrayal, its claims would override those of parents.

91 *Diogenes says yes, but Antipater says no*: for the two Stoics who are the spokesmen here and earlier in Hecato's dialogues, see 3. 51 n. Diogenes is represented throughout as the more permissive, abiding by the letter of the law. Sulla had introduced a new court to deal with forgery of coins (and forgery of wills) in the 80s BC, but passing counterfeit coins off after unwittingly accepting them did not contravene the law.

as required by civil law: see 3. 71 and n.

92 *brass when it is actually gold*: like the problem of the two men contesting tenure of the one plank in shipwreck (§ 89), this dilemma had been advanced by Carneades and incorporated by Cicero into his *Republic* (3. 29, part of the fragment supplied by Lactantius).

§§ 92–95: Promises and agreements are not always binding

have been made without compulsion or malicious deceit: this formulation is incorporated in expanded form later in the *Digest* (2. 14. 7. 7).

93 *should dance openly . . . in the forum*: like the previous instance of the man with the dropsy, this example borders on the absurd, the equivalent in Stoic disputation of esoteric controversies in the schools of rhetoric. For Roman repugnance at such undignified behaviour as singing or dancing in a public place, see 1. 145, 3. 75. Tacitus similarly condemns members of the nobility for performing on the stage (*Annals* 14. 20).

94 *Phaethon asked to be taken up in his father's chariot*: for an extended account of this celebrated myth, see Ovid, *Met.* 2. 31 ff.

the promise which Theseus exacted from Neptune: see 1. 32 n. Cicero joins this example to the Phaethon myth also at *N.D.* 3. 76, but for a different purpose.

95 *Agamemnon . . . sacrificed Iphigenia*: Cicero follows the version of the story in which Agamemnon and the Greek fleet were delayed at Aulis by contrary winds, which induced him to vow the sacrifice of the fairest thing born in that year to obtain fair weather. His daughter

Iphigenia proved to be that 'fairest thing'. The story passed from Greek tragedy into Roman literature, most memorably in Lucretius' condemnation of religious superstition at 1. 84 ff.; see also Ovid, *Met*. 12. 14 ff.

it would be a sin to give it back: This example derives from Plato, *Rep.* 331 C in the first discussion of the nature of justice: does it consist simply of speaking the truth, and paying what you owe?

should you return what he had entrusted to you: Cicero implicitly suggests that such money when returned would be used to further the destruction of the country.

§§ 96–115: The apparently useful and the third virtue of greatness of spirit

96 *We have already discussed prudence . . . we have discussed justice*: Cicero refers here not to the lengthy discussions in Book 1, but to his review of the relation between the useful and the honourable in Book 3. From 3. 40 onward he has cited a series of examples in which the apparently useful has either overridden the claims of justice, or has been rejected in the interests of justice. Some of the unjust practices have been cloaked by bogus appeals to prudence. Cicero has not discussed them systematically under the separate headings of the two virtues.

97 *Ulysses thought it a useful ploy*: the contrast between the Homeric Odysseus (= Ulysses) and the character as portrayed later in tragedy is well brought out by W. B. Stanford, *The Ulysses Theme in Literature* (Oxford 1962). The tradition that he tried to evade military service at Troy by feigning madness, and that his chicanery was exposed when as he ploughed the beach he swerved to avoid his baby son Telemachus planted in his path by Palamedes, is a frequent theme in Greek and Roman literature.

98 *this was the dressing-down he received from Ajax*: since Ajax is addressing the assembled host ('As you all know'), the extract is presumably from the *Armorum Iudicium* of either Pacuvius or Accius.

99 *not only with the foe but also with the waves*: against the foe 'throughout the *Iliad* he is both brave and sagacious' (*OCD*); the *Odyssey* recounts his ten-year struggle with the waves as he makes his way home.

Marcus Atilius Regulus: for Cicero, Regulus is the supreme example of the hero who opted for the honourable course in preference to the

apparently useful. The celebrated legend of Regulus' peace mission to
Rome and subsequent return to Carthage to face torture and death is
accepted by Cicero as historical. But Polybius (1. 35) makes no mention of it, an extraordinary omission had he known of it. Most scholars
assume that the legend was created to efface the cruelty of Regulus'
widow, who tortured two Punic prisoners so severely that one of them
died. If this theory is sound, Regulus died in captivity at Carthage
having made no such journey to Rome.

99 *the Spartan Xanthippus . . . Hamilcar, father of Hannibal*: during his
second consulship in 256 BC, Regulus took sole command in Africa.
Having defeated the Carthaginians and captured Tunis, he offered
such harsh peace terms that they were rejected, and in the spring of
255 the spirits of the Carthaginians revived with the arrival of Spartan
mercenaries under Xanthippus. He defeated the Romans not in
ambush, as Cicero claims, but in the open field, and Regulus was taken
prisoner. Cicero is mistaken in assuming that Hannibal's father was in
overall command; he becomes prominent only in 247 BC. It is another
Hamilcar who was commander in 255 (see Polybius 1. 24. 3, 1. 44. 1
with Walbank's nn.).

100 *deprived of sleep and thus slowly killed*: Cicero's version squares with the
oldest extant account of the legend, that of the middle annalist Sempronius Tuditanus (consul 129 BC): 'Tuditanus records that Regulus
was for long prevented from sleeping, and in this way was deprived of
life' (Gellius 7. 4. 4.). See also Cicero, *Fin.* 2. 65, 5. 82 (this last passage
adds starvation as an additional cause of death).

101 *Can any action be useful . . . if it is not useful to the state?*: see 3. 27 above.

102 *All philosophers . . . share the view that God is never angry*: Cicero here is
contrasting the rational attitudes of philosophers of all schools with
the superstition endemic in Roman religious cults. He draws particular attention to the Epicureans (the statement that 'God experiences
no trouble himself and imposes it on no other' paraphrases Epicurus,
Principal Doctrines 1; see Cicero, *N.D.* 1. 85) and to the Stoics, who
proclaim the benevolence of a Providence which smiles on man and
provides for all his needs (*N.D.* 2. 154 ff.).

'Take the least of evils': for the proverbial phrase, see 3. 3 n.

as voiced by Accius: in Accius' play *Atreus* (fr. 192–3 Warmington)
Pelops had laid a curse on his sons Atreus and Thyestes. When Atreus
claimed the throne on Pelops' death, Thyestes seduced his brother's
wife Aerope, and stole the ram with the golden fleece which was said to

give the right to rule. In revenge, Atreus pretended to be reconciled to him, pledging good faith, but then served Thyestes' sons up to him on a platter. Hence Thyestes' rhetorical question, 'Did you break your faith?' Atreus' reply asserts that no promise to a faithless person is binding, and this is the relevance of the extract to Regulus' promise to the Carthaginians to return, for they were traditionally regarded as perfidious.

103 *the compulsion of enemy violence ought not to have been sanctioned*: Cicero earlier (1. 32) states that a promise forcibly extracted by fear ought not to stand, but at § 108 below he asserts that this did not apply in Regulus' case.

104 *As Ennius so splendidly says*: the citation may be from his *Medea* (cf. the similar expression in Euripides, *Medea* 168ff.) or from *Thyestes* (as comment on Atreus' treachery).

on the Capitol, as a speech of Cato attests: Livy (1. 21. 4) states that Numa established a shrine there, but Fides had not been incorporated into the Roman Pantheon so early. Cato's speech (now lost) presumably referred to its erection by Atilius Caiatinus (censor 247 BC); Aemilius Scaurus restored it in the early first century BC (Cicero, *N.D.* 2. 61).

105 *pain is not merely not the greatest evil, but is not an evil at all*: it was the unanimous view of the older Stoics that pleasure and pain were 'things indifferent', and the doctrine was maintained by Panaetius and Posidonius (see 2. 37n.). For discussion of the problems associated with the teaching, see Rist, *Stoic Philosophy*, ch. 3.

106 *philosophers of more intense views . . . those who are less stringent*: Cicero refers to Stoics and Peripatetics respectively.

he had to adhere closely to the character: since Atreus was an unscrupulous king, he presents an unscrupulous argument.

107 *Even warfare has its code of law*: justice in warfare is discussed at 1. 35ff.

108 *what you have sworn with sincere intent*: the phrase *ex animi sententia* is the traditional formula for a solemn oath; see Livy 22. 53. 10–11. (the oath sworn by the young Scipio after Cannae), 43. 15. 8; Quintilian 8. 5. 1.

Euripides expresses this well: in his play *Hippolytus* (612), the pious hero in dialogue with the nurse says that he will reveal his stepmother's sacrilegious proposal to his father Theseus, in spite of the oath to secrecy which he has unwittingly sworn.

108 *our entire fetial law*: see 1. 36n.

109 *Titus Veturius and Spurius Postumius*: the two men held their second
joint consulship in 321 BC in the course of the Second Samnite War.
After a humiliating defeat at Caudium, they were compelled to make
peace with the victors. It is generally agreed that this was a treaty (*foe-
dus*; so Claudius Quadrigarius cited by Livy 9. 5. 2), and not a pledge
with guarantors (*sponsio*; so Livy himself). The detail as recounted
here of the heroic self-sacrifice of Postumius, so similar to that of
Regulus earlier and to that of Mancinus later (see the n. below), is
highly dubious, especially as according to Livy (9. 11. 1f.) the
Samnites declined to accept his surrender. For the controverted
details, see *CAH* 7. 2^2, 370–1.

Tiberius Minucius and Quintus Maelius: in Livy the plebeian tribunes
are named as L. Livius and Q. Maelius, the version of his source
Valerius Antias; Cicero's version, following Claudius Quadrigarius, is
the more reliable. It is not clear why the plebeian tribunes are cited as
guarantors of the peace; possibly there is confusion with the military
tribunes who are named (Livy 9. 5. 4) among the guarantors.

*Gaius Mancinus had made a treaty with the Numantines without senator-
ial authority*: as consul for 137 BC he was assigned the command in
Nearer Spain. While withdrawing his forces from the walls of Numantia, he was surrounded and surrendered, promising peace with a
solemn oath 'on equal terms' (Appian, *Hisp.* 347). L. Furius Philus
and Sex. Atilius, consuls for 137 BC, proposed that he be surrendered
to allow resumption of hostilities. The Numantines declined to accept
him, and Mancinus returned to Rome, resuming his political career
there. Numantia eventually fell to Scipio Aemilianus in 133 BC.

Mancinus behaved more honourably than Quintus Pompeius: the behaviour of the two commanders is earlier contrasted by Cicero at *Rep.*
3. 28. Pompeius as proconsul in 139 BC was compelled to make a
similar treaty with the Numantines, but later disowned it. He
persuaded the senate not to surrender him. His conduct was similarly
censured by Cicero at *Fin.* 2. 54.

110 *the prisoners would certainly have been restored*: assuming for a moment
that Regulus' return to Rome was historical, we may be more doubtful
than Cicero was that the Roman senate would have agreed to the
exchange, when we recall the defiant stance in similar circumstances
after Cannae (see 3. 114).

111 *This is shown by the laws of the Twelve Tables . . . and by the . . . penalties*

imposed by the censors: Gellius 20. 1. 53 laments that the punishment prescribed by the Twelve Tables for giving false testimony has fallen into abeyance. The 'sacred' laws were those reinforced by an oath which if contravened rendered lives and property forfeit. Livy's moralizing history repeatedly ascribes national disasters to the failure to observe good faith. For an example of penalties imposed by the censors for contravening sworn oaths, see 1. 40.

112 *Lucius Manlius . . . was indicted by the plebian tribune Pomponius*: in 363 BC L. Manlius Imperiosus was appointed dictator to avert a plague by driving a nail into the wall of the sanctuary of Jupiter Capitolinus, a procedure hallowed by ancient practice. He exploited tenure of the office to raise a military levy to make war on the Hernici; according to Livy (7. 3. 9) not only Pomponius but all the tribunes compelled him to lay down the office. Thereupon Pomponius indicted him for violent assaults on citizens while he was raising the levy. Livy, like Cicero, states that the virtual enslavement of the son was added to the charges (7. 4. 4ff.); his account of how the young man exacted an oath from the tribune is so close to Cicero's that they must have drawn on the same source, Claudius Quadrigarius or Valerius Antias.

the man who acquired his surname at the river Anio: Livy's celebrated account of the duel between Titus Manlius and the Gaul in 361 BC is told to underline the virtues of *disciplina* (Manlius seeks the permission of his commander before joining battle) and *clementia* (after killing the Gaul, he robs the corpse only of its collar (*torques*), the gesture which gained him his surname Torquatus (Livy 7. 10. 11–13). He later held the consulship three times in 347, 344, and 340 BC; in his third consulship he defeated the Latins at the river Veseris close to Mt Vesuvius (Livy 8. 19. 1 ff.). Earlier in the fighting of that year, his son had engaged in a duel with the Tusculan cavalry commander Geminus Marcius, contrary to his father's orders (Livy 8. 7. 1 ff.), and his father had him publicly executed to underline the importance of military discipline; hence here 'bitterly harsh towards his son'.

113 *the ten Romans sent by Hannibal to the senate . . . deserve rebuke*: after the Roman defeat at the hands of Hannibal at the battle of Cannae in 216 BC, the Carthaginian leader attempted to raise funds by offering to release the Roman prisoners on payment of a ransom. He sent ten of the Roman captives to Rome to negotiate, having compelled them to swear an oath to return to him if they failed. As Cicero reports, one of our two main authorities, Polybius (6. 58. 3ff.), 'an outstandingly good source' who in Mommsen's words is 'like the sun

that shines on the field of Roman history', reports that nine of the
ten did return of their own free will, and the tenth, who had tried
to avoid having to return by adopting the ruse described here, was
put in irons and escorted back to Hannibal. Livy's lengthy account of
the episode (22. 58ff.) initially agrees with Polybius, but then
recounts another version, that all ten remained in Rome until three
more delegates arrived. When the Roman senate dismissed the
proposed plan to ransom the captives, the three duly returned to
Hannibal, but the ten stayed in Rome claiming to have absolved themselves of their oath. The next censors condemned them in such harsh
terms that some of them committed suicide, and the rest never
thereafter ventured out in daylight. In spite of Polybius' eminence as
historian, this version, deriving from Acilius (see § 115 below) has
the ring of truth; it clearly lies behind Cicero's first sentence in this
paragraph.

114 *the really significant part of the story is this*: for the 8,000 troops left to
guard the Roman camp, see Polybius 6. 58. 2. The 'small payment',
according to Polybius, was three minae per captive; according to Livy
(22. 58. 3) it was 500 *quadrigati nummi* for each cavalryman, 300 for
each footsoldier, and 100 for each slave (*quadrigati nummi* were later
coined as denarii; a mina was roughly equivalent to 100 denarii). The
Roman senate was indignant that the 8,000 men had surrendered
without a fight or without attempting to escape; hence the refusal to
ransom them. For Hannibal's dejection when he heard of this outcome, see Polybius 6. 58. 13.

115 *Gaius Acilius*: the earliest Roman annalists wrote in Greek in order to
parade Roman achievements before the Greek world. Acilius, fluent in
Greek (he interpreted for the group of Greek philosophers who visited
Rome in 155 BC) published his history in the late 140s BC. He could
have discussed the senate's reaction to Hannibal's proposal with par-
ticipants in the debate or with their sons.

§§ 116–20: The apparently useful and the fourth
virtue of temperance

116 *the Cyrenaics . . . and the Annicerii so-called*: for the two Aristippuses,
see 1. 148n. It is uncertain which was the founder of the Cyrenaic
school, though the close association of the elder with Socrates makes
him the less likely candidate. The Cyrenaics argued that bodily pleasure is the goal of life; they rated it higher than mental gratification.

Diogenes Laertes 2. 93 ff. states that there were three subgroups of Cyrenaics, one of them being the Annicerii, founded by Anniceris of Cyrene, who appears to have espoused a less extreme form of hedonism.

Epicurus . . . the supporter and sponsor of virtually the same doctrine: in fact the Epicurean doctrine of pleasure, as Cicero concedes at *Acad.* 2. 131, differs greatly from that of the Cyrenaics. In particular whereas for Aristippus the absence of pain was no pleasure, for Epicurus it was the height of contentment. For fuller accounts, see Rist, *Epicurus*, 100 ff.; Long, *Hellenistic Philosophy*, 61 ff.

117 *as Metrodorus has written*: Metrodorus, pupil and friend of Epicurus, seemed destined to succeed him as head of the school, but he died before his master in 278/7 BC.

For to begin with: Cicero in this paragraph sets the Epicurean ideal of pleasure against three of the four virtues—prudence, courage, and temperance—which together with justice form the four subdivisions of the honourable in Book I. In § 118 he concedes that Epicurus sought some accommodation with each of the three in his ethical teaching, but as climax he argues that pleasure as the highest good can certainly not be reconciled with justice.

119 *Callipho and Dinomachus*: these little-known philosophers may belong to the Academics or the Peripatetics. Callipho exercised considerable influence over Carneades the *doyen* of the Academic school, especially with his thesis that the *summum bonum* was the combination of virtue and pleasure (so Cicero, *Acad.* 2. 139, where the image of 'mating a brute beast with a man' also appears). Dinomachus is closely associated with Callipho in that doctrine; see *Fin.* 5. 21. The *floruit* of both is probably the early second century BC.

at greater length elsewhere: Cicero refers to his *De finibus*, in which the first two books are devoted to a critique of the Epicurean highest good, the second two to that of the Stoics, and the fifth to a review of the tenets of the Academy.

§ 121: Postscript

121 *among the lecture-notes of Cratippus*: see 1. 1 n.

If I had visited Athens . . . when I was on my way: Cicero left Tusculum to sail from Pompeii at the end of June 44 BC, and crossed to Sicily. But contrary winds detained him at Syracuse, and letters from Atticus and a meeting with Brutus convinced him that it would be unpatriotic to quit Italy. Shortly after returning he delivered on 2 September the *First Philippic*, a justification of his conduct since Caesar's assassination combined with temperate criticism of Antony's recent activities.

Index and Glossary of Names

the plan and returns to torture and death, 1. 39; 3. 99, 111, 113, 115

Atilius Serranus, Sex. (cos. 136), supports surrender of Mancinus to Numantines, 3. 119

Atreus, father of Agamemnon; in Accius' tragedy *Atreus* takes revenge on brother Thyestes by killing his children and serving them up at table, 1. 97; Thyestes had falsely sworn allegiance to him, 3. 106

Attic comedy, elegant and witty, 1. 104

Atticus *see* Pomponius

Aufidius Orestes, Cn. (cos. 71), gives public dinners as tithe-offerings, 2. 58

Augustine, Christian apologist, praises *Hortensius*, Introd. 2; knowledge of *De officiis*, Introd. 6

Augustus, Introd. 6; *see also* Octavius

Aurelius Cotta, C. (cos. 75), as aedile refused to mount public shows, 2. 59

Bardylis I (*c*.448–358), Illyrian king who disrupted Macedonian northern border until killed by Philip II; fair distribution of booty, 2. 40

Basilus *see* Minucius

Bede, his knowledge of *De officiis*, Introd. 6

Boethius, his knowledge of *De officiis*, Introd. 6

Brundisium, Cicero's detention in, Introd. 1

Bruno, Leonardo, his citation of *De officiis*, Introd. 6

Brutus *see* Iunius

Brutus, Cicero's history of Roman oratory, Introd. 2

Buchanan, George, Introd. 6

Caecilius Metellus Macedonicus Q. (cos. 143), his differences with Scipio Aemilianus harmoniously expressed, 1. 87

Caecilius Metellus Numidicus (cos. 109), insidiously undermined by Marius, 3. 79

Caelian hill, house on it obstructs the auspices, 3. 66

Caesar *see* Iulius

Callicratidas, Spartan admiral who after victory at Mytilene was defeated and drowned off the Arginusae islands, 1. 84; impetuous rather than crafty, 1. 109

Callipho, obscure philosopher proclaiming virtue and pleasure as the highest good, 3. 119

Calpurnius Lanarius, P., purchaser of house on Caelian hill, 3. 66

Calpurnius Piso Frugi, L. (cos. 133), as tribune passed first law against extortion, 2. 75

Calypso, nymph who detained Ulysses for seven years on Ogygia, 1. 113

Canius, C., Roman knight tricked into buying a house at Syracuse, 3. 58–60

Cannae, scene of Rome's greatest defeat (216), 1. 40; 3. 47, 113

Capitol at Rome, 3. 104

Carneades (214–129), founder of Third Academy; scepticism, Introd. 2; highest good, Introd. 5

Carthage/Carthaginians, destroyed by Rome, 1. 35; broke treaties, 1. 38; captured Regulus, Introd. 3; 1. 39; levelled by Aemilianus, 2. 76; Regulus and, 3. 99f., 110

Cassander (*c*.358–297), lieutenant of Alexander later governor of Macedonia and Greece; his father's letter of advice to him, 3. 48

Catilinarian conspiracy, Introd. 2

Catiline *see* Sergius

Cato *see* Porcius

Cato Maior, Cicero's treatise on old age, Introd. 2; 1. 151

Catulus *see* Lutatius

Catulus, first book of *Academica*, Introd. 2

Caudium, scene of Roman debacle in Second Samnite War, 3. 109

Celtiberi, intermittent wars with in north-central Spain 195–133, 1. 38

Chartres, school of, Introd. 6

Chremes, character in Terence's *Self-tormentor*, 1. 30

Chrysippus (*c*.280–207), third head of Stoa and most influential authority; his *Peri Kathekontos*, Introd. 3; epigram on pursuing self-interest, 3. 42

Cicero *see* Tullius

Cilicia, governorship of Cicero, Introd. 2

Cimbri, German tribe defeated in Po valley by Marius, 1. 38

Cimon, fifth-cent. Athenian statesman; his legendary hospitality, 2. 64

and orator at Athens, pupil of Plato but did not write philosophy, 1. 4; accomplished orator while a youth, 2. 47

De oratore, its philosophical content, Introd. 2

De senectute see *Cato Maior*

Diana, Roman goddess identified with Greek Artemis; Agamemnon sacrifices Iphigenia to her, 2. 95

Dicaearchus of Messene (fl. 326–296), Peripatetic philosopher, pupil of Aristotle, admired by Cicero; his *On the Extinction of Human Life*, 2. 16

Dinomachus, (prob. early second-cent.), little known philosopher who posited virtue and pleasure as the highest end, 3. 119

Diodotus (d. *c*.60), Stoic teacher and friend of Cicero, Introd. 2

Diogenes of Babylon (*c*.240–152), Stoic philosopher, pupil of Chrysippus and teacher of Panaetius, Introd. 4; permissive towards vendors, 3. 51 f., 55; and to passing counterfeit coins, 3. 91

Dion of Syracuse (*c*.408–354), uncle of Dionysius II whom he sought with Plato's guidance to make a philosopher-king; instructed by Plato, 1. 155

Dionysius I of Syracuse (430–367), extended Syracuse's hold over areas of Sicily and southern Italy; his fear of assassination, 2. 25

Dionysius II, tyrant of Syracuse 367–344; ousted for a decade 357–347, he surrendered to Timoleon in 344; his treatment of Damon and Phintias, 3. 45

Drusus *see* Livius

Ennius, Q. (239–169), father of Roman literature; poet of several genres, above all *Annales* (verse-history of Rome) and tragedies (free adaptations of Greek masters); citations from unknown plays, 1. 26 (*Thyestes?*), 51 f.; 2. 23 (?*Thyestes*), 62; 3. 104 (?*Medea* or *Thyestes*); citation from *Medea*, 3. 62; from *Annales*, 1. 84

Epaminondas (d. 362), celebrated Theban general and statesman; crushed the Spartans at Leuctra, 1. 84; schooled by the philosopher Lysis, 1. 155

Epicureans attacked, Introd. 3; doctrine of the highest good, Introd. 5

Epicurus of Samos (341–270), founder of the Epicureans *c*.307; taught that pleasure was life's chief aim, 3. 116 f.

Epigoni, play by Accius, 1. 114

Erasmus, his knowledge of *De officiis*, Introd. 6

Erillus (correctly Herillus), third-cent. heterodox Stoic, 1. 6

Eteocles, son of Oedipus; his words in Euripides *Phoenissae* cited, 3. 82

Euripides (*c*.485–*c*.406), Greek tragedian, author of *Phoenissae*, 3. 82; citation from *Hippolytus*, 3. 108

Fabius Labeo, Q. (cos. 183), his subterfuge when assigning boundaries, 1. 33

Fabius Maximus Verrucosus, Q. (cos. five times 233–209), hero of the Hannibalic war; his policy of non-engagement praised by Ennius, 1. 84; his techniques of dissembling and ambushing, 1. 108

Fabricius Luscinus, C. (cos. 282, 278), hero of the war with Pyrrhus; sends back the traitor to him, 1. 40; 3. 86 f.; just, but no sage, 3. 16

Faith, goddess, 3. 104

Fimbria *see* Flavius

Flavius Fimbria, C. (cos. 104), pro-Marius and anti-Sulla; his refusal to pronounce Lutatius Pinthia a 'good man', 3. 77

Frederick the Great's approbation of *De officiis*, Introd. 6

Fufius, L. (fl. 100), orator of moderate ability; prosecutes M'. Aquilius, 2. 50

Furius Philus, L. (cos. 136), proposed surrender of Mancinus to Numantines, 3. 109

Gallia Comata, Province of Antony, Introd. 1

Gorgias, tutor of Marcus at Athens, Introd. 3

Gracchus *see* Sempronius

Gratidianus *see* Marius

Gregory the Great, Christian apologist, Introd. 6

Grotius, Hugo, draws on *De officiis*, Introd. 6

Gyges, king of Lydia *c*.685–657, Introd. 3; murdered his predecessor Candaules and married his widow, 3. 38; his stratagem condemned, 3. 78

The Oxford World's Classics Website

www.worldsclassics.co.uk

- Browse the full range of Oxford World's Classics online

- Sign up for our monthly e-alert to receive information on new titles

- Read extracts from the Introductions

- Listen to our editors and translators talk about the world's greatest literature with our Oxford World's Classics audio guides

- Join the conversation, follow us on Twitter at OWC_Oxford

- Teachers and lecturers can order inspection copies quickly and simply via our website

www.worldsclassics.co.uk

American Literature

British and Irish Literature

Children's Literature

Classics and Ancient Literature

Colonial Literature

Eastern Literature

European Literature

Gothic Literature

History

Medieval Literature

Oxford English Drama

Poetry

Philosophy

Politics

Religion

The Oxford Shakespeare

A complete list of Oxford World's Classics, including Authors in Context, Oxford English Drama, and the Oxford Shakespeare, is available in the UK from the Marketing Services Department, Oxford University Press, Great Clarendon Street, Oxford OX2 6DP, or visit the website at www.oup.com/uk/worldsclassics.

In the USA, visit www.oup.com/us/owc for a complete title list.

Oxford World's Classics are available from all good bookshops. In case of difficulty, customers in the UK should contact Oxford University Press Bookshop, 116 High Street, Oxford OX1 4BR.

The Anglo-Saxon World

Lancelot of the Lake

The Paston Letters

The Romance of Reynard the Fox

The Romance of Tristan

GEOFFREY CHAUCER   The Canterbury Tales
Troilus and Criseyde

JOCELIN OF BRAKELOND   Chronicle of the Abbey of Bury
St Edmunds

GUILLAUME DE LORRIS   The Romance of the Rose
and JEAN DE MEUN

WILLIAM LANGLAND   Piers Plowman